UNDERSTANDING AUDIENCES

Learning to Use
the Media Constructively

(

LEA's COMMUNICATION SERIES
Jennings Bryant/Dolf Zillmann, General Editors

Selected titles in Mass Communication (Alan Rubin, Advisory Editor) include:

Alexander/Owers/Carveth • Media Economics: Theory and Practice, Second Edition

Harris • A Cognitive Psychology of Mass Communication, Third Edition

Moore • Mass Communication Law and Ethics, Second Edition

Moore/Farrar/Collins • Advertising and Public Relations Law

Sohn/Wicks/Lacy/Sylvie • Media Management: A Casebook Approach, Second Edition

Van Evra • Television and Child Development, Second Edition

For a complete list of titles in LEA's Communication Series, please contact Lawrence Erlbaum Associates, Publishers

UNDERSTANDING AUDIENCES

Learning to Use
the Media Constructively

Robert H. Wicks
University of Arkansas

LEA LAWRENCE ERLBAUM ASSOCIATES, PUBLISHERS

2001 Mahwah, New Jersey   London

Lawrence Erlbaum Associates, Inc., Publishers
10 Industrial Avenue
Mahwah, New Jersey 07430-2262

Cover design by Kathryn Houghtaling Lacey

Library of Congress Cataloging-in-Publication Data

Wicks, Robert H.
Understanding audiences : learning to use the media
constructively / Robert H. Wicks.
p. cm.
Includes bibliographical references and index.
ISBN 0-8058-3647-0 (pbk. : alk. paper)
1. Mass media—Audiences. I. Title.

P96.A83 W53 2000
302.23—dc21

00-034757
CIP

Books published by Lawrence Erlbaum Associates are
printed on acid-free paper, and their bindings are chosen for
strength and durability

Printed in the United States of America
10 9 8 7 6 5 4 3 2 1

Dedicated to Jan and Ian

Contents

PART II: CONSTRUCTING MEDIA MESSAGES

5 Framing Media Information   75

PART III: USING MEDIA MESSAGES

6 Fundamentals of Media Information
Processing   99

7 Children as Audience Members   118

8 The Radio and Television Talk Show Audience   142

Preface

As the 21st century begins, people are spending more time than ever before using media. The contemporary media environment includes traditional media such as films, newspapers, radio, and television as well as relative newcomers such as the Internet and the World Wide Web (WWW). *Understanding Audiences* is intended to help people recognize the important role that media play in their lives and to suggest ways that they may use media constructively.

Understanding Audiences invites scholars and students of mass communication to consider how media messages interact with attitudes, beliefs, opinions, and predispositions to produce conceptions of social reality among audience members. This book most heavily relies on social science theory and research from communication, psychology, and sociology. Many of the ideas, however, parallel recent work that has been produced by critical and cultural scholars of communication. It suggests that a wide range of methodological approaches should be used to help understand the nature of media audiences. To learn much about the processes associated with constructing social reality, students and scholars should appreciate the merits of both humanistic and scientific approaches.

Two primary questions are explored in this book: (a) How do people use media to develop attitudes, beliefs, and opinions in the course of constructing social reality? and (b) How may people learn to use media constructively to enhance the quality of their lives?

To answer these questions, one must understand the nature of the media as they relate to audience members. Media companies depend on attracting audiences for their survival. Newspapers without readers, television programs without viewers, and Internet homepages without visitors do not last for long. For this reason, media organizations continually experiment with new and innovative ways to attract and engage the audience members. People should understand why the media present the kinds of messages they do and how these messages interact with cognitions and emotions.

The first step in this inquiry is to consider the relationship between the media and audiences. To do so, one must understand what is meant by the term *audience*. The mass audience composed of a vast, anonymous, and

heterogeneous collection of individuals is rapidly giving way to segmented audiences. Media fare is produced to appeal to segments or subgroups of the mass audience that are composed of people with similar
needs and interests. These multiple audiences are often categorized based
on demographics, psychological profiles, geography, social class, or membership within a cultural group. Programmers and advertisers target these
audience segments by providing specialized media fare containing advertising that is tailored to fit the segment identified.

The second step is to consider how the media contribute to the formation of attitudes, opinions, and beliefs. Media professionals deliberately
construct messages to achieve desired outcomes. News professionals
frame information to spotlight certain issues. Advertisers use persuasive
strategies to encourage people to purchase a product or adopt an idea. Media audience members should understand the techniques that are employed when professional communicators produce media messages. They
should also recognize that, under certain conditions, messages can reinforce or alter existing belief systems.

The third step is to consider how audience members contribute to the
process of constructing social reality when they interpret media messages. Audience members do not simply receive media messages. Although the media may be instrumental in shaping attitudes, opinions,
and beliefs, people actively process and interpret media messages in the
context of stored knowledge. Psychological theory is especially useful in
explaining how the mind works when messages are encountered and processed. Specifically, an understanding of the mechanisms associated with
memory and the use of cognitive schemas may explain why people interpret messages as they do.

The fourth step is to consider how audience members use media to satisfy cognitive needs. People use the media to learn news and information
about social, political, cultural, and economic events or to find out about
interesting or important people. Professional communicators develop
messages that are intended to engage audiences and make them think.
The process of thinking about media content in the context of stored
knowledge may ultimately contribute to the reinforcement of beliefs or
the formulation of new ideas. Media consumers should be aware that
they can develop the skills to analyze the quality of media messages effectively as they generate cognitive representations of the world in which
they live.

Next, it is important to discover how audience members use media to
satisfy emotional needs. A situation comedy or compelling dramatic program may make people laugh or cry. Watching an interview with a Hollywood personality on the *Oprah Winfrey Show* may enable viewers to feel
closer to the celebrity. Witnessing a dysfunctional relationship, which
erupts into a brawl on *The Jerry Springer Show*, enables people to feel better

about their own life circumstances. Although these programs may satisfy different kinds of emotional needs, media consumers should learn to understand their own psychological makeup and recognize why they are drawn to certain types of media messages.

The final step in the inquiry is to consider how audience members should learn to use the media constructively to enhance the quality of their lives. Understanding how and why messages are crafted as they are help audience members assess the quality of media messages. An understanding of their own cognitive and emotional reactions to these messages will also help them become literate media consumers. Citizens should recognize that the media can be used as tools that educate and entertain. Used properly, the media may even facilitate social interaction and civic engagement. Therefore, one primary objective is to learn how to maximize the benefits of these tools. Doing so will enable audience members to take advantage of the media at their disposal.

ACKNOWLEDGMENTS

Many people contributed to the development of this book. First, I thank the graduate and undergraduate students at the University of Arkansas who helped shape the ideas that guide this volume. I also thank the Fulbright College of Arts and Sciences, former Dean Bernard Madison and former Department of Communication Chair, Jimmie Rogers, for investing heavily in this project. My departmental colleagues also offered valuable commentary during the development of this book. Bill Christ of Trinity University provided insightful advice on various drafts of this book. To each of these people, I am indebted.

Acquisitions Editor Linda Bathgate at Lawrence Erlbaum Associates provided exceptional feedback on the various drafts. She also identified superb reviewers who recommended content, organizational, and structural changes that helped frame and illuminate the arguments and concepts presented.

Most important, I thank my wife Jan and son Ian for their love, support, advice, and encouragement throughout the course of this project.

—*Robert Wicks*

I   Beyond Media Effects to Constructing Social Reality

Part I considers the interaction between members of the audience and the producers of media messages as they relate to the construction of social reality. Each person possesses a unique set of attitudes, beliefs, and opinions that is different from every other person. Some of these are passed onto children from parents, whereas others may be learned from teachers and friends. The media also contribute to the ways in which we view our world. The first two chapters consider the relevance of media in the process of assisting us to construct meaning about the world in which we live. As is seen in these chapters, representations of social reality develop when media messages interact with existing knowledge and predispositions held by audience members.

1 Interpreting Media Messages

SUMMARY

- People *interpret* media messages.
- The media encourage the audience to become *engaged* with messages.
- Interpreting messages contributes to the *construction of social reality.*
- Audience members and professional communicators should understand the *implications* of constructing social reality.
- Understanding *how and why* media messages are produced along with an understanding of *how we process these messages* will make us literate members of the media audience.

DISTORTING REALITY

On an April evening in 1977 an ABC News camera crew photographed Ruby Clark, a Black woman, walking down the street of her Ferndale neighborhood near Detroit, Michigan. The clip was used to promote *Sex for Sale: The Urban Battleground*—a program that aired as part of the ABC News Close-Up series. Shortly before her appearance on television, the narrator reported that most of the women in the neighborhood were prostitutes, stating: "According to residents, and Detroit police records, most of the prostitutes' customers or johns were white; the street prostitutes were often black. This integrated middle class neighborhood became a safe meeting place for prostitutes and 'johns.' "

Ms. Clark, her husband, and her son were watching the promotional spot when ABC presented frontal close-ups that included facial shots. She appeared to be in her early to mid-20s and was attractive, slim, and stylishly dressed. She wore large earrings and had long hair that was pulled up above her head. In the clip, Ms. Clark appeared to be unaware that she was being photographed. As a result, the wife and mother with no connection to prostitution whatsoever was shunned by acquaintances, church members, and potential employers. Although ABC did not intend to portray Clark as a prostitute, that is the meaning that many viewers

constructed from the combination of visual and auditory messages provided by the network (Grimes, 1990; Smith & Magee, 1980).

The way in which people reacted to Ruby Clark after viewing the clip
was not entirely unpredictable. During the 1970s, audience members held
the media in high esteem as a consequence of their coverage of events such
as Watergate by the *Washington Post*.[1] News organizations at the time presented reasoned analyses of important issues such as the Vietnam war
and the civil rights and women's movements. The credibility enjoyed by
the media—in this case ABC—may have persuaded viewers and even
friends of Ruby Clark that the promotional spot was accurate. At that
time, viewers undoubtedly failed to recognize that television news producers deliberately frame message content to accentuate emotion, conflict, and suspense to attract the attention of the largest possible audience
(e.g., Berkowitz, 1996; Gamson, 1992; Gamson & Modigliani, 1989). Instead, most probably concluded that they had simply seen Ruby Clark as
a prostitute with their own eyes.

Ruby Clark did something that few people would have done in the
1970s. She responded to ABC by filing a lawsuit alleging the news story
had harmed her reputation. In the defamation and invasion of privacy
suit brought against ABC, lawyers for Clark maintained that she was li-
beled because the combination of pictures and sound led many viewers to
the incorrect conclusion that she was a prostitute. The ABC legal team
contended that the text was accurate and therefore not libelous. The appeals court eventually ruled that the broadcast was "capable of defama-
tory meaning" and that Clark "was either portrayed as a prostitute or
could reasonably be mistaken for a prostitute."

The Ruby Clark incident caused people following it to recognize the
possibility that what one sees on television does not necessarily reflect reality. In his 1970 book, *How to Talk Back to Your Television Set*, former Federal Communications Commission (FCC) Commissioner Nicholas
Johnson encouraged citizens to take control of their media environment,
calling for "instantaneous, ubiquitous and no-cost access for all information" (Johnson, 1970, p. 122). The Commissioner foresaw a time in which
telephone lines would provide access to libraries, time and weather reports, and stock market reports. He believed telephone lines would connect computers "with the rapid increase in number, character and
simplicity of terminal devices for the home and office" (Johnson, 1970,
pp. 123–124).

---

[1]Although the media may have been perceived as highly credible at the time, researchers
also point to this period as the time in which the media started to become increasingly negative and cynical toward democratic institutions (M. Robinson, 1975, 1976, 1977).

Commissioner Johnson argued that citizens need to become engaged in the evolution of the electronic media establishment if they want such a system to contribute to the growth and vitality of an enlightened society. The public, he asserted, must challenge the FCC and other regulatory bodies to protect the quality of through-the-spectrum programming. This could be accomplished by careful monitoring to ascertain that the media establishment operates in a socially responsible and constructive way. In other words, in his view, people should become active participants in the formation of the entertainment and information systems if they would like to witness the development of a healthy media environment.

THE INTERACTION BETWEEN PEOPLE AND MEDIA

We live in a world surrounded by media. Television programs inform and entertain. Movies make us laugh and cry. We can now choose from dozens of radio formats to make the commute to and from work more enjoyable. We can travel the globe or keep in touch with friends and family through the Internet. Unquestionably, the media can contribute to the quality of life of citizens and societies. Therefore, it is not surprising that using media is now a favorite worldwide pastime.

People around the globe spend more than 3.5 billion hours watching television each day, and the average American spends about half of his or her leisure time viewing (Kubey & Csikszentmihalyi, 1990). Add to this all other media, including the Internet, and one can easily see that understanding the relationship between people and mass communication is an important and interesting undertaking. However, understanding the relationship between people and media goes well beyond simply adding up the amount of media that people use. We must also understand why people are so attracted to media and consider the implications of this attraction (Robinson & Godbey, 1997).

Sociologists were among the first to observe that the more we use media, the less we interact with other people. Watching it on a cable access channel or reading about it in the morning newspaper has largely displaced the social experience of attending the town hall meeting. Although these may be efficient and viable ways to develop knowledge about civic issues, they also reduce the kinds of interpersonal debates that took place before the media became so pervasive. As media remain a primary information and entertainment source, many scholars express concern that interpersonal discussions about important social topics will continue to decline leading to accelerated civic and social disengagement of the audience members (e.g., Becker & Whitney, 1980).

Some researchers also believe that the Internet may have a similar narcotizing effect that will interfere with human discourse about contemporary social issues. As with television, a possibility exists that excessive usage will erode time that people once spent engaged in interpersonal discussions. Although the Internet may appear to be inherently interactive, recent research reveals that excessive usage can lead to feelings of loneliness and depression. In severe instances, evidence suggests that people can actually become addicted to the Internet.

Although it is tempting to blame the media for the many social ills, audience members should recognize that the media can be used constructively by providing an open forum in the marketplace of ideas. The media are neither inherently good nor bad. Programs like *Sesame Street* on PBS as well as news and documentaries contribute to the knowledge base of children and adults. Countless films, magazine articles, and newspapers stories have served to entertain and enlighten members of the audience. The media are simply tools that we use either to enhance or diminish the quality of life. As with any tool, however, media audiences need to learn how to use them properly to take full advantage of what they have to offer. Thus, the point of *Understanding Audiences* is not to pass judgment on the media. Rather it is to help audience members understand how to make the best use of the media offerings at their disposal.

UNDERSTANDING THE NATURE OF MEDIA INDUSTRIES

To use media constructively, people must first understand the nature of media institutions. Literate media consumers should recognize that both older media entities (such as newspapers) and newer ones (like the Internet) have a vested interest in attracting and maintaining the attention of the audience. Media content is produced and disseminated by large organizations to make a profit either through direct sales to consumers or through the sale of advertising to sponsors.

The *political economy* approach, as it is known, considers the interplay among political, economic, and technological factors as they relate to the dissemination of media programming and messages. This approach focuses on understanding the objectives and motivations associated with attracting and engaging the media audience. Because contemporary media corporations (which own everything from theme parks to television stations to baseball teams to wax museums) exist to generate profits and prosper, they must continually attract the attention of audiences. Therefore, they are always on the lookout for new and different entertainment and information content, programming genres, or interesting presentation styles to accomplish their goals.

In the past, media have attracted audiences by specializing in the production of one-way messages. For example, television producers supplied programming that was intended to be received by the audience. Programmers presumed that a satisfied audience would be reflected in terms of rating points. Although the ratings remain the mainstay of success in broadcasting, new strategies are being tested that make audience members participants in the communication process.

Instead of receiving information or entertainment programming, citizens are now encouraged to respond to media content. On July 20, 1999, for example, more than 31,000 viewers of *Dateline NBC* acted as *online jurors,* voting to acquit a mother who was taken to court by her daughter after the mother had taken disciplinary actions against the girl. Producers at *Dateline* recognized that audience members enjoy becoming participants rather than bystanders in the communication process. Producers of game shows also recognize that many audience members prefer the opportunity to interact with the action on the screen (see Box 1.1). Therefore, designing media to engage audiences by emulating interpersonal interaction appears to be a priority in the contemporary media environment.

BOX 1.1. Interactive TV's New Approach

Beginning in October 1999, television audience members were able to play along with contestants of *Jeopardy!* and *Wheel of Fortune* using new interactive technologies. WebTV afforded audience members the chance to play the games in real time along with the television contestants. Using remote controls, viewers select letters for *Wheel* and choose from multiple-choice answers for *Jeopardy* (L. Anderson, 1999).

Players begin by submitting their name, address, phone number, password, and e-mail address and then download a game engine into the WebTV receiver. The game package includes encoding hardware as well as software. Home players answer questions and solve puzzles along with the TV contestants and other at-home users as they watch the program on the same screen and even compete for prizes.

The game shows represent Sony/Columbia TriStar's first efforts to develop an audience for interactive television (ITV). Mixed Signals Technologies developed the technology for Columbia TriStar using the Microsoft WebTV plus system software. Sony is the parent company of both Columbia TriStar TV and the Game Show Network, which manufactures the WebTV boxes. WebTV's owner, Microsoft, is also investing in a competitor to spearhead a move toward open standards for ITV platforms.

Members of the media audience should also be aware that the messages they receive are often orchestrated to generate enthusiasm and cultivate audiences. In the concentrated media marketplace, it hardly seems a coincidence that ABC sponsored a weeklong extravaganza on *Good Morning*

America, World News Tonight, and *Nightline* celebrating the opening of Disney's Animal Kingdom in Orlando. The theme park and ABC are both part of the Disney media empire: ABC was merged with Capitol Cities Broadcasting in 1986 and the network was sold to Disney in 1996 for $19 billion. Peter Jennings concludes his evening news program by urging viewers to visit the *World News Tonight* Web site at www.abcnews.com. Should audience members be tempted to abandon network television in favor of surfing the Web, they may still remain members of the ranks of the Disney audience if they follow the advice of Jennings.

Audience members should also recognize that programmers are now experimenting with aggressive new techniques aimed at shocking them. For example, television talk shows that would have tested the limits of *The National Enquirer* a decade ago now routinely present graphic sexual topics and fist fights between guests as a means to engage audience members. In the summer of 1998, *The Jerry Springer Show* actually moved into first place for television talk shows—attracting even higher ratings than *The Oprah Winfrey Show.* Viewers should try to discern what they find interesting or appealing about different programs and how these shows satisfy certain human needs.

UNDERSTANDING THE NATURE OF MEDIA AUDIENCES

Although scholars in the political economy tradition consider the nature of media industries and the products they produce, other researchers focus on how people interpret messages. Understanding how and why media messages are produced should enable audience members make better self-assessments of why they find these messages interesting or compelling. Developing this skill may help them see how various messages satisfy certain cognitive and emotional needs. Hall (1980) asserted that audience members should learn to assess the quality of messages. They should develop critical thinking skills that enable them to: (a) accept the meaning intended by the producer, (b) accept aspects of the message, or (c) reject the intended meaning.

Interpreting media implies an understanding of the dynamics that occur when people encounter messages and struggle to understand them and place them in proper context. As Allen (1987) explained in his description of *reception theory,* "meaning should no longer be considered as the result of immutable property of a text but must be considered as the result of the confrontation between reading act and textual structure" (p. 75). Using media in this context focuses on the principle that meaning is a negotiated process between specific audiences and texts.

This book encourages audience members to consider and understand the ways in which contemporary media organizations structure textual, graphic, aural, and visual messages to maintain their attention. It urges readers to consider how media messages interact with their own knowledge, beliefs, and attitudes in the process of shaping their conceptualizations of social reality. People must understand how their own predispositions and knowledge influence the reception and interpretation of mediated messages.

This book also urges students of communication, journalism, advertising, public relations, and telecommunications to learn how to use the tools of media wisely. Many of these students will ultimately engage in the creation of messages that will contribute to the development of economic, political, and social belief systems among audience members. An understanding of the potential impact of messages is essential in this endeavor.

Finally, this book is intended for media practitioners. As the Ruby Clark example illustrates, professional communicators often fail to consider how their reports is received, processed, and interpreted by members of the audience.

OVERVIEW OF THE BOOK

Part I: Beyond Media Effects
to Constructing Social Reality

The book is divided into three parts. Part I, containing the first two chapters, provides a framework outlining the principles associated with the construction of social reality.

Chapter 2 traces the historical roots of the media effects tradition in mass communication theory leading to the evolution of a developing meanings paradigm. This paradigm proposes that people actively participate in the process of constructing social reality. Media messages are believed to stimulate psychological processes that utilize existing knowledge as people negotiate meaning. Measurement strategies used in the past may not be sensitive to the kind of learning that takes place when this interaction between people and the media occurs. This is because we are only beginning to understand the mechanisms related to the interpretation of media messages and the construction social reality. The chapter stresses the importance of using quantitative and qualitative methods in tandem and recommends greater emphasis on the use of multiple-method research strategies.

Part II: Constructing Media Messages

Chapters 3 through 5 focus on the media and the construction of messages. In the contemporary media environment, literate audience members should understand why they are so valuable to media companies. Chapter 3 considers how media institutions now employ new and innovative ways to capture and maintain the attention of the audience. Partnerships and cross-marketing strategies between entities within these large multinational media corporations are designed to entice and engage the audience. The chapter also examines regulatory trends and considers the growing importance of the Internet and the WWW as media institutions.

Chapter 4 explains how people interact with persuasive messages. Virtually all advertisements, public service announcements, promotional messages, and infomercials are produced with the express intent of persuading the members of the audience to accept an idea, buy a product, or adjust a behavior. In this chapter, we will consider public communication campaigns to illustrate how professional communicators strategically communicate information to influence human behavior. These strategies try to engage audiences by making rational claims, appealing to emotions, or employing some combination of the two.

Chapter 5 illustrates how journalists and editors frame media messages to transmit a perspective or viewpoint. Frames allow journalists to process large amounts of information quickly and to package it efficiently for transmission to their audiences. However, professional communicators operate from their own attitudes, beliefs, and opinions, which may influence or distort the information selection, production, and distribution processes. Furthermore, it is important to recognize that media organizations may cause communicators to consciously or unconsciously construct messages in certain ways. These processes can have a significant impact on the messages that audiences receive.

Part III: Using Media Messages

The remaining chapters of this book analyze the ways in which audiences use media messages to construct social reality. Chapter 6 provides an overview of information-processing theory in a media context. The chapter suggests that prior knowledge and interpretive frames guide the ways in which people construct social reality. It also points out that incoming information is capable of stimulating the retrieval of associated stored knowledge. This process contributes to the construction of representations of reality because new information is interpreted in the context of existing attitudes, beliefs, and opinions stored within knowledge structures known as *schemas*. Finally, social group membership, message structure, and the influence of media practices and norms may affect how audience members process and interpret media messages.

Chapter 7 considers children as media consumers. Recent research indicates that watching television news can upset elementary school children so effectively that they begin to see the world around them as much scarier that it is in reality. Graphic visuals of murders, wars, and natural disasters lead to nightmares, sleep disturbances, and other lasting reactions in children. To understand how children process and interpret media messages, we consider what causes them to pay attention to it, how well they understand it, and what causes them to remember it. The chapter evaluates the processes associated with social learning from the media and how children use schemas. It also considers whether media messages may cultivate distortions of social reality. It concludes with an examination of the findings about the incidence of violence on television. Finally, it reports that certain media programming can have a healthy or beneficial influence on children.

Chapter 8 illustrates the increased utility of the uses and gratifications theory by considering the impressive rise in popularity of both radio and television talk shows. Talk shows have become extremely popular during the past several years, with different types seeming to provide different gratifications to members of the audience. Televised talk programs like *The Oprah Winfrey Show* present discussions with interesting guests. Shows such as these also pursue controversial topics in a responsible fashion and introduce new books to the audience. Radio programs like *The Rush Limbaugh Show* can reinforce political attitudes and opinions held by the listeners. Shows like these enable people to monitor the perspectives of other members of society. *The Jerry Springer Show*, by contrast, maintains a band of burly security guards that possess a keen sense of timing to intercede just milliseconds before the punches fly. The rise of talk shows provides an opportunity to reevaluate the uses and gratifications model in a new light.

Chapter 9 evaluates the Internet and the WWW by considering the gratifications that audience members receive when they use chat rooms, use e-mail, or go cybershopping. The Internet has been likened to the printing press in terms of social importance. The interaction between older media and the Internet may also be having a profound impact on our economic, cultural, and political institutions. For example, stock purchases are made as buyers monitor the stock market on cable television (see Box 1.2).

The Internet also provides opportunities for social interaction and greater efficiencies in time management. Databases such as Lexis/Nexis or UMI ProQuest Direct enable students and scholars to download news or legal information while writing a term paper or journal article. The

---

BOX 1.2. Influences of CNBC on the Stock Market

The Dow Jones industrials fell 150 points after 3:30 P.M. on August 4, 1998, when Prudential's chief technical analyst, Ralph Acampora, one of the market's most prominent Wall Street bulls, appeared on *CNBC's Street Signs* and declared that he had decided to become a bear. CNBC President Bill Bolster said: "It's a flattering observation. But we can't take credit [for the market decline] because we just don't know" (Lieberman, 1998, p. 3b).

Later in the month, on August 31, the Dow Jones index plummeted 512 points culminating in a loss of 20% in value from the previous month. The technology-based Nasdaq Composite Index also lost almost 9% of its value on the same day—much of it in the final, frantic minutes of trading—to post its worst decline since the October 1987 stock crash. Volume on the New York Stock Exchange was a near record, with 916 million shares changing hands.

The following day, the Dow Jones rallied for a 300-point gain, and a new all-time record for volume of shares changing hands was set. On both days, people viewing CNBC or monitoring the market through other online sources made many of the trades through the Internet on computer terminals from homes and offices around the nation and globe. The advent of online trading is having a profound effect on global economic markets and investing strategies. An off-the-cuff remark made during a luncheon by Federal Reserve chairman Alan Greenspan hinting that U.S. economy's growth rate may not be sustainable is capable of causing wild fluctuations in the stock market as investor traders buy and sell stock with the click of a mouse.

Internet can link millions of people simultaneously and even provide instantaneous timely information about controversial or interesting topics and (see Box 1.3). Some have even theorized that the Internet will bridge the classes as it fosters interaction and communication among members of the global community.

As with any new technology, it is important to understand its strengths and limitations. Although the Internet may offer information and entertainment gratifications, some researchers believe a correlation may exist among depression, stress, and loneliness and the amount of time spent online. Furthermore, some researchers now believe that some Internet users may find it as addictive as illicit drugs, alcohol, or tobacco. As with any new medium, it is important to recognize the most productive ways of utilizing this new tool.

Chapter 10 summarizes the central ideas in this book. The book concludes with a detailed bibliography useful to mass communication scholars, students, and media practitioners interested in understanding more about how audiences use media to construct social reality.

Box 1.3. Internet Visits Following the Release of the Starr Report

Relevant Knowledge Returns Overnight Results About Visitation to the Starr Report

Atlanta, September 14, 1998—During a 2-day period when the posting of the lurid details of the Kenneth Starr report caused an Internet-surfing frenzy, RelevantKnowledge, which tracks Internet traffic, reported that 24.7 million unique visitors to various sites posting the document. News and governmental sites had the highest percent increases from week to week. Six million unique visitors viewed the text of the report and/or the Clinton rebuttal on government, news, and portal web sites.

Across an aggregation of sites that published the works, 10 times more Web users visited the Starr Report, released Friday, September, 11, than President Clinton's rebuttal, RelevantKnowledge said. The company also found that most Web users viewed the Starr Report on national news sites and portals rather than the government sites, where the report was originally published.

"The frenzy to see the Starr Report is like nothing we've ever seen before," said Jeff Levy, CEO of RelevantKnowledge. "The government sites, which were less equipped with bandwidth to deal with the sheer volumes of visitors, sent many Web users to the major news sites and portals."

News sites, both regional and national, had a 95% increase in visitors on Friday, September 11, and Saturday, September 12, compared with the same days a week before, over 7 million unique visitors during the 2-day period. Fifty-four percent of total traffic to these sites viewed some portion of the Starr Report.

National news sites, however, attracted the lion's share of visitors, as 6.4 million different Web users viewed these sites. This volume represents an increase in users of 127% over the same days the week before. Men ages 35 to 49 and women ages 18 to 34 accounted for the largest portion of the Starr Report audience.

Web users also relied on regional news sites to read the Starr Report, which, on an aggregated basis, attracted 1.6 million unique visitors on Friday and Saturday—a 13% increase from the Friday and Saturday the week before. Of this total traffic, 22% went to the text portion of the Starr Report.

Although they did not receive the brunt of Web traffic on Friday and Saturday, the government sites that originally published the report saw their audience increase nearly twentyfold to 1.3 million unique visitors versus fewer than 70,000 the week before.

"These government sites, which aren't accustomed to receiving manifolds of traffic like they did on Friday and Saturday, are very much like what we saw with the British Monarchy site when Princess Diana died August of last year. It shot up within the Top 30 of our rankings," Levy said.

Source: http://www.Mediametrix.com/PressRoom/RKarchives/09_14_98.html
Used with permission of Media Metrix. Relevant Knowledge and Media Metrix announced a merger between the companies in October 1998. The new company is named Media Metrix with the tag line, the Power of Relevant Knowledge.

2 From Media Effects to Constructing Social Reality

SUMMARY

- Early communication researchers believed that *media had powerful and immediate influences* with respect to shaping the attitudes, beliefs, and opinions of audience members.
- Newer theories assert that *media effects are minimal* and mitigated by a host of other variables.
- The media have the ability to *spotlight* certain issues.
- Under certain conditions, the media may *cultivate* a view of the world that is inaccurate.
- The interaction between message *content and structure* may influence interpretation of media messages.
- The development of *cognitive theory* helps to explain the processes that occur when people encounter media messages.
- *Schemas* influence the interpretation of messages and the construction of social reality.
- The term applied to an understanding of how people construct meaning from media is *constructionism.*
- *Literate audience members* understand how they construct meaning about the world.

EARLY COMMUNICATION THEORY

Early communication theorists attempted to explain what caused reporters and editors to include certain stories in newspapers (e.g., Breed, 1955; White, 1950). These researchers were mainly interested in determining the characteristics of information that makes news salient because they assumed a one-way linear relationship between the message sender and receiver. Specifically, they suspected that if they understood the criteria employed by media gatekeepers in the process of selecting, collecting, and disseminating media information, they would then be in a better position

14

to understand something about the opinions, beliefs, and attitudes of the society (Converse, 1964).

Attitudes constitute the evaluations held toward objects, issues, or other people (Petty, Cacioppo, & Kasmer, 1988). They are related to positive or negative feelings, information and knowledge, or behaviors that manifest themselves when people encounter other people or issues (Cacioppo & Petty, 1982; Petty & Cacioppo, 1986a). Most of the early research concluded that media messages contributed to the development of attitudes because a passive and unquestioning audience absorbed them.

Early communication research was also largely influenced by the behaviorist tradition (i.e., stimulus–response theory) in psychology. The basic premise was that people were essentially irrational and that emotional impulses caused them to behave as they did. This perspective was consistent with research in the 1920s that indicated that media channels could be used for propaganda purposes to alter attitudes and beliefs (e.g., Lasswell, 1927, 1934, 1948). However, early propaganda researchers also pointed out that such attitude shifting generally occurred over time when carefully constructed ideas and images were developed and presented as part of an overall persuasive campaign. In other words, attitude shift is possible under certain conditions, but mere exposure to a message is no guarantee that it will occur.

Nevertheless, thinking along behaviorist lines prevailed for quite a while producing naive perspectives such as the magic bullet (Schramm, 1971) or hypodermic needle theories (Berlo, 1960). The basic premise of these theories was that the media were capable of having immediate and direct influences on individuals, and messages emanating from media institutions have the ability to manipulate human behavior. Examples of this manipulation were the supposed effectiveness of political advertising campaigns or the ability of politicians to shape public opinion by staging events designed to attract news media coverage (Kern, 1989; Lazarsfeld & Merton, 1948).

MEDIA'S LIMITED EFFECTS

The magic bullet theory was attractive to parents, teachers, and political leaders because it provided a handy and simple explanation for antisocial behavior in children. However, as early as 1960, Joseph Klapper cautioned against assuming that television was capable of direct and immediate effects on individuals. In his volume, *The Effects of Mass Communication*, he systematically analyzed the available evidence to offer a more conservative assessment of what was known with respect to media influences over people (Klapper, 1960). To do so, he compiled virtually all of the relevant media effects research produced until 1960 by media scholars employed at universities as well as that of broadcast industry analysts working in the private sector.

Klapper argued that empirical research does not demonstrate that media are all powerful in influencing behavior. When a media message does produce a direct effect, he suggested, it is a departure from the norm. Klapper also distinguished between the potential for instantaneous and powerful influence of media over individuals and the likelihood that media effects may be subtle and occur over time. Klapper contended that media effects are mitigated by many variables including: (a) message content; (b) the manner in which communicators construct messages; and (c) the knowledge, attitudes, beliefs, and predispositions an individual held prior to exposure.

Klapper's limited effects model may have been benchmark at the time, but it was not an entirely new idea. As early as 1922, journalist Walter Lippmann wrote that people are all captives of the "pictures in their heads" (p. 3). He explained that, in the "buzzing confusion of the outer world, we pick out what our culture has already defined for us, and we tend to perceive that which we have picked out in the form stereotyped for us by our culture" (p. 81). This statement implies that human beings tend to process information in the context of previously stored knowledge for the purpose of reinforcing beliefs and stereotypes. Lippmann also recognized that the selective portrayal of the world by the newspapers of the 1920s contributed to the construction of social reality by spotlighting certain news items while ignoring others. Issues that obtrude, he wrote, tend to attract the attention of the news media. These obtruding issues present themselves in the forms of hurricanes, earthquakes, fires and other natural disasters, economic downturns, and political upheaval or scandal.

The work by Lippmann and others to follow (e.g., Burke, 1968; Goffman, 1974; McLuhan, 1964; Schramm, 1971) was important because it represented a shift away from considering the media as an environmental stimulus to an analysis of the media as a dynamic cultural system deserving of study. The central theme became what people do with media information rather than how media messages affect people.

THE 1970s AND 1980s: ALTERNATIVE PERSPECTIVES

By the mid-1970s and into the 1980s, researchers were training their focus on television to assess whether the new medium was having an influence on individuals and society (e.g., Gunter, 1987; Katz, Adoni, & Parness, 1977; Neuman, 1976; Stauffer, Frost, & Rybolt, 1983). The studies often concluded that television seemed to have little, if any, impact on viewers, and that lack of retention of television information had to do with the transitory nature of the visual medium. With respect to television news, J. P. Robinson and Levy (1986) concluded that compressing as many as 20 news stories in a 22-minute newscast, combined with the processing challenge of simultaneously interpreting audio and video, makes the retention of information nearly impossible.

Other researchers, however, were skeptical of these findings and simply did not believe that media effects were truly so minimal. How could the media have so little influence when we are immersed in them on a daily basis? The problem, some researchers concluded, was that some of the studies evaluated by Klapper and others to follow were not effectively measuring what had been retained through the television viewing experience. As early as 1964, in his now classic article "The Obstinate Audience," Bauer characterized media users as active and goal-oriented. By 1974, Katz, Blumler, and Gurevitch had formulated a statement on media uses and gratifications intended to (a) explain how people use media to gratify their needs, (b) explain motives for media behavior, and, (c) identify functions or consequences that follow from needs, motives, and behavior (for a review, see Rubin, 1994). These researchers explained that ample evidence exists to suggest that people go out of their way to utilize the media to accomplish certain goals and derive specific gratifications. In short, information and entertainment needs significantly drive the behaviors of media audiences.

Coinciding with the emergence of uses and gratifications research, McCombs and Shaw (1972) introduced the agenda-setting research tradition, which also argued in favor of the active audience. Agenda-setting scholars believe that effects may be more pronounced than Klapper believed because the media have significant influence in deciding which information is presented in newspapers and on television. Using survey data, these researchers reported that correlations existed between how important respondents perceived issues to be and the amount of coverage they received. Conceding that the media were not necessarily capable of telling people what to think, they asserted that the media may be capable of encouraging people to think about certain issues.

Discontent with the limited-effects model continued to grow as scholars demonstrated that the media appeared to have an influence on people under certain circumstances. Cultivation theorists argued that fictional crime programs seemed to have the ability to cultivate the beliefs and attitudes of viewers concerning the incidence and type of crime prevalent in society (for reviews, see Gerbner & Gross, 1976; Gerbner, Gross, Morgan, & Signorielli, 1980; Hawkins, Yong-Ho, & Pingree, 1991; W. J. Potter, 1991a). People may also remain silent when the media present a view contrary to their own. This is because people may perceive that they hold a minority viewpoint when they may, in fact, be in the majority. As a consequence, the minority perspective advanced by media outlets may ultimately become the majority perspective (for a discussion of the spiral of silence, see Noelle-Neumann, 1984). Although neither the spiral of silence nor cultivation theory are in opposition to the limited-effect perspective, both suggest that interaction between the media and people may ultimately produce effects that are not so minimal.

As the 1980s progressed, it became clear that the uses and gratifications approach, agenda setting, cultivation research, the spiral of silence, as well as other developing theories of persuasion were individually incapable of explaining human interaction with media. Although each approach provided pieces of the puzzle on how people interact with the media, none offered a coherent model that integrated psychological processes and effects of media messages as well as the influence of broader social, anthropological, and environmental factors. Such a model would require mass communication theorists to evaluate both media content and the psychological composition of the audience members in tandem to explain how people construct social reality through interacting with media content (Shapiro, 1991, Shrum & O'Guinn, 1993).

THE COGNITIVE REVOLUTION OF THE 1980s AND 1990s

By the mid-1980s, rapidly expanding information-processing research in the field of psychology prompted Gardner (1985) to assert that a cognitive revolution had taken place (for a review of scientific revolutions, see Kuhn, 1962). This cognitive revolution profoundly and directly influenced the development of mass communication theory prompting scholars to consider the relationships emerging among information-processing theory, agenda setting, persuasion, the spiral of silence, and uses and gratifications and cultivation theories. Furthermore, collaborative research between communication scholars and psychologists accelerated leading to significant cross-pollination between the allied fields (e.g., Bryant & Zillmann, 1991, 1994; Reeves & Anderson, 1991; Reeves & Thorson, 1986; Thorson, Reeves, & Schleuder, 1987).

Consequently, the use of cognitive theory has become commonplace in communication scholarship. This theoretical approach is helpful in explaining the interaction between dynamic structural variables (e.g., video pacing, type of music, video editing procedures, gender or race of actors) and content genres (e.g., news, entertainment, or sports programs). Cognitive theories have also been used to evaluate how message content may interact with the viewer's mood or emotional state, which in turn may influence message reception and interpretation (Zillmann, 1983a, 1983b, 1991a, 1991b). These studies have generally focused on the internal microlevel processes that take place when people encounter media information. Such inquiries have yielded significant insights as to what causes people to pay attention to media and what they remember from exposure to media information (e.g., Anderson & Burns, 1991; Brosius, 1993; Chaffee & Schleuder, 1986; Grimes & Meadowcroft, 1995; Schleuder, White, & Cameron, 1993; Thorson, Reeves, & Schleuder, 1987).

Within the sphere of political communication, a parallel political cognition revolution took place during the 1980s and 1990s. W. A. Gamson (1988) asserted that a change in focus evolved in which the voting behavior and political attitudes of citizens became secondary to an understanding of the interpretive processes associated with the construction of political meaning. "It draws on concepts rooted in cognitive psychology—schemata, constructs, cognitive maps, frames, script and mode of political thinking" (Gamson, 1988, p. 164). Specifically, the focus had shifted to the viewpoint of citizens actively creating political meaning through the process of elaboration (i.e., evaluating or interpreting new information in the context of previously held attitudes, beliefs, and knowledge).

Political communication researchers have tended to focus on the construction of political meaning as a consequence of variables such as (a) the manner in which messages are packaged, (b) the influence of sponsors such as public relations specialists, and (c) media practices and professional norms. The cognitive revolution described by Gardner (1985) is fundamentally anchored in an attempt to understand the psychological microlevel cognitive processes of individuals. As a result of these two complementary research orientations, a more global picture of how people come to understand the world around them has begun to emerge. The effect has been a shift toward research strategies that attempt to relate the message, the media, and the individual to explain the processes associated with the construction of social reality.

COGNITIVE THEORY

Cognitive theory maintains that people do not literally encode and retrieve information. Rather, they interpret new information in the context of existing knowledge, beliefs, and attitudes. The process is continual and interactive as the mind uses sounds, images, and any other available stimuli to comprehend information (Hoijer, 1989). In effect, new information is checked against stored knowledge enabling an individual to understand it based on previously held beliefs and predispositions.

Schemas are collections of organized knowledge or frameworks that guide comprehension, memory, and other processes associated with interpreting messages. Schemas, which are based on past information and experience, may be organized around objects, events, people, or roles. As a result, people may infer a great deal that was not provided when they encounter new information because the schemas they access contain ideas that were established in the past. As we grow older, schemas become more complex and new schemas constantly develop. People rely heavily on four types of schemas in the course of processing information (Fiske & Taylor, 1991; W. J. Potter, 1998; Wicks, 1992b):

1. *Self-schemas* comprise all of the images and ideas that one has about oneself. People probably have more schemas about themselves than about anything else.

2. *Person schemas* are knowledge clusters about other people. They contain all of the information about gender, race, physical properties, personality traits, and other characteristics. Person schemas are important in film and television presentations because they enable audience members to quickly categorize actors. Furthermore, as is seen later in this volume, it is common for people to attempt to emulate actors that people admire, like, or trust.

3. *Role schemas* are intended to provide cues as to how people should behave in certain situations. A newscaster mentioning that a candidate for public office is a Democrat may cause audience members to infer that he or she is liberal. As with all schemas, these shortcuts that enable us to quickly categorize and classify may also send us down the wrong path by contributing to stereotyping. Habitually casting certain social groups as poor, lazy, aggressive, or as fugitives from justice may have undesired social consequences.

4. *Scripts*, also called event schemas, guide everyday behavior. Social norms encourage cheering and applause when your favorite football team scores a touchdown. Such behavior in a library would be entirely inappropriate. With respect to media, certain recurring themes or scripts enable film or television viewers to follow stories and make inferential leaps when certain information is not provided. Scripts enable us to draw on past experience to understand story-telling devices that communicators employ.

Using scripts is especially important for a variety of reasons. First, they enable audience members to pick up stories in midstream. This is especially true for news reporting in which events may carry over several days, weeks, or years. Children also learn appropriate or inappropriate behavior through the presentation of habitually repeated themes. As is seen later, criminals often escape punishment in television dramas. Researchers question what influence this will ultimately have on the scripts that develop in childhood. Conversely, researchers have demonstrated the benefits of exposing children to programs such as *Barney, Sesame Street,* or *Mr. Rogers*, which contain recurring positive social scripts.

MEDIA LITERACY

The 1990s were a period in which media literacy became an important concern. Becoming media literate implies empowering people to understand the extent to which messages may influence them (for discussions of media literacy, see Aufderheide, 1993; W. J. Potter, 1998). Furthermore, people need to understand the inherent strengths and weaknesses of the media to assess the quality of the information and entertainment programming available to them. In effect, media literacy implies taking charge of one's media environment to use it most effectively. This control comes from understanding the nature of media messages and how we approach, interpret, and ultimately assimilate or discard these messages.

To be media literate, people need to understand what motivates the media to construct messages in the ways that they do. An understanding of how messages are produced and the psychological processes that take place when people encounter messages enable citizens to make the most of media. Developing these skills enable people to operate from a high degree of media literacy. This implies that people should recognize that media messages may have multiple meanings. Therefore, media users should learn how to use broad-based schemas in a sophisticated fashion to deduce the best possible meaning from the messages they encounter.

W. J. Potter (1998) explained that people with poor or limited media literacy skills have greater difficulty interpreting meaning from media messages.

> These people are also habitually reluctant or unwilling to use their skills, which remain underdeveloped and therefore more difficult to employ successfully. As a result, it is unlikely that people at lower levels of media literacy will construct multiple meanings from a media messages, so they are much more likely to accept the surface meaning of the message itself. Thus, low literacy people are much less able to identify inaccuracies, to sort through controversies, to appreciate irony or satire, to develop a broad, yet personal view of the world. (p. 5)

There are "four inter-related dimensions of media literacy: the cognitive, emotional, aesthetic, and moral dimensions" (W. J. Potter, 1998, p. 7):

1. The *cognitive domain* denotes an awareness of the processes associated with thinking. It implies a recognition that messages are crafted in various ways by professional communicators with specific agendas. Understanding the cognitive domain also means that an individual is aware that new information is always interpreted in the context of stored knowledge. From an intellectual standpoint, this domain enables people to rationally assess and process the information. In so do-

ing, the communication may enhance a knowledge base or even be discarded as erroneous or irrelevant.

2. The *emotional domain* denotes an awareness that media messages can interact with feelings. The need for stimulation may cause an individual to crave the vicarious thrill of an action-packed movie or television program. Television viewers may attempt to elevate their spirits by watching television talk shows featuring bizarre guests engaged in dysfunctional relationships. In these instances, viewers should recognize that media satisfy specific emotional needs. Understanding the ways in which we interact emotionally with media may help us to use it with care and discretion and to better understand ourselves and why we need the type of emotional stimulation that the media provide.

3. The *aesthetic domain* denotes an ability to evaluate media from an artistic point of view. As media consumers, we should strive to develop the same skills at distinguishing quality as we do in art and literature. Producers of media messages recognize that audience members are the ultimate judge and jury of what will succeed and what will fail. If citizens demand excellence, producers will be forced to comply. As such, citizens should develop an appreciation for excellence in the writing, directing, and producing of media content.

4. The *moral domain* denotes an ability to infer values contained within the messages. Situation comedies such as *M*A*S*H* contained messages about the futility of war. *All in the Family* broke new ground by raising the issues associated with racism and sexism in a comedy format. *Married with Children* mused about the dysfunctional family in contemporary American society. In dramatic or action television programs or films, situations are frequently resolved using violence that goes unpunished. Audience members should recognize that moral messages are often contained within all kinds of media messages.

Literate audience members should realize that interacting with media is a dynamic multidimensional process. This process involves interpreting media content using cognitive skills, emotions, an ability to assess artistic value, and an understanding of underlying moral themes. As W. J. Potter (1998) explained:

> The purpose of media literacy is to give us more control over interpretations. All media messages are interpretations. Journalists tell us their interpretations of what is important and who is important. Entertainment storytellers show us their interpretation of what it means to be human, to develop relationships, to engage in conflict, and to achieve happiness. Advertisers try to convince us that we have problems and that their products help us quickly overcome these prob-

lems. Also, as audience members we can construct our own interpretations of those messages. (p. 9)

INTERPRETING AND MISINTERPRETING MEDIA INFORMATION

Media in contemporary society are instrumental in providing us with information that exists beyond our daily experiences. Our system of language provides a mechanism by which we may communicate concepts that are shared by other members of our culture. These may represent concrete concepts such as house, car, and office or they may represent abstract ideas such as democracy or atheism. The essence of the concept is more important than characteristics such as size or color. Thus, the ability to communicate ideas among members of society is dependent on concepts in which there is an agreed upon shared meaning. Although these communication conventions may afford us a means of communicating, differences among people remain in their conceptions of social reality.

Drawing on cognitive theory, Lowery and DeFleur (1988) asserted that the time had come for researchers to begin considering the interrelationships between message contents and characteristics to develop a meanings paradigm. Such a paradigm would be concerned with the "relationship between internal and subjective representations of reality (meanings) and the influence that knowledge had on human conduct" (DeFleur & Ball-Rokeach, 1989, p. 234) to advance our understanding of how people construct social reality. The term commonly given to this is *constructionist theory* or *constructionism* (for detailed reviews reflecting historical evolution of constructionism, see Delia, 1976; 1977; Delia & O'Keefe, 1979). The central feature of the constructionism approach is an understanding of the ways in which people interact with media to construct social reality as opposed to how media affect or influence people (Gamson, 1988).

Because the media serve as a primary conduit through which ideas, attitudes, and beliefs flow, it is important to understand how we construct meaning as a result of encounters with these messages. As we saw earlier from the Ruby Clark incident, even professional communicators produce messages that may distort meaning and adversely influence message reception and interpretation. The problem is certainly not new. Greek philosopher Plato recognized this long ago in his well-known Allegory of the Cave (Plato, 1945).

In it, Plato described a scenario in which men were chained at the bottom of a cave with a long entrance that allowed only minimal light to enter. These men had been chained since childhood so that they could see only a wall in front of them. Behind them was a parapet with a parallel road behind it. Behind the wall that the men are facing is a fire burning that casts light on the it. People behind the parapet may hold up shapes and objects that cast shadows on the wall. The men may also hear movements or discussions behind them but they may interpret them only through the images cast on the wall in front of them. Plato theorized that such an arrangement would lead the men to construct reality that may be at odds with the true reality that exists behind them. Although the shadows enabled them to construct a reality, the constructed reality did not accurately represent the true reality of the events taking place behind them.

In many respects, media audiences confront the same problems as did the men in Plato's cave. We receive images, sounds, and other stimuli from the media. People working within certain logistical or organizational constraints produce communication messages. Complex information must be compressed to accommodate the structure of television newscasts. Personal agendas and biases may further influence how messages are constructed. The media routinely present messages that will attract audiences rather than those that may educate and enlighten. Finally, the receiver will interpret these messages based on individual predispositions, attitudes, and beliefs. Given this, there is no theoretical reason to believe that messages will be uniformly processed and interpreted by media audiences. In fact, the opposite assumption is much more logical.

THE CONSTRUCTIONISM MODEL

Although the term *constructionism* has most commonly been applied to negotiating meaning when people interact with media, many of the principles are adapted from interpersonal constructivist theory.

> Constuctivism defines communication as occurring when two or more people, with a mutually recognized intention to share, exchange messages. Moreover, the sharing process is goal driven. The organization and quality of the verbal and nonverbal behavior employed in that process can be seen fruitfully as a rationally organized means to some end. (Applegate & Sypher, 1988, p. 45)

Constructivism is concerned with communication that is intended to accomplish goals such as persuading, communicating ideas, or comforting people. The intent of the constructivist approach is to understand the influence of the communication process on social and cognitive development.

Constructionism in a media context departs from the minimal effects model both in theory and method. Gamson (1988) and Neuman, Just, and

Crigler (1992) identified the central features of the emerging constructionism model:

- Constructionism assumes the presence of an active audience that is actively working to construct meaning from multiple information sources. Studying this audience requires a shift from measuring attitudes to a focus on concepts rooted in cognitive psychology, such as schemas, cognitive maps, and scripts. Attitudes may remain relatively stable, whereas constructing meaning represents a dynamic and creative process. As such, the effect of a message on an individual may be quite minimal, but the processes associated with assimilating the message may be much more important. The emphasis, therefore, is on the creation of meaning rather than the degree to which communication may influence behavior.
- Constructionism considers differences in the types of messages presented. Producers and consumers find media messages salient for a wide range of reasons including prior knowledge, opinions, attitudes, beliefs, and cultural orientation. There is no reason to believe, therefore, that people will uniformly interact in the same ways with media messages. We must recognize that different kinds of issues presented in different ways will guide the ways in which they are interpreted.
- Constructionism is sensitive to differences in the information and entertainment media and distribution systems. Significant differences may exist in the ways that people interact with aural, visual, and textual content. The fundamental issue is how effectively these different media engage the audience and whether some of these differences are due to differences in cultural orientation.
- Constructionism is concerned with the development of common knowledge rather than public opinion. Neuman and his colleagues (1992) explained that the fundamental issue focuses on

  what people think and how they think about public issues rather than the narrowly defined valence-oriented "opinions" concerning an issue or a candidate. The use of "knowledge" rather than "opinion" emphasizes the need to organize information into meaningful structures. The phrase "common knowledge" emphasizes that the structuring and framing of information is not unique to each individual but aggregates into the cultural phenomenon of shared perspectives and issue frames. (p. 18; see chap. 5, this volume, for a discussion of framing)

- Constructionism considers the three-way interaction among the individual, the medium, and the message. The best way to study constructionism is to employ multiple methodologies ranging from experimental and content analysis to surveys, panel studies, and focus groups. There is also a shift away from survey instruments that employ precoded response categories to open-ended questions in an effort to draw on the processes that take place when people encounter media fare.

STUDYING CONSTRUCTIONISM

The study of constructionism begins with the assumption that truthful and objective messages do not exist. The messages that are produced by the media are interpretations that have been crafted to reflect the reality that the producer sees. Audience members then interpret these messages in the context of knowledge that is stored in schemas. New information may alter a schema, which in turn may influence the interpretation of future messages. This explains why people may change the way they think about the world as a result of encountering new information.

The first step in studying the construction of meaning is to identify an issue or set of topics that produce different kinds of belief systems in different people. Journalists typically report political issues using a specific set of ideas and symbols that aid in the construction of meaning. At the core of any news report is a central organizing frame that is employed to provide focus to the news report. Throughout the report, alternative perspectives are presented that are intended to provide context and coherence. Journalists would call this process of providing a set of alternative opinions on an issue *fairness and balance*.

Gamson and Modigliani (1989) illustrated the process of constructing meaning using the example of nuclear power. Nuclear power was initially portrayed through the media as an economical alternative to polluting power sources such as the burning of fossil fuels. However, nuclear accidents at Three Mile Island in Pennsylvania in 1979 and Chernobyl in the Ukraine in 1986 undermined public confidence in nuclear plants as clean, cheap, safe, and reliable power producers[1]

Few people in the 1970s or now have the scientific knowledge to assess the risks versus advantages of nuclear power. People depend on the media to learn new information and knowledge (Ball-Rokeach & DeFleur, 1976, 1982). This knowledge about various topics accumulates over time ultimately producing schemas. In the case of nuclear power,

---

[1]Ironically, *The China Syndrome,* a film released in 1978, depicting a nuclear accident, actually contained a line in which an actor speculated that a meltdown might produce a hole the "size of Pennsylvania."

information repeated about Three Mile Island, the Chernobyl accident, as well as opposition to nuclear power by the late baby doctor, Benjamin Spock, and nagging questions about where to store nuclear waste, contributed to the belief that nuclear power is bad. Framing by journalists may have influenced attitude and beliefs systems of audience members. As a result, a commodity that once had a promising future quickly fell into public disfavor.

USING MULTIPLE METHODOLOGIES

Studying something as complicated as how people construct knowledge about nuclear power may best be accomplished using multiple methodologies. The most commonly used approaches are content analysis, surveys, interviewing techniques, and experiments (Graber, 1988; Just et al., 1996; Kaid & Bystrom, 1998; Neuman, Just, & Crigler, 1992).[2] Multiple methodologies enable researchers to understand the dynamics that take place when attitudes, beliefs, and opinions are galvanized and meaning is constructed. The use of multiple methodologies is intended to produce results that contain a high degree of both internal and external validity.

- Content analysis enables researchers to investigate the symbols and messages that people encounter. As chapter 5 explains, journalists are trained to find ways to identify a problem and recommend a solution. Through the use of content analysis, it is possible to investigate the ways in which information was presented to the public. Depending on the issue, researchers may wish to focus on media messages including editorials, political cartoons, and standard news reports. Well-executed content analyses may produce a high degree of external validity if appropriate procedures are employed (see Krippendorff, 1980; Riffe, Lacy, & Fico, 1998).
- Interviews of citizens are used to assess what people know or believe about certain issues. The idea is to enter the actual living environment and allow people to express themselves in a natural and comfortable setting. The questions are open ended and recorded for transcription afterward. These sessions pro-

---

[2]Studies published during the 1990s exemplify the strengths of the multimethod approach. In their book, *Common Knowledge: News and the Construction of Political Meaning*, Neuman, Just, and Crigler (1992) utilized combinations of content analysis, depth interviews, surveys, and experiments to assess the construction of meaning of five issues during the middle 1980s. *Crosstalk: Citizens, Candidates and Media in a Presidential Campaign* (Just et al., 1996) employed similar strategies to interpret the construction of meaning during the 1992 campaign and election.

vide a sense of flow that may explain underlying thought processes. Interviewing strategies can provide a wealth of
information about the processes that take place when people
construct meaning. They have a high degree of external validity because they are conducted in naturalistic settings.
- Surveys are usually conducted over the telephone making it
possible to include a large and random sample of respondents.
The responses are coded using standardized categories that are
based on responses to open-ended questions. In some cases, researchers have also employed standard scaling procedures to
generate data. The ability to reach a large sample makes it possible to compare the opinion and attitude data to the results of
the content analysis. Surveys provide a moderate degree of external validity and "some internal validity from the
intercorrelated responses to questions about media usage,
knowledge of issues and personal characteristics" (Neuman,
Just, & Crigler, 1992, p. 27).
- Experiments enable researchers to investigate messages that
may produce changes in attitudes, opinions, beliefs, or knowledge. If subjects are randomly assigned to different media
stimuli and changes in belief systems take place, it is reasonable to infer that the communication produced an effect. The
unnatural experimental environment, however, may produce
attention levels that are higher than might be expected when
using media at home. Although internal validity for experiments is high, external validity is low due to the effects that
are attributed to the experimental environment.

CONCLUSION

Media institutions play an enormous role in our lives by offering products
that entertain and inform us and may contribute to the quality of our
lives. Increasingly, the process of using media involves a reciprocal relationship between the members of the audience and the offerings presented. This relationship requires an understanding of how people
negotiate meaning in the course of constructing social reality. Therefore,
it is an important and fertile research direction for mass communication
scholars and students.

The constructionism perspective advocates viewing communication
as a dynamic and constructive process. Media messages are capable of
producing effects on individuals and societies, but we must also understand the contribution of the audience members in the construction of social reality. Messages are not be uniformly understood and interpreted by
different audience members. Rather each audience member uses commu-

nication to build on knowledge stored in cognitive schemas in the course of interpreting messages and developing new knowledge.

Constructionism is best studied using a range of methodologies because a single methodology is incapable of analyzing texts, images, or sounds as they relate to the members of the audience. It is essential to study the communication produced by media institutions with a recognition that differences between individuals and social groups will influence how new information is processed and interpreted. As consumers of media, we should realize that our own psychological composition influences the meanings we construct from media messages. Media practitioners should learn to anticipate how the messages they produce will interact with different members of society in their construction of social reality.

II Constructing Media Messages

Part II evaluates how message structure and content interact to attract and maintain the attention of audiences. Media organizations vie for our attention and endeavor to keep us engaged with various products ranging from books and newspapers to television and the Internet. Literate media consumers should consider the ways in which large media corporations use cross-media marketing strategies to capture audiences. The chapters in this section also consider the principles associated with persuasive communication and analyze how professional communicators frame messages to help audiences construct meaning about the world around them. As is seen in these chapters, the media strive to play an instrumental role in attracting people's attention and shaping their attitudes, opinions, and beliefs.

3 Attracting and Maintaining the Attention of the Audience

SUMMARY

- Media have traditionally sought to attract the largest possible mass audience.
- The mass media include products intended for heterogeneous audiences as well as narrower audience segments.
- Contemporary media focus on attracting *segmented audiences.*
- The media establishment is composed of many large and wealthy multinational corporations.
- These media corporations seek to produce large profits.
- These media corporations are *vertically integrated* in which production, distribution, and presentation are centrally controlled.
- Media corporations employ *cross-marketing strategies* to attract and maintain audiences.
- New and developing forms of media products will continue to vie for the attention of the audience.

REDEFINING MASS COMMUNICATION

Mass communication has traditionally been defined as messages distributed by book publishers, Hollywood studios, record companies, newspapers, and television and radio stations to a large and heterogeneous audience. The ultimate goal of most media corporations is to maximize profits. To do so, they must attract a large number of readers, viewers, and listeners to generate economic returns in the form of advertising revenues. Alternatively, profits are garnered through the sale of media products such as compact disks (CDs and DVDs) and videotapes or to generate revenue in the form of the box office receipts. The Internet and the WWW have also become important sources of mediated information, entertainment, advertising, and commerce as the virtual shopping mall continues to evolve. Direct mail, telemarketing, and outdoor advertising may also be considered mass media, although they do not fit the classical definition (Folkerts, Lacy, & Davenport, 1998).

Media outlets competed for nearly $201 billion in advertising revenue in 1998 (see Box 3.1). Much more money exchanged hands if one considers revenues from books, cable subscriptions, videos, CDs, and other products that do not rely directly on advertising. Media industries have taken aggressive action to attract and retain audience members—especially boomers (45–55 years old), bloomers (25–44 years old), and tooners (25–44 years old with children who watch cartoons).

THE PROFIT MOTIVE

It may sound cynical or unfair to suggest that media organizations exist solely to return profits to stockholders. Aspiring Hollywood actors, actresses, script writers, and directors live on the edge of poverty hoping to produce high-quality films and establish their careers. Musicians and bands roam the country sleeping in their vans at truck stops while trying to break into the highly competitive record business. Journalists at local newspapers, television, and radio stations often work long hours for low wages because they see a civic duty in apprising the public of current events or because they simply enjoy the practice of journalism. Few members of the news media, however, get rich. In 1998, the median annual pay for an entry level television news employee was less than $18,000. Beginning radio journalists fared slightly better, earning nearly $21,000 annually (Stone, 2000).

Media companies may be committed to the creation of quality information and entertainment programs. Every year, the media produce films, books, and television programs that receive critical praise. The ultimate measure of success is the quarterly profits that are tied to box office receipts, circulation figures, Nielsen ratings, and other measures of audience size. Although many media companies strive to produce quality products, the name of the game is capturing and retaining the attention of the audience.

THE MASS AUDIENCE

The notion of the mass audience is about a century old. Early social philosophers argued that members of the audience would interpret the content of newspapers, magazines, and books in roughly the same way. The mass

Box 3.1. U.S. Advertising Expenditures—All Media

Media	1997(1) (millions)	% of total	1998(2) (millions)	% of total	% Change
Daily Newspapers					
Total	41,341	22.1	43,925	21.8	6.3
National	5,322	2.8	5,721	2.7	7.5
Retail	19,257	10.3	20,331	10.1	5.6
Classified	16,762	8.91	7,873	8.9	6.6
Magazines	9,821	5.2	10.518	5.2	7.1
Broadcast					
Television	36,893	19.73	9,173	19.4	6.2
Cable Television	7,237	3.9	8.301	4.1	14.7
Radio Total	13,491	7.21	5,073	7.5	11.7
Other					
Direct Mail	36,890	19.7	39,620	19.7	7.4
Yellow Pages	11,423	6.11	1,990	5.9	5.0

(Continues)

Box 3.1. (Continued)

Media	1997(1) (millions)	% of total	1998(2) (millions)	% of total	% Change
Miscellaneous (3)	23,940	12.8	25,769	12.8	7.6
Business Papers	4,109	2.2	4,232	2.1	3.0
Outdoor	1,455	0.8	1,576	0.8	8.3
Internet	600	0.3	1,050	0.5	75
Total—National	110,538	59.0	119,285	59.3	7.9
Total—Local	76,662	41.0	81,942	40.7	6.9
TOTAL—All Media	$187,299	100.0	201,227	100	7.5

(1) Revised data.

(2) Preliminary data.

(3) Includes weeklies, shoppers, pennysavers, bus, and cinema advertising.

Estimates include all costs: time and talent, space, and production

Note. U.S. Advertising Expenditures is a comparative chart indicating both the amount of advertising expenditures (in millions of dollars) brought in by each of the various media as well as the percentage of total ad dollars by each medium. The Newspaper Association of America (for newspapers) and McCann-Erickson Worldwide (all other media) supplied the data for this chart. Used with permission.

audience is most often viewed as heterogeneous collection of individuals who are separate from one another and behave independently. The members of this audience are anonymous to the messages producer. Little interaction takes place among the people that make up the mass audience, and the messages are presumed to have a uniform influence of each member. Interpreting Blumer (1946), W. J. Potter (1998) explained that this conceptualization of the audience assumes the mass is "very loosely organized and is not able to act with the concertedness or unity that marks a crowd. The mass is not organized as a social unit and does not adhere to any set of established social rules or conventions" (p. 244).

This conceptualization of the mass audience paralleled the rise of the magic bullet theory (also known as the hypodermic needle perspective), in which messages were assumed to reach everyone in roughly the same way and that each person processed the messages in a similar fashion. Observers pointed out that Adolph Hitler effectively utilized the radio spectrum to mobilize support in Germany. The 1939 broadcast of "War of the Worlds" presented by Orson Welles is also cited as an example of the media's ability to influence the behavior of the mass audience. Many listeners actually believed that the earth had been invaded by Martians and panicked.

By the 1950s, however, the idea of the mass audience as originally conceived was beginning to fade. Friedson (1953) criticized this perspective by arguing that going to the movies, listening to the radio, and watching television included significant interpersonal interaction. Media content often sparks discussions and debates before, during, and after exposure. Furthermore, the audience consciously decides which medium or programming it will use. Therefore, the mass audience is actually a highly developed social order in which networks of individuals continually move between various media options and interact with others about what they have read, heard, or seen.

Webster and Phalen (1997) reconceptualized the idea of the mass audience as a social unit in which people are bound together by something that attracts their attention. This social group forms when

> a multitude of individuals select something as the focus of their interest. This art of choice making defines individual membership in the mass and, in the aggregate, makes the mass a powerful social force. (Webster & Phalen, 1997, p. 7)

To accommodate this growing populace, the producers will meet audience demand for specific genres and content. As such, the audience serves as judge and jury of what will survive in the media environment.

Webster and Phalen (1997) contended that, despite slippage in the ratings, broadcast television networks still attract millions of viewers each night during primetime hours–making the mass audience the dominant model. These viewers are geographically, demographically, and socioeconomically quite diverse. Cable networks attract considerably smaller audiences who are also geographically spread out, but many of these audience members share many demographic or socioeconomic traits. Cable networks, which specialize in slicing away part of the overall mass audience by providing specialized programming that may appeal to certain audience segments, still capture large audiences. According to this perspective, the erosion of the network audience to cable does not justify redefining the media audience.

THE SEGMENTED AUDIENCE

Some have argued, however, that the notion of the mass audience is outmoded because the new media environment offers so many more media products than in the past. Until the mid-1980s, for example, television was dominated by the three main networks, ABC, CBS, and NBC, which attracted a mass audience garnering more than 90% of all viewers. During the 1990s, with the rapid proliferation of cable networks, pay-per-view, Fox, WB, and UPN, the combined ratings of the big three networks slipped to less than 50%. This, together with the phenomenal growth of video stores, changes in radio formats, multiscreen theaters, the advent of CDs, and of course the Internet, led many to proclaim that the age of the mass audience had come to an end. The age of the segmented audience, enabling people to program their own media environment, had arrived.

In the contemporary media environment, identifying audience segments has become an increasingly sophisticated undertaking. Segmenting the audience makes sense from both a practical and economic standpoint (Wicks, 1989a). Daily newspapers and local radio stations have geographical boundaries that dictate the membership of the segments. With respect to radio, however, the format offered attracts a narrower segment of the overall audience. The daily newspaper, by contrast, attracts as many readers as possible from the segment (Wicks, 1989b).

Media outlets also segment audiences based on demographic variables such as gender, ethnicity, age, income, and education. In a segmented media environment, broadcast and cable networks provide a dizzying array of outstanding programs designed to educate, entertain, and enlighten. Conversely, E!, the cable entertainment network, routinely employs gimmicks intended to engage viewers by appealing to their prurient tastes. Viewers of *The Howard Stern Show* witnessed the bizarre spectacle of seemingly inebriated exotic dancers, recruited from go-go bars in New York's Times Square district, wiggling, giggling, and squirming as the talk show host tickled them. Throughout the ordeal, the dancers were confined in a contraption Stern called the *laughing stocks*. Alternatively, audiences may vicariously experience the thrill of being in a fistfight by tuning into *The Jerry Springer Show*. Programs featuring profanity, violence, and sexism have large constituencies.

Media executives are primarily interested in boosting ratings, increasing box office sales, or selling more books. The implication is that they want audience members to pay attention exclusively to their products. If the media can successfully attract the attention of the audience and then maintain high levels of interest, the likelihood increases that the audience will stay longer and return again in the future. As such, getting the attention of the audience is a crucial first step in maintaining an audience.

Attention to media is maintained by manipulating the content and structure of the messages produced (Geiger & Newhagen, 1993; Geiger & Reeves, 1993a, 1993b). Structural devices such as eerie music in a thrilling movie cue the audience to pay attention because danger lurks. Short clips prior to a commercial promoting upcoming news items warn the audience to *stay tuned*. The content is intended to attract audience members by promising information and entertainment or by offering them the opportunity to adjust their emotional state. Situation comedies, for example, produce joy and laughter, whereas a professional football games offers the thrill of combatants in action.

The objective of attracting the audience's attention is to find the right combination of content and structure that attracts and engages enough people to make the media programming profitable. In certain circumstances (e.g., Super Bowls, presidential debates, and even interviews with prominent personalities such as Monica Lewinsky), programs continue to produce large and heterogeneous audiences. Increasingly, these programs with broad-based appeal are a departure from the norm. The trend toward producing programming with ever-narrower audience segments is clear.

MEDIA AS BIG BUSINESS

From an economic standpoint, media corporations have never had more people using their products. If you spend a day at a theme park followed by a movie, a trip to Blockbuster, and watching MTV in the evening, you may have spent the entire day engaged with Viacom International products. Other large media concerns like ABC/Disney are just as efficient at attracting the attention of the audience. As such, declining network ratings may not be the nail in the coffin if these corporations attract the attention of the audience in other ways. If ABC cannot entice you to watch television, they may be able to persuade you to visit Disney World.

The giant media companies began forming in the 1980s and continued throughout the 1990s. The Disney merger with Capital Cities/ABC in 1995 produced a media empire that includes TV stations, TV networks, magazines, newspapers, and theme parks including Disneyland and Disney World. Disney was already in the book publishing, film production, and video businesses prior to the merger. Enormous media corporations try to enhance their economic position by expanding their holdings and offering more media products to attract even larger audiences. Increasingly, this is accomplished through mergers and acquisitions that produce international media concerns with holdings in a vast range of media and allied enterprises.

PUBLISHING HOUSES, MOVIE STUDIOS, AND CABLE NETWORKS

At first glance, books, films, and cable networks may appear to be odd bedfellows. However, they have much in common both in terms of their ability to attract segmented (i.e., specialized or narrow) audiences and with respect to their economic role within media corporations.

Books are the oldest forms of written mass communication dating back to the 1400s, when the printing press was invented. Films date back to the 1800s, but became more sophisticated with the addition of sound and color in the 20th century. Unlike television and radio, books and films may be produced for relatively narrow segments of the overall audience. For example, younger people tend to go to the movies more than older people do. More educated people read more books.

Unlike media, which rely heavily on advertising, consumers pay directly to acquire books, videotapes, and DVD's and to view films. Subscribers of pay cable networks such as ShowTime or HBO also pay for the films and specials they receive through subscription fees. Cable networks such as MTV and Nickelodeon are relatively inexpensive and usually come bundled as part of an overall cable or satellite package. However, like books and movies, they cater to fairly narrow audience segments. In short, these media are probably more alike than different. It should come as little surprise then that the largest media corporations own publishing companies, Hollywood studios, and cable networks.

Book publishing is no longer a cottage industry in which small publishing houses provide writers with a forum for their work. Although many university presses and some small publishing houses continue to flourish, the book industry of today is dominated by four multinational firms that own and operate everything from wax museums and theme parks to cable networks and film studios. Books in today's media environment invite users to interact through the use of CD-ROMs. E-books, unveiled in 1998, enable consumers to download books at home. Publishers are forming alliances with other specialized media such as cable networks to establish product awareness and stimulate sales.

At first glance, the book industry may appear to be in a bit of a rut. Critics lament that "nobody reads anymore" because television stole the audience or people are too busy surfing the Internet to sit down and read a book. Hard data appear to bear this out. Estimates released by the Association of American Publishers (AAP) show only a 2.4% increase in book sales in 1997 to $21.28 billion. The increase was below the 4.2% gain reported in 1996 and was also less than the 4.7% compounded annual growth rate recorded between 1992 and 1997. The only real bright spots in 1997 were the 13% gains for the elementary/high school (Elhi) category and the 7.4% increase for higher education books. AAP President Pat Schroeder explained that disappointing trade sales "reflect a period of transition for the industry as publishing houses seek new ways to deal with old problems such as returns" (Milliot, 1998).

Despite reports of less than stellar earnings during the latter half of the 1990s, the book industry is alive and thriving. Fifty years ago, book publishing was a relatively small business producing comparatively few books for an "elite readership whose access to bookstores was limited by geography" (Baker, 1994, p. 36). Between 1947 to 1997, annual sales volumes increased from $435 million to more than $21 billion. More than 50,000 titles are now published each year. Today, the book industry is experimenting with provocative new products intended to stimulate sales and spark interest anew in publishing.

PERSONALIZED MEDIA IN A GLOBAL COMMUNICATIONS ENVIRONMENT

In 1996, seven publishing houses dominated the industry. As a consequence of buyouts by large multinational media companies, the number dwindled to four by 1998. Germany's Bertelsmann AG owns Random House, Doubleday Dell, Bantam, and Knopf. The company has 57,000 employees involved in more than 300 individual companies, which provide information, education, and entertainment in 50 countries. It owns book clubs, literary and scientific publishing companies, daily newspapers, consumer magazines, trade journals, radio and television stations, online services, printing shops, and service companies as well as other technical firms. The Bertelsmann Music Group owns the Arista, RCA, and Windham Hill record labels. Sales in 1996 and 1997 amounted to about $14 billion. Jointly with America Online, Bertelsmann also owns Compuserve.

British media conglomerate Pearson PL, the owner of the *Financial Times,* which is published in 12 locations around the globe, owns Penguin USA, Addison Wesley Longman, and Putnam Berkley. In November 1998, Pearson paid $4.6 billion to acquire the Simon & Schuster education, reference, and business and professional divisions, which include Prentice-Hall and Allyn & Bacon Publishers. The conglomerate also owns Pearson Television, the world's largest television production company, with more than 150 programs currently in production in 30 countries around the world and library sales to more than 100 others with an annual turnover well in excess of £200 million.

Viacom International, which announced plans to merge with CBS in September 1999, owns MTV networks, Nickelodeon, Paramount's film and television units, the Blockbuster Entertainment video rental chain, theme parks, and a dozen television stations. Viacom and CBS shareholders approved the $47.9 billion acquisition of CBS, the largest-ever purchase of a media company. The merger was expected to be complete at the end of the first quarter or early in the second quarter of 2000. Viacom retained the Simon & Schuster imprint and its mass-market affiliate, Pocket Books, for fiction and nonfiction offerings. It also owns Scribner, one of America's oldest trade publishers, and Simon & Schuster Interactive, which spearheads the company's expanding efforts in digital multimedia. Viacom also owns The Free Press, which specializes in social and political commentary, and Simon & Schuster's Children's Publishing Division. Viacom's media revenues for 1997 were reported to be nearly $2.7 billion.

Rupert Murdochs' News Corporation owns HarperCollins publishing. The Australian-turned-American media mogul owns controlling interest of Fox Home Entertainment, Fox Interactive, Fox Movies, Fox Studios, *TV Guide*, the *New York Post*, the Family Channel, and 22 television stations reaching a sizable percent of all American homes as well as many other media enterprises. Media revenues for 1997 were reported to be in excess of $5.5 billion—an increase of more than 23% from 1996.

In 1999, the Time Warner media empire included Warner Books, Little, Brown, CNN, the WB television network, HBO, Comedy Central, Atlantic Records, Elektra, East West Records, *People, Time, Fortune, Sports Illustrated, DC Comics*, Six Flags Theme Parks, Atari Games, *World Championship Wrestling,* and Castle Rock Pictures to name but a few. Time Warner finished at the top of the list of media companies in 1997 with $13.3 billion in revenues—up 12% from 1996 and nearly doubling the $6.9 billion volume of the runner up, ABC/Disney.

On January 10, 2000, America Online, Inc. and Time Warner announced the largest corporate merger in history, creating a fully integrated media and communications company worth $350 billion. Under the new name of AOL Time Warner Inc., the media giant planned to deliver information, entertainment, and communications services across rapidly converging media distribution systems and the Internet. The merger combined Time Warner's huge inventory of entertainment and news offering and its technologically advanced delivery systems with America Online's extensive Internet franchises including the consumer online brands, cyberspace community, and e-commerce capabilities[1]

PARTNERSHIPS AND CROSS-MEDIA MARKETING STRATEGIES

The book industry is in an excellent position to develop partnerships with other media such as cable networks and program producers to cross-promote various media products. Many of the partnership were reached through traditional licensing agreements, whereas others involve sister companies. Pocket Books introduced a Comedy Central South Park book. Viacom, the owner of Pocket Books when the deal was struck, owns Comedy Central jointly with AOL Time Warner Entertainment. Through book publishing, cable networks are creating awareness and promoting their image by developing relationships with other media. Publishers stand to benefit from these arrangements by gaining marketing clout, brand recognition, editorial and graphic content, and incremental distribution (Raugust, 1998).

A prime candidate for partnerships between cable networks and publishing is in the youth sector. In 1997, sales of children's paperbacks slumped nearly 19% to $470 million. AAP President Schroeder said that new initiatives aimed at encouraging adults to read to children will translate into an upswing in children's sales. For example, *Rugrats* and *Blue's Clues* appear on Viacom-owned Nickelodeon during the day. Under the Nickelodeon imprint, Simon & Schuster distributes the books to major retailers such as Barnes & Noble. More than 20 million units of *Rugrats* and *Blue's Clues* were shipped to retailers during a 15-month period between 1997 and 1998 (Raugust, 1998).

Companies have also begun to promote children's books and programming through the presentation of live touring theatrical repertoires. In October 1999, Blue's Clues kicked off a 10- month, 38-city national tour that included a 2-week run at Radio City Music Hall in New York, five shows at the Universal Amphitheater in Los Angeles, and a week-long run at the National Theater in Washington, DC. The tour, entitled "Blue's Clues LIVE!" is intended to interactively engage preschool children. The shows, which feature puppets and costumed actors and actresses, target

---

[1]AOL Time-Warner properties include America Online, CompuServe, Netscape, ICQ, AOL MovieFone, AOL Instant Messenger, Digital City, HBO, CNN, TNT, Cartoon Network, Time, People, Sports Illustrated, Warner Music, Warner Bros., The WB, Looney Tunes, and Time Warner Cable.

children between the ages of 2 and 7. Gateway Computers, Sears Portrait Studio, and Teddy Grahams produced by RJR-Nabisco are sponsoring the concert tour.

ELECTRONIC PUBLISHING

Book publishers are vigorously pressing for new electronic forms of multimedia products that allow consumers to interact with books through computer terminals. Publishers of educational texts benefited in recent years as strong state and local economies accelerated textbook sales and college enrollment have remained stable. To promote growth in the elementary, high school, and college sectors, publishing houses are introducing educational CD-ROMs either bundled with textbooks or as stand-alone products. The CD-ROMs include audio and video clips and interactive links to related homepages on the Web (see Box 3.2). Publishing houses also sell CD-ROMs for relaxation and entertainment pur-

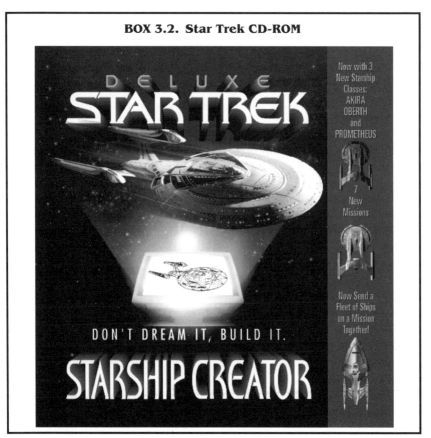

BOX 3.2. Star Trek CD-ROM

poses. For devout "trekkies," Simon & Schuster offer the Star Trek Emissary Gift Set and the *Star Trek Encyclopedia* (interactive edition), which allow users to write their own entries, articles, or fiction about Star Trek and add hyperlinks.

ELECTRONIC BOOKS

The newest direction for book publishing is electronic books known as *E-books*. Having debuted in science fiction films in the 1940s, the electronic book has appeared in episodes of *Star Trek* and in the film *Alien Resurrection*. The E-books, introduced in late 1998, weigh less than three pounds, have clear and readable screens, and can hold many volumes simultaneously. Buying an electronic book through NuvoMedia is similar to purchasing one through an online bookstore like Amazon.com. Instead of having a hard copy sent to you, an electronic version is downloaded either directly into the E-book or into a computer where it may be stored.

Three competitors first introduced the E-books by offering reference texts and journals, followed by textbooks for the educational market. The product sold by Everybook Inc., unveiled in the summer of 2000 with a two-screen color reader, cost $1,600. Softbook Press offers a device about the size of a thick 8 1/2-by-11-inch notebook for $299, and customers must also agree to buy $10 to $20 books or other reading material every month from SoftBook's online store for 2 years (Vinzant, 1998). NuvoMedia Inc. markets a paperback device dubbed the *Rocket e-book* for $199. Softbook and NuvoMedia, both California firms, were acquired by Gemstar International Group in January 2000. Gemstar is a provider of electronic guide services that enable viewers of cable and satellite television to view program information. Box 3.3 illustrates differences in electronic book formats.

BOX 3.3. The E-Books

Photos courtesy of NuvoMedia, Inc. and Everybook Inc. Used with permission.

Publishing houses are rushing to embrace the E-book. Michael Lynton, chairman of Penguin Publishing, and Jonathan Guttenberg, vice president for new media at Bantam Doubleday Dell, believe that the public will be quick to accept the E-book (Vinzant, 1998). NuvoMedia's approach to designing E-books appears particularly suited to the publishing industry because it has attracted financial backing from Bertelsmann Ventures and Barnes & Noble.

In sum, publishing houses, which are parts of large multinational conglomerates, are seeking new and innovative ways to attract and retain audiences. Although books remain the core product base, partnerships with allied concerns such as cable networks enable publishers to develop new markets and reinforce visibility of products that appear on bookstore shelves. CD ROMs will continue to play an important role in the educational and entertainment sectors of the publishing industry. E-books appear to be an important new direction for major publishing houses.

SELLING BOOKS, FILMS, AND VIDEOS

The retail sector of the book industry is no less concentrated than the publishing side of the business. A trip to a modern bookstore has little in common with a visit to the dimly lit, dusty shops that we nostalgically remember. The new 30- to 40-thousand square foot stores create a sense of place where consumers can browse in a comfortable environment, sip on cappuccino, nibble on a croissant, or lounge in comfortable couches and chairs. Four firms—Barnes & Noble, Borders Group, Books-A-Million, and Crown Books—dot the bookstore landscape. Independent retailers accounted for 17% of U.S. book sales last year—down from 32.5% 1991 according to New York-based Book Industry Study Group. The major chains claimed more than 25% of book sales, and online book sales could grow to an estimated 25% by 2004 (Alexander, 1999). Profits for the nation's four largest chains rose more than 14% in 1997 to nearly $5.7 billion.

Video stores did not enjoy the same prosperity as bookstores in the late 1990s. Viacom's Blockbuster chain, for example, was in financial trouble. However, by the summer of 1998, Blockbuster was again on firm financial ground. The turnaround was the result of a creative new sales strategy. First, Viacom entered into joint production of *Titanic*—the largest grossing film of all time—with Rupert Murdoch's News Corp. In addition, Viacom's chairman Sumner Redstone (who is the 15th wealthiest individual in the nation, with personal assets totaling $6.4 billion, according to *Forbes Magazine*) recognized that the problem plaguing video stores had to do with cash outlays for tape purchases. The studios charged as much as $65 a copy for new releases, which limited the number that a store could afford to acquire. Consumers, frustrated by their inability to obtain a recent release, began to purchase their own copies for as little as $10 or simply wait for the film on pay-per-view, HBO, or on network television.

To reverse the trend, Viacom's Redstone approached Disney Chairman Michael Eisner with a new idea on how to market video. The approach involved a partnership between Blockbuster and the Disney studios in which the videos are provided at a cost of about $7 to $8 each—or about one tenth of the old price. In return, the studio would receive between 30% and 40% of the rental charges until the revenue stream dwindled. Then Blockbuster would be free to sell the video to recoup the initial cost. Other studios including Warner have signed onto the new agreement.

Besides new partnerships aimed at maintaining a steady stream of customers into video stores, Viacom is busy creating new cable outlets for the inventory of programming it owns. TV Land, which blends a nostalgic look at classic programming like *Gunsmoke, Hogan's Heroes,* and the *Ed Sullivan Show,* was the country's fastest growing new cable channel in 1998—attracting 30 million subscribers in 2 years. Cable programmers also welcomed the arrival of Noggin, a network that was jointly developed by Viacom and the Children's Television Workshop, which produces *Sesame Street.*

The reach of international media conglomerates goes well beyond U.S. borders. Viacom-owned MTV is seen in more than 86 million Asian homes on regional services such as MTV Mandarin, which appears in China and Taiwan, MTV India, and MTV Asian for Indonesia, Thailand, and the Philippines. In 1998, MTV launched a service for 10 million households in Moscow and St. Petersburg, representing the first time Western television has been produced for a Russian market. MTV now contributes a reported $636 million in cash flow to Viacom or a 41% return on its $1.5 billion revenues.

In summary, media corporations are finding creative new ways to attract national and global audiences. The future would seem to suggest a greater interplay between publishers and retailers of books, E-books, CD-ROMs, films, and videotapes. More cross-media marketing between cable networks and these related media industries is expected in the future.

NEWSPAPERS, RADIO, AND TELEVISION

Unlike books, films, or cable networks, which often appeal to specialized audience segments, television and newspapers are almost always produced to attract a broad spectrum of viewers and listeners. Radio stations typically target audience segments based on demographic variables.

The number of daily newspapers declined from 1,509 in 1997 to 1,489 in 1998. Newspaper circulation has declined since 1970, when readership approached 78 million. By 1998, the number of daily readers was down to less than 59 million despite a much larger population. In the 1920s, more than 40% of all American cities had competing newspapers. Today only about a dozen out of the more than 1,500 papers compete with other papers that are separately owned and operated in the same city. On the surface, the scenario appears quite grim for newspapers.

As with the book publishing industry, the picture is greatly exaggerated. About three quarters of all newspapers are parts of chains or groups. The largest of these, Gannett Inc., is a worldwide media conglomerate operating in 45 U.S. states, the District of Columbia, Guam, Great Britain, Germany, and Hong Kong. The company's 84 daily newspapers have a combined paid circulation of more than 6.7 million readers including *USA Today*, the nation's second largest selling daily newspaper. With a circulation of approximately 2 million, *USA Today* is now available in 60 countries worldwide. Gannett also owns *USA Weekend*, a weekly magazine with a circulation of more than 21 million delivered in 534 Gannett and non-Gannett newspapers. Gannett owns 21 television stations covering 17% of the United States and owns cable systems in major American cities. The company also owns the Gannett News Service and other companies that specialize in direct marketing and advertising.

Gannett, although the largest, is similar to many other chains. Thomson Newspapers owns 62 papers, Hollinger International owns 54, MediaNews Group owns 34, and Knight-Ridder owns 33. The top 20 newspaper companies own 488 papers, and the trend toward consolidation continues each year. Advertising revenues continue to increase, approaching $44 billion in 1998, despite somewhat lethargic readership numbers. On the magazine side of the industry, there were 10,466 consumer magazines and thousands of specialty magazines for businesses and trade associations in 1996. In short, newspapers and magazines appear to be financially healthy.

More than 12,000 radio stations presented programming in the United States in 1997. More than 1,500 full-power television stations were licensed, of which 1,150 were commercial and 365 were educational in nature. In addition, more than 1,600 low-power broadcast stations provided programming within a limited area.

Television continues to be the most used of the media industries, with more than 98% of all American homes owning a color set. Thirty-eight percent of the households have two sets, and nearly one third of all households have three sets. In the average household, a set is turned on for more than 7 hours and the average person watches nearly three and one half hours daily. People over the age of 55 use television the most, averaging more than 5 hours a day (Nielsen Media Research, 1995).

WINDS OF CHANGE AND THE *TELECOMMUNICATIONS ACT OF 1996*

The 1980s and 1990s were a pivotal period not only for television, but also for electronic media industries generally. The stage was set in the 1980s when President Ronald Reagan appointed Mark Fowler to serve as the Chairman of the Federal Communication Commission (FCC). Fowler advocated free market competition for broadcasters, pushing aside proceedings on the regulation of children's programming and advertising. Instead, he chose to focus on eliminating regulatory underbrush about which broadcasters had long complained. The time-consuming license renewal process was scrapped in favor of a simple postcard application in 1984. In essence, broadcasters were no longer required to present evidence of meeting community needs (Head, Sterling, & Schofield, 1994).

Ownership rules also changed in 1985, raising group ownership caps from 7 to 12 stations. In 1987, the FCC also eliminated the Fairness Doctrine, which had enabled citizens free access to the spectrum to refute political opinions. The move gave rise to partisan programming such as *The Rush Limbaugh Show* and may have propelled the development of radio/cable talk shows such as *The Howard Stern Show*. Slackening of content rules gave broadcasters more freedom to decide what their stations may carry. Programs that would have pushed the limits of network censorship decency a decade ago are now commonplace.

With the passage of the Telecommunications Act of 1996, a single broadcast group can now own stations covering up to 35% of the national audience. As a result, large media corporations are purchasing more and more stations. The Act also eliminated the barriers that prevented telephone companies from entering the programming arena to compete against broadcast and cable networks. Another important development was the sunset of the Financial Interest and Syndication (Fin–Syn) rules in 1996. These rules once prevented broadcast networks from producing much of their own programming in an effort to ensure a diversity of voices in the media marketplace. The elimination of these rules opens up an entirely new avenue for broadcast networks to generate revenues by entering the domestic and international production and syndication markets.

Changes in regulation resulting from the Telecommunications Act of 1996 have fueled a consolidation that even surprises industry experts, leading some to contend that the ranks of television station owners have become "a shockingly exclusive club" (Lafayette, 1998). Pioneers of the airwaves sold out to megacorporations in the late 1990s as these conglomerates bulked up to provide leverage against networks, syndicators, and advertisers through their ability to wield clout. In May 1994, there were 658 owners of full-power television stations in the United States. By the summer of 1998, the number had dwindled to 425, but this figure included PBS stations, which are often licensed to universities. Among the four largest commercial networks (ABC, CBS, Fox, and NBC), the number of station owners declined from 290 to 189—or a drop of 35%. Industry experts predict that the number could shrink to about 100 within a few years. If Congress decides to let companies own more than one station per market, consolidation will occur even sooner.

Group owners contend that they are well suited to serve the communities in which they operate. They assert that deeper pockets enable multistation groups to invest in new technology as well as expensive programming such as news and high-quality syndicated shows. Group size also has its advantages in negotiating terms for syndicated programs for large companies like Hicks, Muse, Tate and Furst, and Hearst–Argyle Television. The locally owned mom-and-pop station, however, has no such leverage. This means that such a station may pay as much for a second-tier program as a group pays for a syndicated episode of *Seinfeld* or *Home Improvement*. From a business perspective, bigger is better because larger groups are able to operate more efficiently. Large groups also avoid redundancy in staff needed to negotiate advertising schedules, syndicated program acquisition, and general oversight of the broadcast stations. This leads to more streamlined management and greater economies of scale. Thus, it is increasingly difficult for locally owned stations to remain profitable. As a result, they are more likely to sell out to large media conglomerates.

REGULATORY CHANGES ON THE HORIZON

ABC, CBS, Fox, and NBC would like the FCC to lift the ceiling that limits broadcasters from owning stations reaching more than 35% of the nation's viewing households. The National Cable Television Association has petitioned the FCC to allow broadcasters to own cable systems in markets where it operates stations. Finally, various broadcasting and newspaper companies have asked the FCC to lift the cross-ownership ban that stops a broadcaster from owning a daily newspaper in the same market. The current ban exempts cross-ownerships if the situation existed before the rule did.

Deregulation in the 1980s and 1990s was predicated on loosening rules because so many outlets for expression existed that increased diversity in the marketplace. However, the 1990s were a time of considerable consolidation in broadcasting. The ability of any individual or firm to develop and maintain a Web site is far from equivalent to the power derived from owning a newspaper, television, and radio station. The problem is compounded if these media properties are located with the same market. The television networks own stations in virtually every large city in the nation and some own stations in smaller cities. Owners of stations and cable operations in the same city would have little incentive to present programming of a competitor if the cable-broadcast ban were lifted.

At first glance, it appears that diversity exists within the cable network industry. Going beyond Liberty Media, AOL Time Warner, Fox, Disney, CBS-Viacom, and NBC, few exist. Further, Liberty's TCI and AOL Time Warner own an enormous number of cable operators of cable systems. Only four major broadcast networks exist, and each of them owns local stations. For example, CBS owns 14 television stations and 155 radio stations in 33 markets. Groups like Capstar own hundreds of broadcast stations around the nation. For better or worse, deregulation has helped those who have to have even more.

THE INTERNET AND THE WORLD WIDE WEB

The Internet, a faint glimmer just a decade ago, now has a profound impact on how audience members allocate their time. Eighteen- to 35-year-olds, who used to spend about 4 hours a night watching television, are now devoting 1 of those hours to the Internet (*Technology Forecast,* 1997). By 1997, more than 50 million people worldwide used the Internet with major service providers reporting as much as a 15% increase monthly in subscriptions.

Advertisers are allocating more of their revenues to the Internet. Technologies continue to merge as consumers using basic Internet operations such as e-mail or the WWW can do so with inexpensive laptop computers. Hand-held computers now provide access to the Internet. Therefore, mass communication in the late 1990s denoted a convergence between traditional media such as television and radio with newer media such as cable, the Internet, and cellular telephones. These communication systems also enabled people to run businesses from the home and to supervise, monitor, and manage business operations from virtually any location.

CONCLUSION

The trend concerning media organizations is unmistakable. Consolidation will continue both within sectors such as broadcast station ownership and across the media as a whole. Companies like AOL Time Warner, with net revenues of $13,270 billion in 1997 will continue to grow larger through mergers and acquisitions. ABC/Disney, with revenues of $6,898 billion in 1997, now owns newspapers, magazines, television and radio stations, cable operations, and theme parks. Gannett, the seventh largest media empire with 1997 revenues of $4,498 billion, grew large through the acquisition of newspapers, but now owns radio and television stations, cable operations, and other media enterprises.

The fact that large media corporations continue to grow is indisputable and troubling to many. However, one must recognize that such a pattern is part of a global trend, as demonstrated by the British media giant Pearson and the German company Bertelsmann. To prosper, these domestic and international media firms will continue to produce media products to satisfy the ever-increasing demands of the audience. We can expect to see greater coordination between allied media industries to produce an appetite for media among us—those who consume it.

4 Persuading the Media Audience

SUMMARY

- Many media messages are expressly designed to persuade people to adopt a specific perspective or behavior.
- People utilize *selective processes* when they interact with media. These processes include selective exposure, selective attention, selective perception, and selective interpretation.
- *Attention* is the amount of mental effort that an individual invests to consider an idea or object.
- Attitude change may occur by way of the *central* or *peripheral* routes.
- Factors that influence *attitude change* leading to persuasion include:

  1. characteristics of the *source*;
  2. *context* of the message and how difficult it is to understand;
  3. how *frequently* a message is presented through media channels;
  4. the *number of arguments* conveyed and the context through which they are presented;
  5. the overall message contents' *salience*;
  6. the degree to which messages *involve* the audience; and
  7. the *mode* through which a message is presented.

- Messages that produce *affective* or emotional responses may influence attitude change.
- Messages that attract attention and produce comprehension lead to learning and attitude change.
- Effective communication campaigns endure over time.
- Effective communication campaigns target audience segments.

PERSUADING THE AUDIENCE

In this chapter, we look at strategically orchestrated persuasive media messages that are produced to encourage people to behave in a certain way or adopt a point of view. To sell products, advertisers use persuasive communication. Candidates for political office use these strategies to convince people to vote for them. Public service campaigns (PSAs) urge people to adopt healthy behaviors or socially responsible behaviors. In this chapter, we consider how professional communicators construct messages that are intended to persuade the audience. To do so, strategies employed in PSAs are analyzed and theories associated with constructing messages that influence the behavior of the audience members are evaluated. These techniques are similar to those used to persuade consumers to purchase a product or vote for a candidate.

COMMUNICATION CAMPAIGNS

Communication campaigns are deliberately created to persuade people to do something such as purchase a product, vote for a candidate, prevent crime, or change behavior. The term *campaign* comes from military parlance and refers to a coordinated effort to achieve a desired goal such as capturing territory from the enemy (Wells, Burnett, & Moriarity, 1995).

Communication campaigns are often viewed as using communication in an organized way to bring about change among a relatively large target audience during a prescribed time period (Jeffries, 1997; Rogers & Storey, 1987). The strategies associated with advertising, political, and public communication campaigns are similar because each relies on the construction of messages that are intended to persuade members of the audience. The message must also be placed where it will be seen, read, or heard by the appropriate target segment(s). It must also be presented frequently enough and contain information that will ultimately produce the desired outcome.

Communication campaigns work best when they focus on specialized segments rather than the overall audience. This is because messages that fit logically with certain demographic or psychographic segments may miss the mark with other audience segments. Demographic variables typically include age, gender, occupation, race, and so on. Alternatively, demographic data may describe people based on membership within a group (e.g., people ages 35–54) or as part of logical groupings such as baby boomers. Psychographic categories are grouped according to psychological variables that define the psychological profile of the audience segment. They most often include activities, attitudes, needs, values, personality traits, decision processes, and purchase behavior (Wells, Burnett, & Moriarity, 1995).

A campaign to curtail drunk driving might be targeted toward males between the ages of 16 and 25 because surveys reveal that they are quite likely to engage in heavy drinking (Atkin & Freimuth, 1989). Although this constituency represents only 5% of the population, the risk is high that they will be responsible for significant harm to themselves, their passengers, or other motorists and pedestrians. Furthermore, 5% represents nearly 15 million drivers, making this a very large and important audience segment. Hence, the campaign designed for this segment must capture their attention and then get them to consider the message in a deliberate and reasoned way. The communication strategy developed would differ considerably if the target audience were defined as working professionals.

BALANCE AND DISSONANCE THEORY

Many of the contemporary models of persuasion can be traced to theorizing that began in the 1920s and continued through the 1950s (Hovland, Janis, & Kelley, 1953; Lasswell, 1948). These models identified the components of the persuasive communication process by posing this question: *Who* says *what* to *whom* in what *channel* with what *effect?* The research concentrated on the characteristics of the communicator, the message, the audience, the modality, and the enduring effects of messages on attitude change. This early work set the stage for contemporary models by defining the components of the communication process that appear to be most crucial in understanding persuasive communication in a cognitive processing context.

Persuasion refers to altering attitudes by getting people to consider the information presented (McGuire, 1969). People feel comfortable when they receive communication that is consistent with their attitudes and beliefs (Heider, 1958) and uncomfortable when information is in conflict with their predispositions (Festinger, 1957). For example, an individual may recognize that smoking cigarettes can lead to cancer but chooses to smoke anyway. Messages that repeatedly stress the risks of smoking make a person uncomfortable while smoking because of the conflict between cognitions (i.e., the individual enjoys smoking but recognizes that doing so poses significant health risks). The tension between these cognitions is known as *cognitive dissonance* (Festinger, 1962). Dissonance is capable of producing behavioral change over time. This person may quit smoking or, to reduce dissonance, may consider alternative resolutions. He or she may decide that to quit will result in gaining weight, making smoking a preferable option. Another alternative would be to avoid the messages because they produce tension related to cognitive dissonance.

SELECTIVE PERCEPTION: EXPOSURE, ATTENTION, AND INTERPRETATION

Selective perception is presumed to have a number of fundamental components. First, people must consciously or unconsciously expose themselves and pay attention to media messages. Selective exposure is a conscious or unconscious attempt by the individual to find information that is consistent with currently held beliefs and attitudes. Selective attention is the process of paying attention to information that is in accordance with beliefs and attitudes once it is encountered. Selective interpretation is the process of translating information to be consistent with beliefs and attitudes held by the receiver of information.

At about the time that cognitive consistency and dissonance theories began to take hold in psychology, Klapper (1960) was completing his meta-analysis on the communication literature that seemed to support theories of selective perception. His analysis revealed that regardless of whether the process is conscious, people tend to expose themselves to those mass communications that are in harmony with attitudes and interests. Because people tend to utilize attitudes and predispositions in the course of information processing, messages incongruent with previously held attitudes and beliefs are most likely to be forgotten. Messages with which they disagree may be ignored or interpreted to conform to existing views. Finally, contradictory information is forgotten more easily than that which conforms to existing attitudes and beliefs.

Selective exposure is especially prevalent in the domain of political communication. Lazarsfeld, Berelson, and Gaudet (1948) reported that voters in Erie County, Pennsylvania, were prone to hear rhetoric from their own party but insulated themselves from propaganda of the opposing party. Furthermore, when participants in the study were asked to explain where they obtained recent information, political discussions were mentioned more frequently than the media. Family, friends, and others were supplying information from the media to those who had not been exposed. This is the two-step information flow theory, in which media messages are transmitted to relatively well-informed individuals who in turn communicate the information through interpersonal channels (for a summary of the two-step information flow theory, see Katz, 1957).

Under certain circumstances, people pay more attention to information that conforms to their beliefs and attitudes (Brock & Balloun, 1967; Olson & Zanna, 1979). Attention is the amount of mental effort that an individual invests to consider an idea or object. Attention to media is associated with the degree to which one is engaged with the messages that are presented through text, audio, visuals, or some combination of the three modalities. As discussed earlier, processing limitations prevent people from maintaining all sensory stimuli in a high state of activation. Because people cannot simultaneously read newspapers, listen to the radio, and watch television, they must select the messages to which they attend.

Apart from selective exposure and attention, people also protect their attitudes through the process of selective interpretation. Vidmar and Rokeach (1974) reported that prejudiced viewers interpreted *All in the Family*'s Archie Bunker's ethnic comments as reflecting reality, whereas unprejudiced viewers considered them to be satirical bigotry (see chap. 6, this volume). Similarly, the attitude one holds toward a candidate may influence perceptions of how well he or she performed in a debate (Fazio & Williams, 1986). Consistent with top–down theories of information processing, prior attitudes, opinions, and beliefs influence the messages to which we expose ourselves, the amount of mental effort we allocate to those messages, and the ways in which we interpret them.

Finally, the process of attending to messages is fluid in that we seem to have the ability to shift information-processing resources as needed between competing messages (Basil, 1994). Certain communication genres such as film tend to focus our attention because few distractions exist. By contrast, an evening at home offers multiple communication possibilities—ranging from the television to the computer to interpersonal communication. People appear to be adept at scanning the information environment and directing attention as needed. As is seen herein, these issues are critical in the formation of a public communication campaign.

THE CENTRAL AND PERIPHERAL ROUTES
TO ATTITUDE CHANGE

Communication campaigns presented through the media attempt to manipulate variables related to the source, message, recipient, and channel to persuade a specific target segment to engage in a particular course of action. However, the degree to which we become engaged with media messages is related to the ways in which they are received and the extent to which members of the audience evaluate them. The elaboration likelihood model (ELM) makes a distinction between the central and peripheral routes to attitude change (Petty & Cacioppo, 1981, 1984, 1986a, 1986b; Petty & Priester, 1994).

According to ELM, the central route means actively and carefully thinking about information and evaluating the merits of the appeal or the arguments presented. The peripheral route to persuasion includes any kind of attitude change that occurs without much thought or elaboration. A commercial for a course intended to teach Web design may stimulate one person to consider whether he or she has the ability to work with computers, whereas another person may consider whether the benefits are worth the financial costs. In the end, a decision whether to take the course results from considering the new information in the context of stored knowledge. In both cases, cognitive energy was exerted to consider the claim encountered in the commercial. This example illustrates the central route to attitude change.

Another person may encounter the same advertisement, be favorably disposed toward learning Web design, and decide to take the course simply because it sounds fun and interesting. Although this individual may also feel positive toward the communication, attitude shift would be less pronounced because the person failed to reflect deeply on the content of the message. In this case, the peripheral route to attitude change was used. Attitude change of this type is assumed to be relatively temporary, susceptible to alteration, and not capable of predicting future behavior. Persuasion by way of the peripheral route occurs when processing abilities are limited or motivation to process is low (see Box 4.1).

INFLUENCES OF THE SOURCE ON ATTITUDE CHANGE

Communication campaigns typically involve manipulating the source, the message, and the channels to produce the desired outcome on the part of the receiver. The source is the person or people that present the message rather than the actual sponsor of the campaign. Factors such as demographics, gender, credibility, and attractiveness come into play when deciding how to encourage effective transmission of communication between the source and members of the target audience. Messages presented may contain a combination of appeals, claims, evidence, or recommendations. The channels include the specific type of medium such as radio or television station, newspaper, magazine, or billboard. The intent is to manipulate the variables so that the receivers of the message are enticed to consider the claims being made and respond by purchasing a product, voting for a candidate, or changing personal behavior.

The characteristics of the source can have a significant influence on the persuasiveness of the message. Expert or attractive sources can elevate or enhance attitudes (Kelman & Hovland, 1953), have no effect (Rhine & Severance, 1970), or even have negative effects (Sternthal, Dholakia, & Leavitt, 1978). The initial predisposition of the receiver and the degree to which the individual is affected by the communication significantly influences whether thought and elaboration occur. If a high-credibility source (i.e., a popular actor or sports figure) advocates a position about which a receiver is neither interested nor involved, then attitude change is viable by way of the peripheral route (see Box 4.2). However, if an issue is important and a high-credibility source advocates a position counter to that of the recipient, the individual may vigorously counterargue the communication. If this source is successful in altering an attitude, then change has come about as a result of the central route.

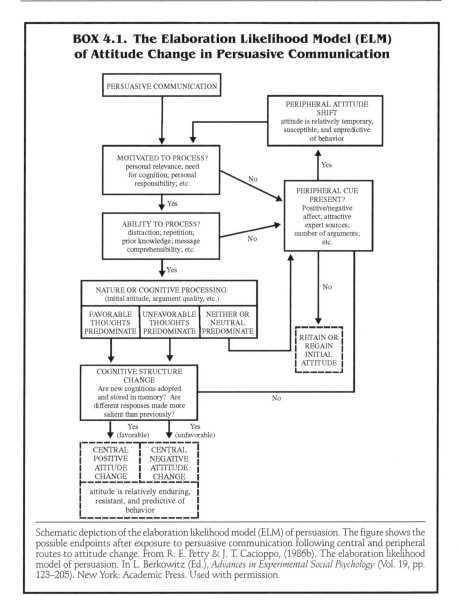

BOX 4.1. The Elaboration Likelihood Model (ELM) of Attitude Change in Persuasive Communication

Schematic depiction of the elaboration likelihood model (ELM) of persuasion. The figure shows the possible endpoints after exposure to persuasive communication following central and peripheral routes to attitude change. From R. E. Petty & J. T. Cacioppo, (1986b). The elaboration likelihood model of persuasion. In L. Berkowitz (Ed.), *Advances in Experimental Social Psychology* (Vol. 19, pp. 123–205). New York: Academic Press. Used with permission.

A communicator's credibility is most important when receivers are not particularly involved with messages and the stakes of the outcome are low. Use of an attractive or credible source to influence attitude change works best when the target audience has little at stake, such as purchasing an inexpensive product or engaging in other low-risk actions (Petty, Cacioppo, & Schumann, 1983).

BOX 4.2. Newman's Own Products

Paul Newman uses his celebrity status to encourage people to purchase a product. Newman reinforces the persuasive appeal by noting that all profits, after taxes, from the sale of Newman's Own products are donated to educational and charitable purposes. Used with permission.

EFFECTS OF THE MESSAGE ON ATTITUDE CHANGE

Effects of the message on attitude change were investigated in the context of: (a) frequency of repetition, (b) how difficult a message is to understand, (c) the number of arguments contained within a message, (d) the use of rhetorical questions to engage receivers, and (e) the number of sources presented within a message and the environment within which a message is presented (Fiske & Taylor, 1991).

One of the most important variables related to message comprehension is the degree to which the message involves and evokes a response from an individual. Arguments in favor of a complicated ballot amendment in a neighboring state that will raise taxes are unlikely to stimulate active processing by the receiver. If an individual learns that he or she is moving to that state, he or she will invest more cognitive effort to understand the pros and cons of the ballot measure. If the arguments presented are strong and relevant, then a person may be persuaded to adopt the perspective advanced. For example, if the individual has school-age children and discovers that the revenue from the proposed tax will be used for education, then he or she may invest the cognitive effort to think about and analyze the issues. If the message is poorly articulated or the person lacks the ability to comprehend a message, then attitude change is unlikely. In the prior scenario, if the media frames the issue as a plan by the state to increase revenue rather than improve schools, then attitude shift is less likely.

The number of arguments contained within a message can influence its persuasiveness. Petty and Cacioppo (1984) found that the number of arguments triggered peripheral processing and attitude change when the message was not highly involving to the receiver. Under high-relevancy conditions, however, the quality of the argument and the number of arguments presented may interact to influence persuasion via the central route. Motivation to understand a message and possessing the cognitive skills necessary to analyze it appear to interact with personal relevance of the message and quality of the argument in producing attitude change (Petty, Cacioppo, & Kasmer, 1988). Increasing personal relevance stimulates additional processing, which may lead to careful reflection and consideration of the appeals contained within the message.

Message repetition has also been correlated with attitude change. Repetition enables people to consider an appeal on multiple occasions, which should lead to acquiring knowledge and reducing uncertainty about the claims being made (Berlyne, 1970; Cacioppo & Petty, 1979; Sawyer, 1981). Repetition in moderation may reinforce a message. However, repetition can produce boredom, whereby people grow tired of the information and begin to discount or doubt it.

Other factors contributing to elaboration include the number of sources delivering the message (Harkins & Petty, 1981), whether the arguments are summarized or posed as a rhetorical question (Petty, Cacioppo, & Heesacker, 1981), and the absence of environmental distractions (Petty, Wells & Brock, 1976). In each instance, the factor that is most influential in persuasion is the amount of cognitive elaboration, both pro and con, that takes place when an individual receives a message. To maximize persuasive effects, a message should provide clear and cogent arguments, be repeated frequently (but not to excess), be understandable, and be presented in a way that is free of distraction (Fiske & Taylor, 1991).

Finally, researchers have considered the distinction between nonlinguistic and linguistic messages. Nonlinguistic messages might be characterized as images like the Coca-Cola logo. Communication of this type is generally processed through the peripheral route. Repeated exposure breeds familiarity that will eventually be transformed into liking Coke. Work by Zajonc (1980) supported this notion as subjects who were exposed to nonlinguistic messages reported higher degrees of liking although they did not recall having seen the stimulus. Because people show the effect of liking a nonlinguistic message "without recognizing the stimulus, without awareness, and without thought," these messages may not stimulate cognitive processes, and therefore represent attitude change via the peripheral route (Fiske & Taylor, 1991, p. 483). Linguistic messages stimulate elaboration because they are often designed to stress pro and con perspectives. As the elaboration likelihood model predicts, the degree to which a receiver is exposed to such communication is mitigated by the message contents.

THE ROLE OF AUDIENCE INVOLVEMENT IN ATTITUDE CHANGE

The source and the content may interact in certain ways with members of the audience to produce involvement with the message. Involvement is the most important variable in predicting that information processing via the central route occurs. Involving communication is information or messages that have personal relevance to the individual (Greenwald, 1981; Greenwald & Leavitt, 1984; Johnson & Eagly, 1989; Petty & Cacioppo, 1979). In the context of the elaboration likelihood model, the most important type of involvement is outcome based, in which audience members clearly recognize the implications of behaving in ways specified in the communication (Johnson & Eagly, 1989).

Consider a scenario in which a Middle East dictator successfully invades neighboring countries leading Congress to reinstate the draft to enlist fighting forces. An 18-year-old high school senior would probably pay close attention to the arguments because his or her future welfare is at stake (LaBerge, 1975; Schneider & Shiffrin, 1977; Shiffrin & Schneider, 1977). He or she may or may not be persuaded by the appeals, but the processing is active and controlled (see chap. 6, this volume). By contrast, an individual well beyond draft age may accept in a fairly automatic way the need to reinstate the draft—especially if the source explaining the military action is well liked or has credibility (e.g., a popular president, a general in the armed forces, or a professor of military history).

In the case of outcome-based involvement, persuasion is possible because the fundamental processes at work are cognitive. The high school senior confronted with the draft may recognize that parallels exist between the actions of Adolf Hitler and the events taking place in the Middle East. Arguments based on humanitarian principles as well as concerns for economic, social, and political stability may persuade this student that serving in the military is the proper course of action. The key is careful and deliberate thought about the persuasive information.

Value-relevant involvement is also important with respect to attitude change and persuasion. This form of involvement is linked to enduring principles that are hard to alter. Another high school senior may believe that any violence is wrong irrespective of circumstances. This individual may intellectually understand the arguments associated with preventing a dictator from expanding into neighboring country. Yet he or she resists attitude change because strongly held beliefs are under siege or the belief systems are so strong that even the most compelling arguments cannot alter them (see Petty & Cacioppo, 1990; Johnson & Eagly, 1990, for discussion of these principles).

PRINCIPLES OF PUBLIC COMMUNICATION CAMPAIGNS

In this section, we consider in detail several successful public communication campaigns that illustrate how effective campaigns operate. Messages designed to promote individual or social welfare are considered public communication campaigns. For example, noncommercial messages urging moderation in the use of alcohol and tobacco are intended to benefit individuals and society. They often contain messages that are reinforced through interpersonal contact with friends, family, and associates.

Those who produce communication campaigns must understand the mechanisms that lead audience members to pay attention to, consider, and ultimately integrate new information with previously stored knowledge. Atkin and Freimuth (1989) asserted that public communication campaigns typically include five fundamental steps (also see Flay, 1981; McGuire, 1989; Rice & Atkin, 1994):

1. Messages must be developed that will cause members of the target audience to pay attention to them.
2. Messages must be produced so that receivers will comprehend and find them appealing. They must produce reactions such as liking and agreement. They should also encourage people to counterargue previously held beliefs.
3. Messages must lead to learning. This implies stimulating thought to produce durable and lasting memory trace on the part of the target audience members.
4. Messages must lead to the formation of beliefs or attitudes and produce genuine intentions to engage in the behavior advocated in the campaign.
5. An effective campaign will lead to long-term continuation of the behavior. Underlying this assumption is the idea that campaigns must successfully stimulate the receiver to construct a new knowledge set (i.e., schema) or alter preconceptions, beliefs, or attitudes.

Adapted from Rogers and Storey (1987) and Rice and Atkin (1989), the following principles are often viewed as fundamental features of communication campaigns:

• Although campaigns are devised to produce an applied outcome, such as discouraging drug use, preventing fires, or encouraging people to volunteer their time, they should be developed in the context of appropriate theories about human and social change.

- Campaign strategists can utilize the media to develop awareness of an issue, stimulate interpersonal communication, and encourage people to assist with a cause.
- Campaign objectives must engage audiences by stressing the concrete advantages that will result by altering behavior or joining a cause.
- Long-term prevention campaigns need to be linked to relevant contemporary values.
- Campaigns should reach a large heterogeneous audience but stress values that are shared universally across cultures.
- Campaign messages should be tailored for target audiences and then placed in the appropriate media outlet that will attract attention. The messages should also communicate specific information and recommend behavior that is feasible and acceptable.
- Behavioral change is most effective when media messages can be reinforced with interpersonal social support.
- Effective campaigns recommend goals that individuals may consider to be obtainable.

EFFECTIVE COMMUNICATION CAMPAIGNS

A number of communication campaigns have used fear appeals in an effort to persuade audiences. Such campaigns linked smoking with cancer by showing images of victims and photographs of diseased lungs. Campaigns advocating seat belt usage presented viewers with images of mangled automobiles at a crash site. Yet the literature reveals that arousal of fear has little or no direct effect on attitude change. In the case of a seat belt campaign, PSAs highlighted the negative consequences of failing to use seat belts by showing motorists who were disfigured in crashes. People avoided watching the PSAs because the images produced anxiety, which interfered with the viewers' attention and retention of information (Lazarus, 1980). The interference created by the unpleasant images may have prevented them from interpreting the messages, which emphasized that seat belts are easy to use, comfortable, and safe (Geller, 1989).

Rather than using images designed to induce fear, communication campaigns should adopt principles of social learning theory (Bandura, 1977; Bandura, Ross, & Ross, 1961, 1963; Bandura & Walters, 1963; Tan, 1986; see also chap. 7, this volume). This theory holds that messages should be structured in ways that will encourage people to cognitively rehearse or think about them. If the receiver sees and understands the advantage of modeling the behavior communicated through the message, then behavioral change may take place.

Several of the most visible and effective communication campaigns were developed to encourage people to think about issues in a new or different light. Since 1942, the Ad Council (originally named the War Advertising Council) has produced many successful campaigns that illustrate how persuasive communication works. During World War II, stark images of life and death and the grave admonition that "loose lips sink ships" were common in the media. The Council also helped raise $35 billion in war bonds by promoting powerful symbols like "Rosie the Riveter." During the war, the song "Rosie the Riveter" encouraged women to help in the war effort. Actor Walter Pidgeon then discovered a real "Rosie" while visiting the Willow Run Aircraft Factory in Ypsilanti, Michigan. Pidgeon recruited riveter Rose Monroe, a widow with two children, to be in the short film. Between 2 and 6 million women were believed to have joined the workforce to help with the war effort as a result of the campaign. "Rosie the Riveter" succeeded because it successfully coordinated use of the media outlets of the day, including a film, a song, and a poster (see Box 4.3). Furthermore, the appeals were personally relevant to the appropriate target audience.

Recognizing the value of public communication campaigns, President Roosevelt asked the Ad Council to remain as a peacetime nongovernment public-service organization to help solve other pressing social problems.[1] In 1998, the Ad Council turned $4.5 million in charitable contributions into almost $1.2 billion in donated media time and space. This space and times were used for issues such as the importance of learning during the ages from birth to 3, domestic violence, raising academic standards in America, antidiscrimination, mentoring, and after-school programs.

THE ENDURING PERSUASIVE CAMPAIGN

The Forest Fire Prevention Campaign featuring the enduring icon, Smokey Bear, was one of the most successful campaigns in history. The Ad Council coordinated its persuasive efforts by employing a wide range of media. The campaign began in 1944 when advertising agency Foote, Cone and Belding, cooperating with the Forest Service and the Ad Council, came up with the idea of using a bear as a mascot. The intent was to

---

[1]The Ad Council now produces more than 35 campaigns a year on issues like education, preventive health, community well-being, environmental preservation, and strengthening families. For a campaign to be selected, it must be noncommercial, nondenominational, nonpolitical, and significant to all Americans. The Ad Council's general operating expenses are funded by donations from over 300 corporations, foundations, and constituent organizations. The nation's top advertising agencies do the creative work. Marketing executives donate their time and expertise, and the media donate millions of dollars in time and space for public service messages. A recent new direction for the Ad Council is supplying Internet banners on social issues that may be downloaded and installed on Web pages.

BOX 4.3. "Rosie the Riveter" Poster

We Can Do It! by J. Howard Miller

This World War II poster, commissioned by the War Production Coordinating Committee, features Rosie the Riveter. The image of Rosie the Riveter was used to encourage women to join the war production work force, thus beginning the women's movement in industry. Courtesy of the National Archives and Records Administration (NARA).

use a comic image to help teach kids and adults about forest fire prevention. The first poster showed Smokey wearing blue jeans and a rangers hat pouring water on a campfire with this message: "Care will prevent 9 out of 10 forest fires." Smokey became a living entity in 1950 when a badly burned black bear cub was rescued from a forest fire in New Mexico and moved to the National Zoo in Washington where it lived until his death in 1977 (Rice, 1989).

The Ad Council, the Forest Service, and the Association of State Foresters continue to promote the campaign. Through the years, Smokey Bear has continued to grow in popularity and visibility. Toys, stuffed Smokey Bear dolls, and clothing became popular with children. About 40 million people have seen the 59-foot tall balloon made for the Macy's Thanksgiving Day/Santa Claus Parade in New York City on television. Millions of people around the world learned about Smokey and his fire prevention message seeing the Smokey float during the Rose Parade on New Year's Day. Thousands of boys and girls have joined the Smokey Bear Junior Forest Ranger Program. Smokey has received so much mail over the years that he was given his own zip code in Washington, DC. In 1984, when Smokey's 40th anniversary was celebrated, a special stamp was issued by the U.S. Postal Service. The stamp included an image of the little burned cub and the image of Smokey that appears on posters.

Smokey also appeared in a movie and a Saturday morning cartoon show that debuted in 1969. The cartoon featured Smokey and his friends teaching children to help keep forests from being destroyed by wildfire. In the town of Capitan, New Mexico, near the place that the little burned bear cub was found, a museum was built in Smokey's honor. Thousands of people visit the museum each year to learn about the history of Smokey and his fire prevention message. Smokey has appeared at thousands of rodeos and amateur and professional sporting events throughout the United States and Canada. Smokey has even been featured in comic books and other children's books. In a recent poster, Smokey stands on the edge of the forest as a city encroaches on what was once forest. His message is always the same - "Remember, Only You Can Prevent Forest Fires!" (see Box 4.4).

BOX 4.4. Smokey the Bear Poster

Courtesy of the USDA Forest Service and the Ad Council. Used with permission.

The number of acres lost through wildfires declined from 30 million per year before the program began to fewer than 5 million by the end of the 1980s. Rice (1989) explained:

> The estimated resource savings over the first 30 years of the Smokey Bear campaign amount to $17 billion, yet the annual program budget is half a million dollars. A public awareness survey conducted in 1976 showed a near-universal 98% aided recall awareness of Smokey Bear. (p. 216)

Smokey Bear, like other successful campaigns, translated an abstract concept into a concrete benefit by placing messages in a variety of media and repeating them over time. As a consequence, those who saw or heard the messages changed their behavior. Other campaigns have had similar success. The slogan "A mind is a terrible thing to waste" (which benefited from the promotional support by Michael Jordan and Spike Lee who have directed several PSAs) helped raise over $1 billion for the United Negro College Fund, which has enabled 150,000 minority students to attend college. Nearly 80% of all Americans report that they prevented someone from driving after consuming alcohol because of exposure to slogans like "Friends don't let friends drive drunk" public service spots. These and other public communication campaigns that attempt to persuade large groups of citizens to change behavior demonstrate that effective communication can result in benefits for both individuals and society.

TAKE A BITE OUT OF CRIME

A sentiment prevailed in the late 1970s that citizens could do little to combat crime. To alter this attitude, a coalition composed of government policymakers, law enforcement officers, and business and labor leaders founded the Crime Prevention Coalition. The objective of the group was threefold:

1. To generate a greater sense of individual responsibility among citizens with the intent of reducing crime.
2. To encourage citizens to take collective preventive measures and work more closely with law enforcement agencies to curtail crime.
3. To enhance crime prevention programs at the state, national, and local levels (O'Keefe & Reid, 1989, p. 210).

Volunteer advertising agency Dancer Fitzgerald Sample designed a campaign around the now famous trench-coated McGruff, the Crime Dog who urged citizens to "Take a bite out of crime." McGruff explained in everyday language the importance of securing homes, avoiding dangerous situations at night, and helping law enforcement officials whenever possible. The national campaign was supported by local materials that were distributed in schools and at public events. The first television and radio spots and newspaper, magazine, billboard, and poster advertisements appeared in late 1979 and were followed up with hundreds of thousands of brochures and related materials that offered specific suggestions on how to avoid and reduce crime.

Follow-up analysis revealed that, by 1981, more than half of the respondents to a national survey had seen or heard at least one McGruff PSA. Most reported seeing it on television. The campaign succeeded in influencing a wide range of demographic and psychographic audience segments. The data based on interviews and panel studies measured the campaign's impact in terms of: (a) individual awareness of how to prevent crime, (b) adjusting one's attitude so that he or she felt one could make a difference, (c) developing a sense that people could personally help prevent crime, (d) degree of awareness of crime, and (e) how much an individual would adopt crime prevention behavior.

The data reveal that people found the campaign likable, with a quarter reporting that they had learned something new and about a half noting that the message caused them to recall forgotten information. The campaign appeared to be most effective in improving household security and encouraging cooperation between neighbors to prevent crime—themes were stressed repeatedly throughout the history of the campaign (O'Keefe, 1985, 1986).

The original partners in the Crime Prevention Campaign decided to create a new home for McGruff in an agency whose sole mission was the prevention of crime. With seed funding from the federal government, the National Crime Prevention Council (NCPC) was created as a nonprofit organization to manage the campaign and coordinate activities of the Crime Prevention Coalition. Like the Crime Prevention Campaign, the NCPC broadened its scope and depth over the years. Its staff grew from 4 to more than 45. It evolved into the nation's communication resource for crime prevention. Aside from coordinating the efforts of the Crime Prevention Campaign, the NCPC provides comprehensive technical assistance and training to communities throughout the United States. The NCPC also disseminates information on effective crime prevention practices to thousands of individuals and organizations every year. It publishes materials that reach millions of readers from virtually all demographic and psychographic categories.

TARGETING AUDIENCE SEGMENTS

As seen in chapter 3, dividing the audience into subcategories has become important in producing information that attract's the attention of the desired audience segment. The NCPC and the Ad Council distribute crime prevention campaigns for four distinct target audience segments—the adult market, the teen market, the children's market, and the Hispanic market. They also produce specialized crime advertising for 31 states. The materials are produced for radio and television, newspapers, magazines, billboards, and, most recently, the Internet.

Adult market public service spots challenge this target segment to invest time and resources in effective delinquency prevention and intervention activities. Adults receive a booklet by calling the toll-free number to learn how to promote positive youth development (see Box 4.5 for an example of a magazine PSA).

The teen market campaign focuses on "Investing in Youth for a Safer Future." It asks teens to get involved in crime prevention and prove adults wrong by doing something right. It stresses that teens can make a difference. It encourages youths to call a toll-free number to receive a free booklet explaining how they can help (see Box 4.6 for an example of a radio PSA).

BOX 4.5. Magazine Crime Prevention Mentoring PSA Targeted to Adults

Courtesy of the National Crime Prevention Coalition and the Ad Council. Used with permission.

BOX 4.6. Teen Crime Prevention
Radio Spot

"Music":	60
TEENAGE BOY:	Okay, so I'm a teenager, right? And everyone's so quick to judge me. On the outside I may look like:
Sound Effects:	HEAVY METAL MUSIC
TEENAGE BOY:	But on the inside I'm all:
Sound Effects:	"FEELINGS" MUSIC
TEENAGE BOY:	Just because I look like:
Sound Effects:	HEAVY METAL GUITAR RIFF
TEENAGE BOY:	Doesn't mean I act that way. In fact, I'm actually involved in crime prevention. That sounds more like this:
Sound Effects:	FUNK "SHAFT" SOUND-ALIKE MUSIC
TEENAGE BOY:	It's really a great way to convince adults that while you may be looking:
Sound Effects:	HEAVY METAL MUSIC
TEENAGE BOY:	You're really thinking.
Sound Effects:	SAPPY/SWEET MUSIC
TEEN ANCHOR:	Call 1-800-722-TEENS to find out how to make your community a safer place for everyone. Get involved. Get the number and call - 1-800-722-TEENS. A public service message from the Crime Prevention Coalition of America, the US Department of Justice, and the Ad Council.

The children's market campaign continues to feature McGruff, but added his nephew, Scruff, to educate children about how to protect themselves against violence, drugs, and crime (see Box 4.7 for an example of a television PSA).

The Hispanic market campaign, the "Unete A La Lucha Contra Crimen," features national and regional Latino celebrities and urges adults to call for free information about preventing crime (see Box 4.8 for an example of a billboard PSA).

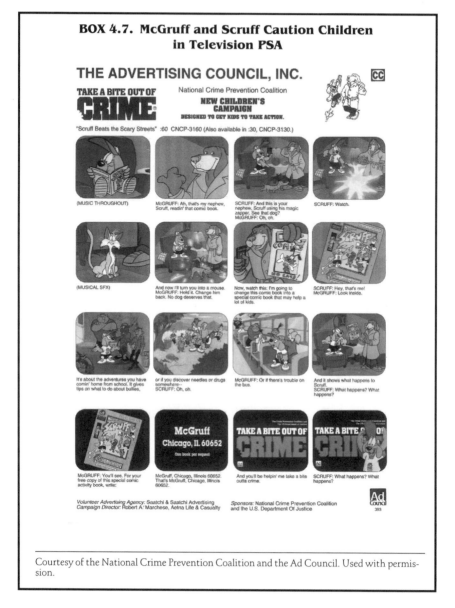

BOX 4.7. McGruff and Scruff Caution Children in Television PSA

CONCLUSION

Communication campaigns manipulate the source, message, and channels through which messages are distributed to attract the attention of the audience. The messages are presented in ways that enable receivers to

BOX 4.8. PSA for Hispanic Audience

Courtesy of the National Crime Prevention Coalition and the Ad Council. Used with permission.

comprehend and recognize their relevance. As such, the quality of the communication is extremely important. Even if a message fails to conform to predispositions of the receiver, it may result in attitude change if the communication is presented in a compelling and thought-provoking manner. Such messages can and often do stimulate rehearsal, which leads to learning and the formation of new or altered attitudes, opinions, and beliefs.

Effective communication depends on structuring messages to appeal to demographic or psychographic variables of the appropriate audience segment or segments. Understanding the nature of the individuals within a target group is essential to creating an effective communication campaign. To stimulate interaction between a source and a message, audience members must first find the message to be interesting and important. If the message succeeds in persuading members of the target audience, then behavioral change may follow. Reinforcement through interpersonal and media channels solidifies the beliefs, attitudes, and opinions formed during the course of the campaign.

Effective communication campaigns rely on the basic principles associated with human information processing. Campaigns must engage members of target audience segments and ultimately cause them to behave in a manner recommended throughout the course of the campaign. To do so, after the messages capture the attention of the appropriate audience segment, they must stimulate thought about the central points or themes. Effective campaigns anticipate the affective or emotional state of the individual or target segment in the course of researching, developing, and executing the campaign. However, scaring the audience normally does not lead to learning. To the contrary, the presentation of information presented in a positive and reasonable manner is likely to lead to the desired modeling behavior.

5 Framing Media Information

SUMMARY

- The media *frame* messages to help people understand issues.
- The media set agendas that contribute to the framing process.
- Messages may be framed either *episodically* or *thematically.*
- *Episodic framing* takes the form of a case study.
- *Thematic framing* presents general or abstract concepts.
- *Schemas, attitudes,* and *beliefs* of professional communicators may influence the ways in which they frame media messages.
- Message framing involves *identifying a problem*.
- Message framing involves *assigning responsibility*.
- Message framing involves *recommending a solution*.
- *Audiences frame messages* when they process information in the context of their own attitudes, beliefs, opinions, and knowledge.
- How a person frames a message is a function of message *issue salience*.
- People *selectively attend* to messages in the course of framing incoming information.
- *Cultural influences* may affect how audience members interpret messages.
- *Constructing meaning* through message framing implies that both the media and the members of the audience play active roles in how people construct social reality.

WHAT IS FRAMING?

The concept of message framing has existed for quite some time. It means that the media choose to focus attention on certain events and then place them within a field of meaning. The Watergate incident that led to the downfall of former President Richard M. Nixon was initially framed by the news media as a partisan issue within an election campaign. Eventually the issue took on broader significance and was framed as widespread corruption within the Nixon White House. Language selected by message producers may also contribute to the framing process. The media initially referred to the *Watergate caper.* This terminology eventually gave way to phrases such as the *Watergate scandal* (Severin & Tankard, 1992).

Frames enable people to evaluate, convey, and interpret information based on shared conceptual constructs. As such, media messages contain contextual cues supplied by professional communicators to help people understand information. The concept of framing is especially crucial to understanding how and why news reporters and editors construct messages as they do. Iyengar (1991) suggested that news messages may supply information in the context of either episodic or thematic frames. Episodic framing is event-oriented coverage of breaking news stories. Thematic framing is presenting issues in context with background information. Analysis of media content is the most common way to study message framing.

The audience also contributes to the framing process. Audience frames are the set of attitudes, ideas, opinions, and beliefs that people employ when they receive information. This type of framing is traditionally investigated using focus groups, interviewing strategies, or panel studies (Graber, 1988; Neuman et al., 1992). By considering media and audience framing simultaneously, a more complete picture of how and why members of social groups negotiate meaning has begun to emerge.

This chapter analyzes both media and audience framing and considers the importance of assigning responsibility within news stories. This implies considering a problem or issue in the context of assessing who or what is responsible for an event or outcome. Finally, the chapter evaluates how audiences negotiate meaning through the framing process by considering how cultural orientation may influence the reception and interpretation of media messages.

MESSAGE FRAMING AND MEDIA AGENDA SETTING

Professional communicators and especially news reporters and editors are trained to communicate information that unfolds across the timeline of history using standardized selection and presentation criteria (Pan & Kosicki, 1993). Journalists use conventional rules to gather information that focuses on the who, what, where, when, and, less frequently, how and why. The intent of news is to link citizens with occurrences in their environment that they cannot experience firsthand (Bird & Dardenne, 1988). As such, news reporting is intended to provide people with an accurate and realistic snapshot of the world at a specific point in time.

The relationship between agenda setting and framing is quite important. Agenda setting research indicates that the media are instrumental in spotlighting certain issues but not necessarily effective in telling people what to think (McCombs & Shaw, 1972). The proliferation of media outlets, however, is causing some to reconsider this assumption. During the 1996 election season, the national press corps often complained that politicians circumvented them, choosing instead to answer questions in user-friendly confines like MTV. The journalists did not assert that one media outlet should have access to candidates to the exclusion of others. Rather, if people receive all or most of their information by listening to *The Rush Limbaugh Show* or viewing candidates on MTV, they may lack perspective to make reasoned decisions in the voting booth. Because these programs do not adhere to the established rules of journalism, people may find it increasingly difficult to make informed decisions about economic, social, and governmental issues.

The premium that news agencies place on speed and reporting the freshest news may interfere with the ability of news producers to produce and transmit the most accurate information. Finally, in the concentrated media environment of the 21st century, it remains unclear whether news agencies will spotlight important social issues or opt instead to report on salacious or sensational news like sex scandals. Media consumers should recognize that their ideas, attitudes, and beliefs may be partially shaped by messages that are designed primarily to attract audiences rather than communicate information.

EPISODIC AND THEMATIC FRAMING

Concrete event-oriented reports, which the news media favor, encourage the production of episodic rather than thematic news stories. Iyengar (1991) explained:

> The episodic news frames take the form of a case study or an event-oriented report and depicts public issues in terms of concrete instances (for example, the plight of the homeless person or a teenage drug user, the bombing of an airliner or an attempted murder). The thematic frame, by contrast, places public issues in some more general or abstract context and takes the form of a "timeout," or "backgrounder," report directed at general outcomes or conditions. Examples of thematic coverage include reports on changes in government welfare expenditures, congressional debates over the funding of employment training programs, the social or political grievances of groups undertaking terrorist activities, and the backlog in the criminal justice process. (p. 14)

In reality, few news stories are exclusively episodic or thematic. Most event-oriented or concrete stories contain some thematic information and vice versa. Nevertheless, most news reports can be categorized as primarily thematic or episodic. Television news relies most heavily on episodic framing because the medium stresses the recency of the information and the speed of transmission (Postman, 1985). The major broadcast television networks try to cram the entire universe of news into 22 minutes each evening, which may interfere with the contextualization of information. Gamson on the Vietnam war and the nuclear energy issue has documented the dominance of episodic framing in television in several articles (Gamson, 1988, 1989; Gamson & Modigliani, 1989).

EVOLUTION OF THE FRAMING CONCEPT

The basic ideas that drive the framing concept can be traced to the writings of Lippmann (1922) on stereotyping, Festinger (1957) on cognitive dissonance, Heider (1958) on cognitive balance, and Freedman and Sears (1965) on selective exposure. Central to the framing concept is the idea that people have a much easier time handling information that is consistent with previously held beliefs and attitudes. Under certain circumstances, people selectively attend to messages or avoid ones they find unpleasant. Even if people tune out messages, there is no reason to believe that cognitive systems simply shut down entirely. Message salience and the way in which messages are presented may encourage people to rethink previously held attitudes and beliefs. As a result, schemas may be altered, leading to adjustments in the construction of social reality.

This contemporary conceptualization of framing is traced to sociological work in the constructionist tradition. Frames provide a field of meaning through which messages about people and events may be understood. Goffman (1974) explained that we actively classify, organize, and interpret our life experiences to make sense of the world. These schemas of interpretation are the frames that enable people to place information in context and make sense of events. Gitlin (1980) explained that frames "enable journalists to process large amounts of information quickly and [enables them to] routinely package the information for efficient relay to their audiences" (p. 7). Gamson suggested that the frame is essentially an organizing mechanism that enables communicators to provide meaning (Gamson, 1992; Gamson & Modigliani, 1989).

The psychological view of framing shares many of the theoretical underpinnings associated with the sociological perspective. Minsky (1975), for example, conceptualized a frame as a template that helps organize knowledge. Iyengar (1991) asserted that framing provides contextual cues to enable people to see where a journalist is going with a story. Journalists utilize scripts to communicate ideas in a shorthand manner.

Scripts are schemas in which story lines are organized involving scenarios or routines with agreed on rules (Rumelhart, 1984; Wicks, 1992b). For example, the dining out script contains entering a restaurant, reading the menu, ordering an entree, dining, and then paying the check. The sequence of events is generally the same each time, therefore there is no need to explain each step in the process when we recount a dining experience to a friend.

FRAMING POLITICAL INFORMATION

Individual journalists construct messages based on their own knowledge, beliefs, and attitudes. These messages are colored by their own predispositions, which may influence both the structure and content of the message (see Geiger & Reeves, 1991, for an analysis of the interaction between these two concepts).

Media organizations also influence the construction of messages. American magazines and newspapers have historically tended to be either conservative or liberal. *U.S. News and World Report*, for example, has a reputation for being more conservative than *Time* or *Newsweek*. Journalists with conservative or liberal leanings tend to affiliate with news agencies that share their attitudes and predispositions. Therefore, the work environment within which journalists and editors operate may contribute to the reinforcement of attitudes and beliefs. Thus, although journalists with liberal or conservative leanings may strive for objectivity, the work they produce will ultimately be influenced by their belief systems, the knowledge they possess stored in cognitive schemas, as well as the culture of the professional environment in which they are employed (see Box 5.1).

These two dynamics—the belief system of the journalist and the culture within which a journalist is employed—are manifested in a variety of ways where framing is concerned. First, although daily media organizations such as television and newspapers may strive to produce issue-oriented coverage of political campaigns, they rarely succeed. Organizational influences such as the sheer number of deadlines on any given day at a broadcast station may prevent journalists from constructing thematic messages. To compound the problem, simply keeping up with breaking news is a formidable challenge that often prevents journalists from reflecting on and analyzing such events. Finally, journalists may consciously or unconsciously frame information to conform to existing biases or beliefs.

The problem of providing analytical news is especially pronounced during the heat of a political campaign. Candidates may schedule numerous events on a single day. This is why critics charge that news reporting

---

Box 5.1. Wag the Dog

On August 17, 1998, President Clinton stunned the nation by admitting that he had an "inappropriate relationship" with former White House intern, Monica Lewinsky, after denying it for 7 months. Four days later, the president ordered strikes on suspected terrorist facilities in Afghanistan and Sudan in retaliation for the bombings of U.S. embassies earlier in the month. The strikes came on the day that Lewinsky reappeared before the grand jury investigating whether the president committed perjury or obstructed justice in an attempt to conceal the affair.

The timing of the strikes caused some journalists and members of Congress to suggest that the strikes were an attempt to divert attention from the Lewinsky affair. In the film *Wag the Dog*, a president caught in a sex scandal tried to distract the nation's attention by fabricating a war with Albania. Video stores in the Washington, DC, scrambled to keep up with skyrocketing demand for the film that was released in 1997. Dale Shaw, assistant manager at Potomac Video, said, "It's been renting like crazy." Copies were also checked out at Washington Video on Dupont Circle. Store manager Erik Evans explained: "People wanted to see what the press is talking about" (Snow, 1998, p. F2).

Indiana Senator Daniel Coats, a member of the Armed Services Committee, questioned whether the strikes were to divert attention from the Lewinsky affair.

> Given the president's personal difficulties this week, it is legitimate to question the timing of this action. . . . Once the president has broken the bond with the American people, as he has done with his repeated lies . . . it raises questions about everything he does or does not do. (Carr, 1998, p. A18)

---

during the campaign season typically follows the horse race rather than focusing on significant issues and presenting reasoned analysis (Graber, 1988; Hofstetter, 1976; Kern, 1989; Neuman et al., 1992). Television stories about candidate rankings in the polls, delegate counts, and the number in attendance at a rally tend to dominate because they are relatively easy to produce (Kern & Wicks, 1994; Wicks & Kern, 1993, 1995). Further, the need for eye-catching visuals and emotional or dramatic oratory lead to the presentation of ceremonial images that contain sound bites of marginal substance and little news value (Buchanan, 1991; Hallin, 1992; Just et al., 1996). Much of the information provided during the campaign season reflects the efforts of political handlers to attract the media to locales that will show a flattering backdrop for events that contain little or no new information.

During a political campaign, framing depends on the development of relationships among sources, journalists, and the audience with each player having a role to execute. To frame a platform, sources may communicate certain keywords or phrases like "we need to hold the line on taxes," hoping that such rhetoric is noted and reported by journalists. Such phrases are scripted to capture the attention of the audience members to persuade them that they and the candidate are allies. These phrases also help to form the schema that an individual may be developing about a candidate. Therefore, the candidate repeats the phrase about taxes often hoping to solidify beliefs in the mind of the audience members. However, such a phrase may actually harm the candidate if audience members perceive that the candidate is insincere or attempting to garner votes by repeating populist themes.

FRAMING OF NONPOLITICAL INFORMATION

Iyengar (1991) made a compelling case to support his assertion that episodic framing dominates television information programming. Because news stories are presented as discrete items or events, television typically fails to provide relationships among issues, people, and events. One problem with this style of presentation is that if citizens believe that social or political problems are solved as quickly in the real world as they are in movies and on entertaining television programs, they may perceive a sense of powerlessness both as individuals or collectively as members of society (Downs, 1972).

The media do not shy away from chronicling the frustrations of the average citizen who confronts the medical establishment, the military establishment, or South African authorities (Neuman et al., 1992). Nor do the media avoid presenting the failures and mistakes of federal, state, or local governments in dealing with social or economic issues. Iyengar (1991) and Neuman and his colleagues (1992) made an important point. Without context between discrete news items, audiences fail to make the proper connections and have little information on which to base their understanding of events and occurrences in the news. The most significant issue with respect to framing is not the identification of a problem or issue. Established news values, which govern the selection criteria, have been well defined. Rather, framing is most crucial in the context of assigning responsibility, considering the morality or legality of an issue, or recommending a solution.

The framing of entertainment and information typically follows scripts that have evolved over time. Scripts are quite common in media presentations of fictional and news programming. Typically, good wins out over evil, lovers resolve conflict (with the notable exception of soap operas, in which the reverse is generally true), the world remains intact for yet another day, and the hero and his or her companion drive off into the sunset to live happily ever after. However, framing may be witnessed during television sports programs and reporting during the news. The script invariably remains the same irrespective of the game or competition with a team or individual emerging victorious at the end. Training, intelligence, and ability combine to help the best prevail. Emotion is also a vital ingredient in sports framing as teams or players demonstrate *heart* while competing. The home run race between Mark McGwire and Sammy Sosa offered all of the possibilities to frame the story (see Box 5.2).

BOX 5.2. Framing a Sporting Event

On September 9, 1998, at 8:18 P.M., Mark McGwire of the St. Louis Cardinals hit an 88-mile-per-hour fastball thrown by Chicago Cubs pitcher Steve Trachsel. The pitcher stood still on the mound as flashbulbs popped, fireworks exploded, and 11 minutes of triumphant celebration unfolded. Following the game, Fox Broadcasting announced that its coverage of Mark McGwire's record-setting baseball game that Tuesday night had set record ratings for the network. The broadcast of McGwire's 62nd home run earned the network a 12.9 rating and a 21 share, making the game the highest rated regular season baseball game in 17 years. Researchers at Fox reported that the game was watched by about 43 million people, enabling the network to win the night. "The whole country has been involved in this," a choked-up McGwire said after he sent a line drive over Busch Stadium's left-field fence and into history. "I'm happy to bring the country together" (Anthony, 1998, p. A1). Watching from the box seats were the sons and daughters of Roger Maris, who broke the fabled record of Babe Ruth by hitting 61 home runs 37 years earlier.

Several years before, fans had abandoned the ballparks in the wake of a divisive player strike. Many agreed that the game had become about money and greed. "'Now there's a reason to come back to baseball," said Sherry Irby, a pharmacist from Florence, Alabama, who drove all night with her husband and two young sons to Chicago to see McGwire. They stood on cardboard mats in the outfield standing-room-only section. "Good role models are few and far between for kids," said her husband, Ken. "The country's been kind of in the doldrums with the Lewinsky thing. We needed something to cheer."[1] Melvin Philip Lucas of Cornell College in Iowa, who teaches a course on baseball's role in American history, explained, "We're in an age of instant gratification. And a home run is instant gratification" (Anthony, 1998, p. A1).

Although home runs may provide *instant gratification* and the country may have been in the *doldrums* on that September evening, the creation of a sense of national community could not have occurred without the help of the media. In 1961, when Roger Maris passed the single-season home run record of 60 set by Babe Ruth, 40,000 seats were empty at Yankee Stadium. The media of the day simply did not hype the event. By 1998, sports journalists recognized that the home run race had all the makings of a great television event. Sammy Sosa of the Chicago Cubs also broke Ruth's record in

---

(Continues)

1998 by hitting 66 home runs. The media framed the race between the athletes as a good old-fashioned American competition among friends.

The intense coverage of the story also enabled it to grow to mythic proportions. As a consequence, the rivalry between Mark McGwire and Sammy Sosa enabled cable and broadcast networks to *pack the house* every time they carried a game featuring either of them. The political establishment recognized the appeal of the drama between Sosa and McGwire. President Clinton invited Sosa to his State of the Union Address in January 1999 and introduced him.

---

[1]Although audience members may have reported that they had grown weary of the Clinton–Lewinsky saga, that did not prevent them from watching an interview with the former White House intern. In March 1999, 48.5 million viewers tuned into ABC to hear Monica Lewinsky talk for the first time to Barbara Walters about her affair with President Clinton. It was the second-most-watched program of the year following the Super Bowl. With such strong ratings, it is no surprise that Walters followed up with a second interview that aired on the last day of a ratings period on November 30, 1999, as part of Walters' *10 Most Fascinating People of 1999* (Johnson, 1999).

FRAMING AIRLINE TRAGEDIES

Several examples of framing are now presented in the context of airline tragedies. Although airline officials may attempt to place the best possible spin on the plane crashes, Federal Aviation Administration (FAA) investigators or spokespersons for the National Transportation Safety Board (NTSB) have little incentive to do anything but provide facts to the media. Aviation disasters are also so sensational in their own right that reporters have little need to hype these stories further. As such, one might assume that reporting would vary little from one news agency to the other. Such an assumption, however, is not always correct because many forces interact leading to message distortion.

Entman (1993) defined *framing* as communicators making salient certain aspects of perceived social reality in a way to "promote a particular problem definition, causal interpretation, moral evaluation, and/or treatment recommendation for the item described" (p. 52). In other words, professional communicators select particular aspects of reality and then highlight them in the messages that they produce. Entman viewed the message framing process in the following way: (a) identify a problem, (b) assess the cause of an event and assign responsibility, (c) consider the issue or problem in the context of legal, ethical, or moralistic principles, (d) identify and recommend solutions to the problem.

Identify a Problem

What causes a professional communicator such as a journalist to identify a specific problem? The most obvious answer is that journalists and editors make unconscious or conscious decisions to explain information based on their belief systems. These belief systems are contained within schemas relating to news values. Because of the institutional nature of journalism organizations and training conventions, these news values would include a set of agreed on rules defined by media practitioners and handed down to aspiring journalists in college. As such, the criteria for defining a problem leads journalists to conclude that a problem worthy of consideration exists irrespective of their own opinions, attitudes, and beliefs. The rules that govern these strategies normally appear in the first few chapters of any undergraduate textbook on news reporting (e.g., Stephens, 1993):

1. the timeliness or newness of a news story
2. the prominence of an individual such as a mayor or president
3. the impact of an event, such as the loss of life in a school bus crash
4. the human interest of the story including gossip about local or national celebrities
5. the conflict and controversy ranging from the debate by a city council to fund a new water treatment facility to the debate on abortion
6. the unusual nature of a story
7. the proximity of the event to the news organization that will cover it

Assess the Cause of an Event and Assign Responsibility

Major airline crashes typically open newscasts and appear on the front page of newspapers because they possess most of the important attributes listed earlier. Once the initial shock of the disaster dissipates, however, questions shift quickly to what went wrong and who was responsible for the crash. The causes of airlines crashes are often quickly identified, enabling journalists to shift the focus to the issue of responsibility. Although most journalists generally agree on a set of rules that define the criteria for identifying a problem, many reasons explain why different journalists might assess cause and assign responsibility.

One incident in which responsibility shifted was the case of the Value Jet crash in the Florida Everglades in 1996. The FAA quickly concluded that SabreTech, a St. Louis-based airline maintenance company, failed to properly package, label, and identify about 125 oxygen containers that exploded in the Value Jet cargo compartment. The jet, which crashed in the Florida Everglades, claimed the lives of 110 passengers and the crew. As the cause of the disaster became apparent, the inquiry shifted to whether ValueJet, SabreTech, or inadequate FAA rules were responsible for the crash. Specifically, did ValueJet and SabreTech violate rules or had the FAA failed to make or enforce rules protecting air travel in the first place?

Two months later, TWA Flight 800, which crashed into Long Island Sound claiming 230 lives, presented journalists with a different type of quandary. Questions concerning the cause of the crash surfaced immediately but remained unresolved for a long time. The probe during the following year looked into three main questions: whether mechanical trouble could be ruled out, whether a bomb inside the plane could be ruled out, or whether a missile or other high-velocity object (such as a meteorite) could be ruled out.

The TWA 800 crash offered journalists and citizens a Rorschach inkblot with which to frame the story. The crash occurred about 8 years after terrorists blew up Pan Am flight 103 over Lockerbie, Scotland. Circumstances were similar in that neither pilot had much time to communicate the problem. Furthermore, numerous terrorist incidents occurred during the 1990s, including the bombing of the World Trade Center in New York City. Therefore, it seemed logical for journalists to question whether the terrorism that had reached American shores made its way to the friendly skies. A definitive answer for the crash was never provided. However, the NTSB suggested that faulty wiring or a mechanical malfunction were likely explanations for the airline disaster.

In summary, journalists frame information in a way to assess cause and assign responsibility. However, stored knowledge, opinions, attitudes, and beliefs may influence how they arrive at their assertions and even conclusions, as was evident in some of the reporting on about TWA Flight 800.

Consider the Issue or Problem in the Context of Legal, Ethical, or Moralistic Principles

Message framing is also an important consideration when journalists consider issues or problems in the context of legal, ethical, or moral principles. In a May 1, 1998, *Wall Street Journal* article, a journalist used legal evidence alleging that SabreTech had broken the law, leading in turn to the ValueJet crash (Daerr, 1998). Reporter Elizabeth Daerr wrote:

> The Federal Aviation Administration is seeking a $2.25 million civil fine against SabreTech Inc., for knowingly shipping explosive oxygen

generators that caused the deadly May 1996 ValuJet crash in the Florida Everglades. The FAA said SabreTech, a subsidiary of Sabreliner Corp., St. Louis, failed to properly package, label and identify about 125 oxygen containers that caught fire in the plane's cargo hold. The FAA also found that employees responsible for handling the containers weren't properly trained. SabreTech, an airplane-maintenance company, and five of its employees involved in the incident were cited with 37 violations each.

The newspaper article stressed that the fine was the largest that could be levied against SabreTech.

With respect to the TWA Flight 800 crash, Elaine Scarry, who holds a professorship in Aesthetics and Theory of Value at Harvard University, wrote a 17-page article appearing in the *New York Review of Books*, entitled, "The Fall of TWA 800: The Possibility of Electromagnetic Interference" (Scarry, 1998). The article contained 106 footnotes and interviews with experts, excerpts from congressional hearings, reports from the NTSB, and information from other credible sources. It also explained that travelers are required to turn off devices such as computers and radios during take-off because they can create electromagnetic interference that can play havoc with the navigational equipment. One explanation for the crash, she asserted, was that 10 military planes and ships were in the vicinity producing high amounts of electromagnetic interference. Citing a NASA study, Scarry wrote:

> electromagnetic interference may also introduce a false command into the plane's electrical system, suddenly instructing its rudder to move, or (at higher power levels) disrupting a plane's control surfaces-its rudder and wing flaps by burning out a circuit. Military planes may themselves at times become vulnerable to interference from other military craft. (p. 59)

The primary point stressed by the author was that all explanations for the disaster must be investigated if future accidents are to be averted.

Journalist Peter Garrison (1998) of the magazine *Flying* found the report written by Scarry to be bordering on the absurd. In attacking the credibility of Scarry, Garrison wrote:

> Scarry-who, by the way, makes no claim of prior experience as an accident investigator, and whose lack of basic familiarity with airplanes, aviation terminology, and the flying environment is evident-attempts to account for the mysterious fuel-tank spark by invoking HIRF: High Intensity Radiated Fields. (p. 111)

He then provided his own set of compelling evidence suggesting Scarry's report could not be considered credible:

> Although I do not think that Professor Scarry made her case, I do admire her courage in wading into so specialized and highly technical an arena so lightly armed. I look forward to her next article in the *New York Review of Books*, which I hope will deal with the measurement of risk and reward in air travel, viewed from the perspective of Aesthetics and the Theory of Value.

Both writers utilized classic persuasive strategies to frame their arguments. Professor Scarry utilized documentary evidence and supported her case with credible citations in an attempt to place the blame (at least potentially) on the U.S. military establishment. She did so by implying that electromagnetic emanations may have been concealed in the investigation to the detriment of public safety. Garrison, by contrast, attacked and ridiculed Scarry's credibility and contended that her lack of expertise invalidated the conclusions she presented. Garrison's conclusions pointed to isolated potential HIRF problems that were inherent to certain types of aircraft such as Black Hawk helicopters but not jumbo jets. In any case, both articles in isolation made a compelling case and tried to explain where the responsibility for the tragedy laid. Scarry and Garrison apparently felt that they had arrived at sound conclusions. To accentuate their beliefs, they framed their articles to persuade readers to see the facts as they saw them (see Box 5.3).

Identify and Recommend Solutions to the Problem

Framing concludes when news reports arrive at a solution or set of recommendations to address the problem or issue. In some instances, it may take considerable time to arrive at a solution. Nearly 10 years after the explosion of Pan Am Flight 103 over Lockerbie, Scotland, the United States and Britain finally agreed to hold the trial of the two Libyans charged with the bombing in a third country. The case would be tried under Scottish law by a Scottish judge but held in The Hague, the capital of the Netherlands. U.S. Secretary of State Madeline Albright and British Foreign Minister Robin Cook said international sanctions against Libya would be removed as soon as the suspects were turned over for trial, but they would work to impose even tougher sanctions if Libya refused. The report essentially brought about closure to the terrorist act (Conan & Montagne, 1998).

By contrast, TWA 800 and Swissair 111, which crashed in the fall of 1998, left journalists unfulfilled and searching for the responsible parties

---

BOX 5.3. Framing an Airline Tragedy

- Excerpt from: "The Fall of TWA 800: The Possibility of Electromagnetic Interference," by Elaine Scarry, *The New York Review of Books*, April 9, 1998

For more than a year, the inquiry into the fall of TWA 800 has addressed three questions: whether mechanical trouble can be ruled out, whether a bomb inside the plane can be ruled out, whether a missile or other high-velocity object (such as a meteorite) can be ruled out. But there is a fourth possibility that has been ignored and that needs to be raised in the inquiry.

To a civilian, the phrase "electromagnetic interference" may at first sound puzzling, even though every commercial flight begins with the instruction to passengers to turn off during takeoff all computers, headsets, radios, and telephones. The power radiated by these objects is tiny. But their emissions can travel out of the cabin windows to the antennas on the outer body of the plane; therefore the FAA regulation requiring airlines to prohibit passenger use of such objects has remained firmly in place. (1) Interference from military equipment can be thousands, even millions, of times as great, (2) and can have much more serious consequences for airborne planes. Because ten military planes and ships were in the vicinity of TWA 800 that night, we need to ask the airmen and sailors on the planes and ships to describe with precision the pieces of equipment that were in use.

- Excerpt from: "TWA 800 and EMI," by Peter Garrison, *Flying*, October 1998

I've often noticed that the print and broadcast media appear to be correct and reliable until they report on something that I know about; then they suddenly turn amateurish, ill-informed, and generally misleading. Nevertheless, when an April cover of the *New York Review of Books* featured the now-famous photograph of a wing tip of TWA 800 floating in the water, I had high expectations of new enlightenment about the mysterious crash. After all, I said to myself, *Time* and *Newsweek* are one thing, the *New York Review of Books* another.

The exceedingly long and heavily footnoted article, entitled "The Fall of TWA 800: The Possibility of Electromagnetic Interference," was written by Elaine Scarry, who holds a professorship in Aesthetics and Theory of Value at Harvard. Scarry has previously written on subjects as disparate as torture and gun control and obviously is not cowed by the technical expertise of others or her own lack of it. Her contention is that the fuel tank explosion that is supposed to have destroyed the Paris-bound 747 off Long Island could have been triggered by stray radio frequency emissions from nearby military aircraft. This possibility, she insists, should be considered by the NTSB alongside all the others. Scarry seems to imply, furthermore, that the military has systematically concealed the extent and magnitude of its electromagnetic emanations to the detriment of public safety.

and a solution to the problem. Because framing could not be concluded in a tidy manner with respect to Swissair 111, William F. Buckley, Jr. (1998) wrote in the *National Review*:

> It's true that in the case of the TWA [800] flight it was thought that the cause of the explosion was a bomb. Why should that not have been pondered [in the case of Swissair 111]? In one sense it's more reassuring to learn that a bomb went off-because bombs are put there by malefactors whose movements human resolve can hope to deal with-than that something went wrong with the air-conditioning duct or in the cargo hold. During that anxious afternoon one would have been grateful for word from flight specialists doing precisely that, speculating on what it is that might have gone wrong in the two fateful moments, the first an hour after take-off when an irregularity was reported; the second 16 minutes later when the plane disappeared into Peggy's Cove. Let the inquest go forward. (p. 67)

Thus, with no evidence to explain the disaster or clues to examine, journalists find it difficult to recommend a solution and bring about closure.

SUMMARY OF MEDIA FRAMING

Professional communicators frame information to provide contextual cues to audience members. These contextual cues are the result of a complex set of individual attitudes and beliefs of the communicator and rules or norms established within the culture of working professionals. In some cases, framing is overt and intentional. Professional communicators recognize the symbiotic relationship that may exist between sources and themselves. Politicians and advertisers, for example, strive to accentuate the positive and dull the negatives. The audience too recognizes that certain forms of communication highlight certain aspects of the message and persuade them to vote for a candidate, purchase a product, or buy into an idea. Framing of news information contains a series of steps in which journalists seek to uncover cause and responsibility of a problem and consider the legal, ethical, and moral implications. The most important element of framing is the assignment of responsibility and recommendations for a solution.

AUDIENCE FRAMING

A newer direction in framing research concerns the ways in which audiences use cognitive frames to interpret new information. Recently, the focus has shifted to studying both communicator and audience frames in tandem to understand the dynamics that take place when citizens process and interpret media.

Communication scholars, sociologists, and political scientists define *audience framing* as the process of negotiating meaning as a result of interpreting new information in the context of previously stored knowledge (e.g., Gamson, 1992; Neuman et al., 1992). The primary issue is how people interpret media information through their own person field of meaning. Further, audience framing is concerned with the degree to which people may construct shared or different meanings as a consequence of using media. Within this domain, it is essential to consider the impact of cultural, social, and economic influences on the construction of social reality. The primary focus shifts away from the possibility or assumption that the manner in which people interact with media is universally similar and that frames presented by communicators are interpreted similarly across a wide spectrum of the audience.

CULTURAL MEMBERSHIP AND COMMUNICATION ABOUT SMOKING

Previously we considered how message framing may influence news content. Now we consider how cultural orientation may influence the reception of messages. We do so by illustrating how one cultural group interpreted news information about the tobacco industry during the 1996 election season.

During the 20th century, the tobacco industry attempted to promote smoking by framing the product in a variety of ways. The fundamental strategy was to target certain groups of people to enssure future markets for the product. In the 1960s, a cigarette company sponsored the *Flintstones*, a children's cartoon, featuring animated cave men and women. At the beginning of each show, Fred and Barney lit up a Winston cigarette to relax while their wives, Wilma and Betty, tended to household chores. Although somewhat less transparent than the Flintstones, Joe Camel was an apparent attempt to capture the attention of the youth audience.

Perhaps the most successful effort to frame smoking as fashionable was a stunt engineered by public relations pioneer Edward L. Bernays. The American Tobacco Company hired Bernays in the 1920s to find new markets for cigarettes at a time when smoking was primarily a male pastime. To break the taboo that prevented women from smoking in public, Bernays contacted a young debutante with whom he was acquainted. He urged her and her friends to march in the Easter Parade in New York City holding up Lucky Strike cigarettes as symbolic torches of freedom (Ewen, 1996). The gesture, he said, would highlight the inhumanity of men toward women in society at that time. He also encouraged her to invite male companions to march along with the debutantes as a gesture of solidarity and support. Finally, Bernays suggested she notify the newspapers of the plan. Within 5 weeks, the smoking parlors of New York theaters abandoned policies preventing women from smoking. In this way, a well-framed message publicized in the media paved the way for change that had significant social impact.

By the mid-1950s, the U.S. medical community was concerned that cigarette smoking and tobacco products in general were harmful. A report from the Surgeon General in 1964 declared that cigarettes cause cancer. This prompted Congress to enact legislation 7 years later banning radio and television stations from accepting tobacco advertising. More recently, federal and state governments took regulatory steps to curb or eliminate smoking in public places and to prevent the sale of tobacco products to minors. Smoking, once considered stylish in movies such as *The Big Sleep* with Humphrey Bogart and Lauren Becall, was rapidly losing favor in American culture. Messages produced by tobacco companies framing smoking as stylish and sexy eventually gave way to others that tried to persuade smokers to quit.

USE OF TOBACCO BY NATIVE AMERICANS

In certain cultures, cigarette smoking and tobacco usage is not viewed as a vice. Native American tribes such as the Cherokees and Keetoowahs use tobacco for religious, cultural, and recreational purposes. During the 1996 presidential election campaign, Republican candidate Bob Dole and, to a lesser extent, the Clinton–Gore ticket became embroiled in a controversy when it was reported that both campaigns had accepted contributions from tobacco interests. The thrust of several news stories that appeared in a wide range of media challenged candidates to respond to charges that accepting funds made them beholden to tobacco interests.

Members of the Cherokee Nation participating in focus groups at the tribal headquarters in Tahlequah, Oklahoma, were asked to view a series of network news stories and discuss them. Two of the stories dealt with the tobacco controversy. One story provided a comment from Bob Dole suggesting that he did not believe tobacco was addictive and a reaction comment from former Surgeon General C. Everett Koop asserting that the statement from Dole was *baffling*. A soundbite from Vice President Al Gore charged that, "The Republicans are addicted to tobacco money . . . and they can't kick the habit." The clear intent of both reports was to suggest that the major tobacco companies have considerable sway with respect to the major political parties (Wicks, Scheide, & Smith, 1999).

The debate on whether candidates should accept contributions from tobacco companies was considered by members of the Cherokee Nation as an affront to their cultural heritage. In one focus group with Cherokees, members preferred to discuss the possibility that tobacco companies tampered with the product to cause smokers to become addicted rather than focus on news about tobacco money financing political campaigns. Although no such discourse was included in any of the news stories, one focus group member demonstrated considerable interest in the topic leading to the following exchange:

> William: Do you feel like the tobacco companies put chemicals in their tobacco to get people addicted?
>
> Elizabeth: I think they did in order to get people addicted. Because, my gosh, you know years and years ago how the Indians smoked and it wasn't an addiction with them. They cured their own tobacco. People would come in and they would have a smoke, men and women would have a smoke and smoked their pipes, maybe in the evening or maybe smoked during the day, but they didn't have to have a smoke every hour, every 30 minutes or anything like that.

Central to Cherokee philosophy is the belief that people must be responsible for their own actions. In keeping with this principle, one focus group member suggested that people should neither blame nor sue tobacco companies if they become ill because the choice to smoke was theirs alone. Another believed that efforts by the two parties to raise contributions from cigarette producers proved each cared only about campaign fundraising and very little about the health of citizens. One participant did not distinguish between the acceptance of modest contributions by Democrats versus the much larger contributions to Republicans, maintaining that families need to teach their own children how to live their lives. Others in the group, however, believed that perhaps the federal government should help regulate the tobacco consumption of children because using tobacco products today may cause a dependency problem later.

Tobacco regulation was also a concern of the United Keetoowah Band of Cherokee Indians—an orthodox branch of the Cherokee tribe. Members of the Keetoowah focus group were not shown any television ads or news stories relating to tobacco. Yet one focus group member brought up its regulation when asked by a moderator if there were issues that they would like to discuss. The participant was concerned that tobacco was unfairly being singled out for criticism during the election, noting that liquor leads to deaths as a consequence of drunk driving and illnesses. He believed that the scrutiny of tobacco by the media represented yet another assault on tribal cultures and values.

The manner in which a message is framed by professional communicators may not match the way it is framed by the audience. In the case of the Cherokees and Keetoowahs, focus group participants recognized that the story was an attempt to link the troubled tobacco industry with the political candidates. Rather than focus on the issue of contributions, some Cherokees and Keetoowahs chose instead to consider the possibility of product tampering by the tobacco companies. Others questioned why the cigarette industry was under such scrutiny when other industries produce equally destructive products. In both instances, tobacco was framed with respect to cultural identify rather than the way it had been presented by the television news reporters.

Evidence from the focus groups suggests that merely mentioning a topic stimulates thinking about the issue in a wide expanse of related cognitive domains. Gamson (1992) also found this to be the case. In a focus group on affirmative action, he reported that members in several groups quoted "the advertising slogan of the United Negro College Fund that 'A mind is a terrible thing to waste' " (p. 118; see chap. 4). The slogan and the affirmative action concepts were cognitively bound together. He also explained that subjects in his study brought up popular films like *Silkwood* and *The China Syndrome* in discussions about nuclear power. These examples suggest that, although media messages may influence what we think, they also stimulate us to construct our own knowledge based on the frames we have constructed over time.

STUDYING COMMUNICATOR AND AUDIENCE FRAMING IN TANDEM

The framing of messages by the news media was studied using a range of methodologies such as field experiments, surveys, content analyses, and correlational data of national surveys (see Gamson 1992; Gans, 1979; Graber, 1998; Hofstetter, 1976; Iyengar, 1991; Neuman et al., 1992; Patterson, 1980). These studied have typically used content analysis in conjunction with other methodologies.

A study conducted in the Boston area in the late 1980s compared media frames to audience frames by analyzing amount of media contact and tape recording depth interviews of people living in the area (Neuman et al., 1992). The content was drawn from the *Boston Globe*, *Time*, *Newsweek*, *U.S. News and World Report,* and the major network newscasts between 1985 and 1987. Forty-three people were interviewed from 1 to 2 hours by trained interviewers who let the subjects do most of the talking. The idea was to draw on the attitudes, opinions, and beliefs of the respondents rather than force them to react to questioning generated by the researchers.

The frames utilized by the media and the interviewees were then compared. The content analysis revealed that the media framed 29% of the news stories in the context of conflict. Only 6% of the discourse from the interviews, however, focused on conflict. The researchers also found that 36% of the discourse focused on human impact, whereas only 18% of the news stories considered impact. Perhaps most important, 33% of the news reports framed events and issues in the context of powerlessness. Twenty-two percent of the discourse focused on whether citizens had the power to alter their situation. Thus, although the media agenda is important in focusing attention on issues, people identify issues that they find important, pay attention, and think about them.

Undoubtedly, the future of framing research rests with using quantitative and qualitative strategies together to discern how citizens negotiate meaning about the world in which they live and how media messages contribute to the process of constructing social reality. The kinds of analyses described in this chapter may help explain the dynamics that take place when people construct meaning from framed media messages.

CONCLUSION

Message framing is the conscious or unconscious act of using contextual cues in the transmission or reception of media messages. Professional communicators use information to guide audience members by introducing problems or issues, suggesting who or what is responsibility for these issues, and recommending solutions. The messages constructed by professional communicators may be objective because they employ the standard criteria of reporting on the who, what, where, when, why, and how. However, the attitudes, beliefs, and opinions of the communicator shape the actual construction of messages. Furthermore, different journalists or professional communicators may arrive at different conclusions as to who or what is responsible for a problem and what the appropriate solution or course of action may be. Finally, the organizational culture of news agencies may foster a collective set of attitudes or beliefs that may lead to the framing of messages.

The audience is also instrumental in the framing process. Audience members interact with information based on their own opinions, attitudes, and beliefs. Individuals do not slavishly absorb the messages as framed by the mass media. "They actively filter, sort, and reorganize information in personally meaningful ways in the process of constructing an understanding of public issues" (Neuman et al., 1992, p. 77). As Gamson (1992) asserted repeatedly throughout his book:

- People are not passive,
- People are not dumb, and,
- People negotiate with media messages in complicated ways that vary from issue to issue. (p. 4)

In summary, the media and people are partners in constructing social reality about the world, country, and community in which they live. This constructed reality is a direct result of the interaction between our own life experiences and what we encounter through the media.

III Using Media Messages

In the first two parts of this volume, we considered the extent to which people interact with media. We evaluated the strategies that producers of media messages employ to attract an audience and persuade people to behave in a certain way. Finally, we analyzed communication messages that frame information to accentuate and highlight certain features of the information. In Part III of this volume, our focus shifts to consumers of media products. We begin by exploring the principles of human information processing. We then consider principles associated with social learning in children. We explore the possibility that media messages may cultivate ideas and attitudes and criticisms of this perspective. Finally, we apply the principles of the uses and gratifications approach to the new media environment.

6 Fundamentals of Media Information Processing

SUMMARY

- Memory processes include the *long-term* and *short-term stores* and *working memory*.
- *Attention* to messages may or may not produce lasting memories.
- Interpreting media information is accomplished either through *automatic* or *controlled processing*.
- Processing interpreted in the context of preexisting attitudes, opinions, and beliefs (i.e., top–down processing) guides message interpretation.
- Media messages *access related stored* information.
- Accessing stored information may produce *common knowledge*.
- Networks of *associated ideas* contained in schemas facilitate construction of common knowledge.
- *Schemas* are instrumental in helping process media messages.
- *Message structure* and *content* influence how successfully and effectively we process media messages.
- *Media practices* and *norms* influence the ways in which professional communicators construct messages.

RECEIVING AND PROCESSING MEDIA MESSAGES

This chapter considers what happens psychologically when people receive media messages. As already seen, the media play an important role in assembling messages that people read, hear, or see. Individuals also play a critical role in the process of deciphering these messages. People interpret information in the context of their life experiences. Many of these experiences are stored in memory and drawn on to make sense of new information. We begin by analyzing the specific processes that take place when we encounter entertainment or information messages.

MEMORY PROCESSES

To explain the process of meaning, theories associated with attending to, and retention of, media messages are reviewed. Although psychologists have yet to agree on a universal memory theory, certain principles are widely accepted. Memory is dependent on stimuli affecting the sensory organs such as eyes and ears (Broadbent, 1958; Craik & Lockhart, 1972; Kellermann, 1985). Variously called the *sensory register* (Atkinson & Shiffrin, 1968a, 1968b), *the sensory store* (Wyer & Srull, 1980, 1981), or the *sensory buffer* (Hastie & Carlston, 1980), this region of the brain receives and interprets external stimuli such as sights, sounds, or smells.

Most memory theorists propose the presence of short-term memory (STM) and long-term memory (LTM) subsystems within the overall memory system of the brain (J. R. Anderson, 1983; Eich, 1982; Guillund & Shiffrin, 1984; Hintzman, 1986; Murdock, 1961, 1982; Ratcliff, 1978; Ratcliff & McCoon, 1989). The STM contains a region known as *working memory* (WM) where current thinking is believed to occur. The STM is believed to have limited capacity because memories within it decay quite rapidly (Baddeley, 1976; J. Brown, 1958; Peterson & Peterson, 1959). The LTM is capable of storing information for indefinite periods of time, even for a lifetime.

In the past, assimilating information into memory was believed to involve a series of discrete stages (Craik & Lockhart, 1972). The preliminary stages involve the evaluation of sensory or physical stimuli such as lines, angles, brightness, pitch, and loudness or perceptual stimuli such as sounds, sights, and smells. If these stimuli generate little cognitive activity, the processing is shallow. If the stimuli generate attention on the part of the perceiver, however, a deeper form of processing occurs. At some threshold, the stimuli may initiate a search whereby the new stimuli are matched against stored abstractions. The individual may deduce new meaning from the search process. Deeper processing leads to elaboration, which triggers associations between new information and information based on the individual's past experience. This new meaning is stored in a relatively permanent fashion in long-term memory as trace.

More recent models of memory (e.g., Basil, 1994; Rumelhart & McClelland, 1986) challenge the Craik and Lockhart (1972) memory model. These newer models, such as multiple resource theory (e.g., Basil, 1994) or the limited capacity model (e.g., Lang, Newhagen, & Reeves, 1996), argue in favor of processing in which distinct mental tasks are performed simultaneously rather than in a specified order. Specifically, humans possess limited information-processing resources but are capable of shifting these resources as needed to assist in processing information. The requirements of the processing task dictate whether resources are concen-

---

BOX 6.1. Using Multiple Streams of Information

During the third week of August 1998, weather forecasters began to notice the formation of the first hurricane of the season off the East Coast of the United States. News accounts on Monday, August 24, indicated that the path of Hurricane Bonnie was so slow and wobbly that it was not clear when or even if the storm would hit land. By Tuesday night, the storm was centered about 200 miles south of Outer Banks of North Carolina. It reached speeds of 115 miles per hour causing the evacuation of more than 500,000 people. By Wednesday, Hurricane Bonnie became a major news story receiving ongoing coverage by CNN and the Weather Channel.

CNBC, which defines the daytime target audience segment as viewers of financial and stock market news, chose to present ongoing live coverage of the storm. As the eye of Hurricane Bonnie moved closer to the Outer Banks of North Carolina, a CNBC reporter at the beach explained that hurricane force winds and torrential rains were approaching the North Carolina coast. As the hurricane report continued, simultaneous video images revealed that the Dow Jones Industrial was down 93.46 points, the Standard and Poors Index was down 9.00, and Nasdaq was down 27.43. Two crawls on the bottom of the screen presented individual stock quotes from the American and the New York Stock exchanges. With the mute button depressed, text of the report on Hurricane Bonnie appeared on the top of the television screen. Seven independent streams of information provided viewers of CNBC with information about the financial markets and a storm in North Carolina.

Audience members also turned to newer media sources to stay informed. When Hurricane Bonnie was at her mightiest, traffic volume was sky high at the Weather Channel's homepage (http://www.weather.com). Todd Walrath, vice president for online services at the Weather Channel, said the Web site received about 40 million page views, including 10 million on August 26, when the hurricane swept into North Carolina. On a normal day, the site received about 3 million hits (Richtel, 1998).

---

trated on encoding, decoding, or retrieval of stored information. Audience members shift resources as needed to attend to and process media messages. Television programmers also appear to recognize that people are adept at monitoring multiple streams of information (see Box 6.1).

Working and Short-Term Memory

The WM is a subsystem of the STM. The WM contains the thoughts or ideas that are actively engaged—those we are currently using (Baddeley, 1986; Gathercole & Baddeley, 1993). Psychologists once thought that people could (metaphorically speaking) maintain about seven chunks of information in an active state at a given time (Bower, 1970; 1972a; 1972b; 1975; Bower & Springston, 1970; Kellermann, 1985; Miller, 1956;

Murdock, 1961; Simon, 1974; Sperling, 1960). A *chunk* is theorized to be a finite set of information such as words or images that decays in 20 to 30 seconds. The problem with this conceptualization of memory is that it does not acknowledge that people are capable of monitoring many environmental stimuli simultaneously (Anderson, 1990; Basil, 1994; Rumelhart & McClelland, 1986).

Consider that one can simultaneously drive a vehicle through city traffic, listen to news on the radio, hear sounds, smell aromas, and plan out activities for the day. The issue is not lack of capacity, but rather the inability to maintain a great amount of information in a high state of activation. The information (e.g., thoughts or ideas) that is in a high state of activation is that which is currently in the WM (Baddeley, 1986; Kintsch, 1972). However, all of the environmental stimuli to which we are exposed comprise the repertoire of information in the STM. Hence, a television news bulletin with surprising or interesting information can catch and shift our attention from the conscious or STM into the WM. Bulletins on the vote by Congress to impeach the president or the bombing of the Federal Building in Oklahoma City are examples of events that may prompt us to shift to WM.

Theorists believe that concepts in the working memory can activate a set of related concepts and associations within the long-term memory. The principles of such activation were well established in a variety of theoretical perspectives, including spreading activation theory by Collins and Loftus (1975), the associative network model of social memory by Hastie, (1986) and the connectionist network model of knowledge by Rumelhart and McClelland (1986). These theories assume that processing one news item in WM may lead to accessing other memories of related news items. Therefore, context is supplied, enabling the media user to make sense of new information. This process may add new content to a schema, which will refine the frame through which interpretation of information occurs.

Long-Term Memory

The long-term memory (LTM) subsystem contains the semantic long-term memory (SLTM) and the episodic long-term memory (ELTM); Rumelhart, Lindsay, & Norman, 1972; Tulving, 1972). The SLTM stores general knowledge that has been accumulated through repeated exposure to information or situations. A weathercaster who predicts rain during the evening newscast may cause an individual to remember to bring an umbrella to work the next day because the individual has fallen into such a habit. By contrast, the ELTM contains information about specific events or episodes. The same weather report predicting rain may prompt another individual to decide to give away tickets to a college football game. In short, the ELTM involves using information to address specific issues. ELTM is constantly changing to accommodate new events and information. The SLTM remains more stable because it pertains to general events, principles, or ideas.

Shortly after exposure to media, humans tend to draw on episodic memory (Bower, Black, & Turner, 1979). As time passes, memory processes become more abstract and constructive as inferential associations and linkages are made between new and stored information (Spiro, 1980). This is because we integrate new information into schemas, which represent general knowledge rather than memories about specific incidents (Branford, 1979; Kintsch, 1978; Neisser, 1976; Royer, 1977).

Reconstructing knowledge implies interpreting new information in the context of stored knowledge. Reconstruction may result in conclusions or interpretations that are incorrect because individuals may not remember where they initially received the facts (Brosius, 1993). For example, people may forget that information about one political candidate did not come from television news or newspapers but rather from an attack advertisement produced by an opposing candidate (Biocca, 1991; Jamieson, 1992; Kern & Wicks, 1994).

A common misconception about memory of media information has to do with attention to messages. Attention often does, but does not necessarily, lead to recall (Collins, 1983; Grimes & Meadowcroft, 1995; Kahneman, 1973; Meadowcroft & Reeves, 1989; Reeves, Newhagen, Maibach, Basil, & Kurz, 1991). Rather, rehearsing or thinking about information in the working memory may lead to the development of stronger and more durable memories. Strong memories are those that are well learned and relatively easy to retrieve from the LTM because they have been regularly rehearsed (Baddeley, 1986).

Automatic and Controlled Processing of Media Messages

People attend to media in either an automatic or controlled way. Automatic processes are unconscious, unintentional, involuntary, effortless, autonomous, and outside awareness (Schneider & Shiffrin, 1977; Shiffrin & Schneider, 1977). They are unintentional because they do not require a specific goal and are effortless because they do not consume significant amounts of processing capacity. Once initiated, they do not need to be controlled because they occur unconsciously (Fiske & Taylor, 1991). Leaving the television turned to CNN while reading, attending to chores, or engaging in conversation represents an example of automatic processing. The viewer may be monitoring the news without much attention or effort.

Certain television programs may require controlled processing if the viewer is to receive benefits from the viewing experience. Consider cooking or carpentry television programs that teach the basics of making a soufflé or building a deck. These programs, which are specifically intended to demonstrate how to execute a task, afford viewers only one opportunity to absorb the material. They must pay careful attention. Thus, controlled processing implies an intense focus on media messages rooted in a motivation to learn. It should be noted, however, that automatic processing implies the presence of active audience members, although the degree to which people attend to the message may be considerably lower.

In summary, if an item encountered in the media is capable of attracting a viewer's attention, and the content presented is maintained in a high state of activation in the WM, the item is more likely to be remembered. This heightened state of activation implies rehearsal, such as thinking about the content or discussing it with other people. The longer the content remains in an activated state, the greater the likelihood that elaboration occurs (i.e., the new information is compared to previously stored knowledge), which increases the likelihood that linkages will develop between new and previously stored knowledge.

DEVELOPING COMMON KNOWLEDGE

Understanding how we interact with media involves the use of cognitive schemas, constructs, cognitive maps, and scripts that contribute to the creation of meaning through the interaction of new and stored information (Nimmo, 1977). Such a perspective argues in favor of the acquisition of common knowledge. Common knowledge is obtained by actively monitoring the information environment with the intent of selectively isolating and abstracting bits and pieces of seemingly novel, important, useful, or interesting information (Graber, 1988, 1990; Neuman, Just, & Crigler, 1992). Integration of information takes place in WM, and the act of rehearsing information strengthens memories as mental pathways between the LTM and WM are deepened producing durable trace (J. R., Anderson, 1990; Baddeley, 1976; Roediger & Challis, 1989; Roediger, Payne, Gillespie, & Lean, 1982; Roediger & Thorpe, 1978). Memories that were stored for quite some time may be summoned if the proper cues are encountered or primed (Raaijmakers & Shiffrin, 1980, 1981; Vanderwart, 1984).

Rehearsing and presenting proper cues are two mechanisms that lead to accelerated recall of stored information (Wicks, 1992a, 1995). These processes are fundamentally psychological in nature. Specifically, they suggest that:

1. Active processing guides attention and reception of media messages.
2. Top–down processing guides message interpretation.
3. Membership within cultural, social, demographic, or psychographic groups may influence meaning construction.
4. Message structure and content can interact to influence meaning construction.
5. Institutional norms and practices at media organizations can influence the production of media messages.

INFLUENCES ON THE PROCESSING OF MEDIA MESSAGES

Active Processing Guides Attention and Reception of Media Messages

Theorists have long attempted to determine whether differences in processing between textual and visual media exist. In the debate, television has often been considered a mindless activity because we simply receive it. Noble (1983) suggested that television viewing is passive because it taps the emotions rather than cognitions or thoughts. Singer (1980) asserted that the process of simultaneously encoding visual and audio channels that may or may not be in consonance (i.e., visual and auditory redundancy) present viewers with a formidable processing challenge. Because people are not presumed to be up to the processing challenge, television viewing tends to be passive.

Some communication theorists believe that reading text forces people to create mental images, whereas visual media such as television and films provide the images to viewers. As a result, human beings expend cognitive energy to interpret text. Visual images are ignored or absorbed depending on motivational circumstances of the individual audience members. However, the process of constructing mental images is not necessarily confined to the print medium. Hoijer (1989) asserted that as we encounter scenes or sequences from television, we must also create mental representations. These mental representations are not photocopies but rather interpretations and impressions that are the result of interaction with cognitive structures in memory. In addition, interpretation may be influenced by affective states of mind or emotions that are tapped during the viewing experience (Zillmann, 1983b). This process of making sense and attaching meaning to incoming stimuli is basically what is meant by *comprehension*.

It is also possible that people simply perceive reading to be active and viewing to be passive (Clark, 1983). Because children either directly or implicitly are taught to believe that reading is more difficult than watching television, they come to assume this is the case. Salomon (1979) found that children expect reading to be more difficult so they expend more mental effort. As a result of the added processing effort, memory for text may be better than memory for viewing because message receivers determine how much mental effort is allocated (Salomon & Leigh, 1984). Equivalent allocation should, however, lead to equivalent processing (Meadowcroft & Olson, 1995).

The fundamental problem with the assumption that watching television is a passive activity is that this assumes serial rather than parallel processing strategies that now dominate the communication and psychological literature (for a review, see Basil, 1994). As noted previously, communication scholars now believe that people can perform multiple processing tasks simultaneously. It is no longer necessary to assume that visual media like television overwhelms the senses and will not lead to higher order processing (Mander, 1978; Winn, 1977). Constructing meaning requires that viewers are active, interpretive, goal directed, and engaged with media (Evans, 1990; Kraus & Davis, 1976). Yet this conceptualization of media usage does not suggest that people are always deeply engaged with televised messages. Instead they are reasonably astute at monitoring messages and tuning in when something interesting, important, or novel is presented (Blumler & Katz, 1974; Graber, 1988; Robinson & Davis, 1990; Rosengren, Wenner, & Palmgreen, 1985).

Specifically, what is meant by the *active audience*? The theoretical components of the active audience can be traced to the work of Bauer (1964), who began to define how audiences become engaged with media messages. The concept of the active audience involves an emotional and intellectual engagement with the message (Biocca, 1988). It implies that media can alter the mood, disposition, and even physiology of the viewer (Zillmann, 1991a). Horror and erotic films, for example, provide frightening or voyeuristic experiences that may affect a person physiologically, causing perspiration or an increase in heart rate (Cantor, 1991; Tamborini, 1991; J. Weaver, 1991).

Televised sporting can also alter the mood of the viewer. A football game may provide a sense of euphoria and even produce outright laughter when a favorite team is beating the opposition (Zillmann, 1983a). Meadowcroft and Zillmann (1987) demonstrated that depressed women experiencing symptoms of premenstrual syndrome (PMS) gravitate toward comedy over serious drama or game shows. Although viewers may not consciously decide to adjust their mood through the selection of media programs, psychological mechanisms encourage them to actively select fare to alter their mental states. In summary, people use certain media and program genres as a means of emotional release (Hearn, 1989).

Structural characteristics of messages may actively engage audience members. For example, the style of music and pacing, shot selection, editing techniques, special effects, and narrative sequencing may lead viewers to become more or less involved with media. The interaction between structure and content can also produce effects that may engage viewers (Geiger & Newhagen, 1993). An advertisement produced on behalf of a candidate might include a hopeful message illustrated with colorful patriotic images and inspiring music. An ad attacking the record of an incumbent opponent on crime might feature gray tones containing images of illicit drugs and police activity placed over a somber narrative describing the ineffectiveness of the administration in power (Kern & Wicks, 1994). Hence, the interaction between message content and structure may influence the degree to which people attend to, process, and store media content.

Active media usage also denotes monitoring the outside world by selectively attending to messages to derive certain gratifications (Blumler & Katz, 1974; Rosengren, Wenner, & Palmgreen, 1985). People select media and program types based on certain gratifications such as the need for orientation or the need to relax. Compelling news events such as the death of Princess Diana focus controlled attention on such news reports. Under these conditions, even subtle features of televised content can have an important impact on the meaning people construct from the message. For example, Newhagen (1994a, 1994b) experimentally studied the impact of censorship disclaimers (i.e., text noting that censors cleared the news items) during the 1991 Persian Gulf war. He found that, although people had difficulty remembering they had seen the disclaimers, they interpreted the news stories quite differently from those had not seen them. Those exposed to the disclaimers were much less likely to trust the credibility of the messages.

Finally, Perse (1990a) examined the audience activity in the context of local television news by testing the relationships among: (1) strength of news viewing motivation and involvement intensity, (2) type of news viewing motivation and involvement orientation, and (3) cognitive and emotional involvement. She found that audience utilitarian (i.e., news that was perceived as helpful or useful) news viewing was associated with higher cognitive involvement and feelings of anger. Diversionary viewing used to relax or escape produced feelings of happiness on the part of the viewers. She found a link between cognitive and affective involvement with the news. The motivations to view largely determine the degree to which the audience members are active.

In summary, the literature does not suggest that people are always active processors of media content. Rather, factors such as message structure (i.e., use of graphics, color, pacing, music, etc.) and message content (i.e., program type or genre) as well as viewing motivation can stimulate active processing (Burnkrant & Sawyer, 1983). Merely attending to a media message is no guarantee that it will be stored in LTM. Without some form of rehearsal or thought about media information, memories decay quickly.

Top–Down Processing Guides Message Interpretation

The Search of Associative Memory (SAM). Top–down processing implies that thinking is a conceptual or theory-driven process in which interpretation of information is based on prior experience or knowledge (Fiske & Taylor, 1991). Bottom–up processing, by contrast, refers to making decisions based exclusively on new data (Bobrow & Norman, 1975; Wyer & Srull, 1981).

Images of a televised baseball game at Candlestick Park in San Francisco may cause one to vividly recall pictures of the earthquake that rocked the ballpark during the World Series on October 17, 1989. Although baseball and earthquakes have little in common, images of the ballpark can stimulate the retrieval of stored memories because they were encountered at about the same time. Alternatively, a news item about a recent earthquake in Tokyo may also cause people to retrieve memories from the San Francisco earthquake because the appropriate content construct was accessed. The explanation for these phenomena may be interpreted in the context of the Search of Associative Memory (SAM; Raaijmakers & Shiffrin, 1981).

SAM may be useful in illustrating processes underlying the construction of meaning from media. Memory is conceptualized as a mental house full of rooms in which related concepts are stored hierarchically and in close proximity. The hierarchy for transportation modes may include categories such as boats, cars, and airplanes. The buses and subways categories would probably be in closer proximity to each other than the buses and boats categories because the former represent forms of commuter transit. Hence, when deciding on a mode of transportation for a summer vacation, one would naturally flow among the cars, boats, and airplanes categories, although buses and subways also provide transportation. The mind thus organizes conceptual domains logically. Concentration on a particular domain will tend to retrieve the contents of that domain rather than other unrelated concepts.

Raaijmakers and Shiffrin (1981) demonstrated that words learned at the same time can be used to cue each other. With successive attempts over time, recall of items encountered concurrently may increase. For example, a dinner conversation may progress through several different subjects such as politics, the economy, and sporting events that appeared in media news reports. At a later time, mention of the political topics touched on during dinner may cue memories associated with the economic topics also discussed. Therefore, cueing is capable of revitalizing stored memories (Ballard, 1913; Brown, 1923).

Human beings are also capable of internal cueing that may result in accessing memories (Tulving, 1974; Tulving & Pearlstone, 1966). This internal cueing represents a kind of networking that ultimately leads to the development of associations between related ideas and concepts. Consider how a television news crime story is encoded and processed. An individual may recall neither the names of murder victims in a drive-by shooting in a certain Miami neighborhood nor any specific details about the incident. However, in the course of running errands, he or she may remember to avoid driving through that neighborhood. He or she may also infer that it is likely that the incidence of rape, burglary, and assault is also high in that neighborhood. Stored information led this individual to infer that he or she should avoid the neighborhood because it had been linked to the schema of crime (i.e., murders, burglaries, assaults, and rapes).

In summary, SAM embraces theories of associative memory and schematic processing that appeared in the 1970s and 1980s (see Brewer & Nakamura, 1984; Hastie, 1981; Markus & Zajonc, 1985; Murdock, 1982, for historical accounts). SAM suggests that incrementing (i.e., the act of recalling an item) makes it more likely to be recalled in the future. Forgetting occurs because the process of retrieving stored information is difficult and grows even more difficult as time passes and new memories are added (Raaijmakers & Shiffrin, 1980, 1981). This is consistent with general information-processing theory, which posits that moving items between long-term memory and working memory strengthens the memory trace, thereby leading to greater access of stored information (J. R. Anderson, 1976; 1983; 1990).

Schemas.   SAM is consistent with the general principles associated with schemas and construct accessibility. Significant interest in schema theory began in 1932 when Frederick A. Bartlett began experimenting to find out how well people remember figures and stories (Bartlett, 1932). He believed that people organize information in logical clusters to make understanding easier and more efficient. This perspective argues against the notion that memory is sequential or that each new bit of information is stored discretely. Such a sequential or linear system would make remembering quite difficult because human beings would be forced to sift through all stored memories until they happened on the correct ones, which facilitate understanding of new information.

A schema is theorized to be a cognitive structure that includes knowledge about a concept, person, or event (Brewer & Nakamura, 1984; Fiske, Kinder, & Larter, 1983; Fiske & Linville, 1980; Fiske & Taylor, 1991; Hastie, 1981; Rumelhart, 1984; Rumelhart & Ortony, 1977; Schank & Abelson, 1977; Taylor & Crocker, 1981; Wicks, 1992b). Schematic thinking helps people to efficiently handle information. This enables people to use information quickly in ordinary human interactions and it assists in making judgments (Cohen, 1981; Tesser & Leone, 1977; Thorndyke & Yekovich,

1979; Yekovich & Thorndyke, 1981). Schemas also serve interpretive and inferential functions because they guide us in our decision making and help us surmise from an incomplete set of facts (Crocker, Fiske, & Taylor, 1984, Crockett, 1988; Wicks, 1992b; Wilcox & Williams, 1990).

Schemas are believed to perform four primary functions (Fiske & Taylor, 1991; Graber, 1988; Wicks, 1992b):

1. They are responsible for assisting us in noticing, processing, and storing information so that it may be retrieved from memory at a later time.
2. Schemas assist us in organizing and evaluating new information. In so doing, they enable us to store related information together making it unnecessary to establish a new conceptual domain for each new piece of information.
3. Schemas enable people to fill in gaps in information by inferring. This makes interpretation possible when incomplete information is encountered.
4. Schemas enable people to solve problems by using information about similar scenarios to assess new information. This helps people decide how to act in certain situations.

Media information is capable of summoning a schema or schemas from the long-term memory to the working memory. As specific new information blends into schemas containing related knowledge, discrete pieces of information become more difficult to retrieve. Instead, people tend to retrieve the set of knowledge on that topic (Dooling & Christiaansen, 1977). When new information is added to a schema, the structure grows in complexity. This implies the evolution of a more cohesive structure with the ability to interact with other related schemas (Taylor & Crocker, 1981). Schema theory also suggests that well-developed schemas are much more difficult to alter than simple schemas. It posits that people are active processors of information and that schematic thinking derives from the need to organize thinking for the purpose of cognitive economy. As is true with the SAM model, very tight linkages associate closely related ideas and concepts. A less organized and cohesive network (see Box 6.2) connects loosely connected concepts.

People are also presumed to assess similarities among objects and then derive an average or central tendency for the category (Rosch, 1978; Tversky, 1977). Hence, when the word *Republican* is encountered in a newscast, it tends to summon concepts associated with conservatism and fiscal austerity, whereas *Democrat* is more likely to summon concepts associated with more liberal leanings and a social conscience. When introduced to a Republican senator, one may assume that he or she supports conservative ideals because they were historically associated with the Re-

BOX 6.2. Graphic Representation of Schemas in Information Processing

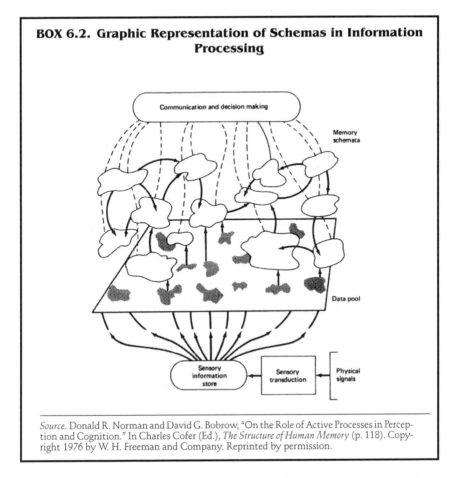

Source. Donald R. Norman and David G. Bobrow, "On the Role of Active Processes in Perception and Cognition." In Charles Cofer (Ed.), *The Structure of Human Memory* (p. 118). Copyright 1976 by W. H. Freeman and Company. Reprinted by permission.

publican platform. This process of assigning objects to categories utilizes both prior experience and inference (J. R. Anderson & Bower, 1973; Hayes-Roth & Hayes-Roth, 1977).

Schema theory presumes that old information affects the manner in which we interpret new information in social settings and elsewhere. Knowledge about others and ourselves guides our responses to new information. This was studied in work on stereotyping (Allport, 1954; Lippmann, 1922), impression formation (Asch, 1946; Bruner & Tagiuri, 1954; Fiske & Dyer, 1985), and attribution (Heider, 1946, 1958). Social schema researchers have built on this foundation to explain how prior knowledge guides attention, memory, and interpretation of social information (Fiske & Taylor, 1991). The selected schemas provide conceptual guidance in determining where one should seek new data and how one should interpret current data (Norman & Bobrow, 1976). The process of moving from schema to schema is quite fluid and many schemas could be linked at any given time.

Images and sounds that stimulate our senses cause us to think about new information within the context of stored schemas. Should a media message catch our attention, we may retrieve related memories from the LTM to make sense of the new information (Carmen, 1985). If we access information stored in these schemas on a fairly regular basis, the schemas become more durable, organized, and easier to access in the future. Thus, the fundamental reason that human beings are able to process information quickly is due to the way in which memory is organized. This may explain why people report that they do not remember much from the morning paper or the evening newscast. Specifically, monitoring the information environment leads to selective retention of isolated bits of information that were then stored in schemas containing previously encountered knowledge rather than stored as episodic memories.

In summary, schema theory maintains that schemas are strengthened by the addition of new, related knowledge. In addition, associations between related schemas are strengthened as individuals evaluate information over time. Further, consistent with the SAM model, retrieval of information becomes easier as a consequence of the deepened memory trace. In other words, the more one rehearses (i.e., thinks about recently encountered information), the more likely one retrieves previously stored knowledge.

Membership Within Cultural, Social, Demographic, or Psychographic Groups May Influence the Construction of Social Reality

Writers and producers of television shows and films may believe that their messages are interpreted similarly by each audience member. Such an assumption is not necessarily correct because such a view is based primarily on the magic bullet or hypodermic needle models of media effects. As noted earlier, these models fell into disfavor largely because they are inconsistent with current research findings suggesting that effects are not universal.

Membership within a cultural, social, demographic, or psychographic group may lead to selective interpretations of television messages. For example, in 1971, Norman Lear unveiled *All in the Family*, a new genre of situation comedy. The lead character, Archie Bunker, was intended to satirize a likable blue-collar bigot and racist. Although most viewers understood the parody, those with beliefs similar to those of Bunker related to him and interpreted the character to be an ordinary and likable fellow (Severin & Tankard, 1992).

Vidmar and Rokeach (1974) conducted surveys of Canadian adults and U.S. adolescents to determine how viewers perceived the program. In neither case did the respondents see Archie as the fool. Rather, U.S. adolescents saw Mike and the Canadian adults saw Edith as the objects of ridicule. In addition, respondents classified as *low in prejudice* were likely to believe that Archie loses in the end, whereas those classified as *high in prejudice* were likely to believe he wins. Additional support was reported in 1976. Brigham and Giesbrecht found that Whites whom were high in prejudice showed a strong tendency to like and agree with Archie and to perceive his racial views as valid.

The construction of social reality based on group membership is a function of the way messages are constructed and the way they are received. News reporting of the affirmative action issue over the years provides an excellent opportunity to illustrate how and why membership within a cultural group may influence meaning construction. The philosophy behind affirmative action was summed up in 1978 when Supreme Court Justice Harry Blackmun wrote that race must be taken into account if institutional racism is to be eliminated from society. In his discourse analysis, Gamson (1992) noted that both Black and White group members believe that everyone should be judged as an individual. On an issue like affirmative action, however, messages framed in certain ways may have the potential of being selectively processed. Some members of certain minority groups attend to, perceive, and retain news information when the story on affirmative action is framed as an attempt to solve a social problem. By contrast, when journalists present the issue as preferential treatment for certain classes of citizens, some Anglo-Americans may be more disposed to perceive the message as an indictment of reverse discrimination.

Psychological and demographic similarities may also contribute to shared meaning construction among certain group members. Soap opera viewing can teach certain groups of viewers how to correctly behave in social situations (Livingstone, 1990a, 1990b). Alternatively, soap operas can also sanction and glorify the incidence of premarital sexual encounters between young adults. The soaps occasionally present episodes on the dangers of teenage date rape and the unenviable pain and circumstances of low-class prostitutes. In so doing,

> the soaps provide a textbook example of the opportunity for selective mechanisms to work. Viewers who seek voyeuristic experiences and activists who wish to condemn this programming as immoral both can have their way by focusing on the prevailing lust. Viewers otherwise motivated may see that sex is pleasurable at times but not at other times. Both messages are available, even if not equally. (Greenberg & Busselle, 1996, p. 160)

In summary, group membership based on demographic, psychographic, cultural, and social groups may influence the way in which media messages are understood and constructed. Television programs, films, or text have the potential to interact with predispositions, attitudes, and beliefs of certain social groups.

Message Structure and Content Can Interact to Influence Meaning Construction

As previously noted, structure and content may influence the degree to which viewers attend to and process media messages (Geiger & Newhagen, 1993; Geiger & Reeves, 1991; Lang, Geiger, Strickwerda, & Sumner, 1993). Structural devices such as placing short visuals of fireworks or the addition of humor in educational programs have been effective in gaining attention and stimulating recall (Bryant, Zillmann, & Brown, 1983). Meadowcroft and Reeves (1989) explained that these devices "facilitate comprehension, because they periodically recapture attention and redirect it to the message. Without them, attention fades and learning suffers" (p. 353).

The interaction between structural and content variables also appears to influence the processing of television news (Lang, 1990; Schleuder, White, & Cameron, 1993). The retention of news items following emotionally charged, disturbing news was quite poor immediately after exposure. Emotional visuals focus attention on specific parts of news items (Mundorf, Drew, Zillmann, & Weaver, 1990; Mundorf & Zillmann, 1991). The reconstruction of the news item afterward is mediated by perceptual judgments rather than retrieval, which may in turn produce errors in recall (Brosius, 1993; Zillmann, 1983a; 1983b). Newhagen and Reeves (1992) reported memory differences before, during, and after the presence of negative compelling images. Memory was worse for material that preceded the negative scenes.

Different types of messages stimulate differences in how much people remember and how the information is processed, stored, and recalled. In one study, experimental participants read a series of news foundation stories. Then subgroups read, viewed, or listened to news stories that were consistent with the foundation stories inconsistent with the foundation stories or unrelated to the foundation stories. Afterward, subjects were tested on their ability to infer and remember. Those in the consistent condition were more likely to draw more inference from what they had seen, heard, or viewed. However, subjects in the inconsistent group tended to remember more facts. This indicates that additional cognitive effort was exerted resulting in a reconciliation of inconsistencies. Therefore, structure and content influenced the ways in which messages were processed and recalled (Wicks & Drew, 1991).

In summary, the structure and content of messages play an important role in how people construct meaning because they may engage viewers and influence the manner in which messages are interpreted. The common practice of teasing stories at the beginning of a newscast or during commercial breaks may generate interest in these stories and stimulate attention. Content consistent with previously held beliefs and attitudes may strengthen predispositions. Information that is not consistent with predispositions may cause people to pay closer attention and perhaps remember more because they find the information surprising. Finally, text superimposed over televised messages can influence how messages are received and interpreted. Emotional messages have the potential to influence processing, retrieval, and storage (Newhagen, 1994a, 1994b).

Institutional Norms and Practices at Media Organizations Can Influence the Production of Media Messages

Television news programs can cause individuals to construct meaning that does not necessarily reflect reality because the basic news formula stresses conflict, controversy, human interest, and suspense (Mayeux, 1991; Stephens, 1993). Producers and journalists also subjectively process news, and these professional communicators can influence how information is interpreted. This mediated information is due to systematic biases such as the personal beliefs of editors and journalists, the institutional conventions of media institutions, and the pure marketability of a news story.

At the institutional level, a television news assignment editor confronts the daily dilemma of generating enough news to fill the newscasts scheduled throughout the day and evening (D. Berkowitz, 1996; Gans, 1979; Powers, 1977; Shoemaker & Reese, 1996; Tuchman, 1978). Furthermore, news stories must have a good likelihood of attracting viewers. Consequently, factors such as the availability of compelling images determines which stories are presented on television. In addition, the assignment editor may decide to send news crews to locations nearby the television station to reduce the amount of travel time needed to cover a story. As a result, the criteria for inclusion may depend more on visual aspects and ease of coverage rather than on the actual importance of the news story. Over time, systematic biases such as these may influence the degree to which news reflects what is truly taking place in the community.

Another institutional factor influencing television news is the role of the consultant (Butler, 1985; R. Powers, 1977). As early as 1968, consultants began experimenting with structural features of newscasts such as eye-catching sets, on-screen graphics, bouncy theme music, and banter between news personalities to get the attention of the audience (Allen, 1997). Consultants tend to recommend accelerating the pace of newscasts to make news seem more exciting and interesting. By the middle of the 1980s, more than two thirds of all commercial television stations employed news consultants (Butler, 1985).

Consultants also conduct surveys and focus groups to determine which topics interest people and assess how much audience members like news personalities in various markets. This research is supplied to station and network executives who use it to increase ratings. Two of the largest consulting firms, McHugh & Hoffman and Audience Research and Development, urged stations to de-emphasize political news and focus more on crime and weather (D. Berkowitz, Allen, & Beeson, 1996). As such, consultants play an important role in determining what content is presented and how the messages are structured.

Factors related to journalistic biases compound the problem. Although journalists are trained to maintain objectivity in their reporting of news, it is impossible to do so entirely. The raw material that is combined into news reports involves individual biases that begin with predispositions, attitudes, and beliefs. Television news presents a set of special problems. The images produced by photographers and edited in video suites by technicians may result in a finished product that contains biases from many people, as demonstrated by the Ruby Clark incident described in chapter 1. Assuming the noblest intentions of journalists, the process of creating television news reality explains why sources often lament that news stories presented on television are more fiction than fact. All of this is compounded by the fact that most viewers are unaware of these influences that contribute to the shaping of the news product.

CONCLUSION

In summary, a myriad of factors contributes to the ways in which we come to know about the world in which we live. Media outlets frame messages and attempt to persuade people to adopt a perspective or purchase a product. Biases held by professional communicators and journalistic conventions can also shape the content of television news stories affecting how and why people construe information as they do (Epstein, 1973; Gans, 1979; Tuchman, 1978).

As media consumers, we must be aware that interpreting media messages is a two-way street. The attitudes, beliefs, opinions, and predispositions we hold inevitably contribute to the construction of social reality. Interpreting media involves complex processes in which the message as produced interacts with each individual receiver. As a result, no two people interpret a media message in precisely the same way, although many people may construct quite similar meanings. In certain instances, strongly held attitudes or beliefs cause different people to attach different meanings to the same message. This process is normal and healthy in terms of constructing meaning. However, to be media literate, we must understand why and how we interpret and misinterpret media information.

7 Children as Audience Members

SUMMARY

- Children *attend* to, *comprehend*, and *retain* much of the media fare they encounter.
- Younger children pay attention to *salient* or obtruding features of media messages.
- Younger children have difficulty distinguishing between fictional and real characters.
- Older children rely both on salient features of the message and *scripts* or plots.
- Older children comprehend more than do younger children.
- Grotesque forms produce fear in both older and younger children.
- The media content that children retain will influence the *interpretation* of future messages.
- Aggression and violence presented on television may *teach* children these behaviors.
- Aggression and violence presented on television may *desensitize* children.
- Aggression and violence presented on television may encourage children to perceive the world as dangerous, thereby producing *unnecessary* fear and *anxiety*.
- Aggressive media messages *interact* with a host of other variables to produce violence and aggression in children.
- *Heavy television viewing* is believed to produce an appetite for violence.
- Most incidents of violence portrayed on television are *not punished.*
- *Advertisers target children* using cross-marketing strategies.
- Examples of *positive or prosocial* on television can produce healthy growth and learning in children.

GLORIFYING KILLING ON TELEVISION

On April 20, 1999, twelve students and one teacher at Columbine High School in Littleton, Colorado, perished when Eric Harris, 18, and Dylan Klebold, 17, went on the worst mass school shooting spree in U.S. history. The teenagers injured 22 other victims before turning their weapons on themselves to claim their own lives. Police found more than 30 pipe bombs around the school, inside booby-trapped cars, and in the suspects' two suburban homes. Some bombs were palm-sized carbon-dioxide cartridges wrapped with nails and BBs to maximize killing power. Other bombs, equipped with timers, were made from propane barbecue tanks.

In the school library, where one gunman died from a gunshot wound to the back of the head and another had a hole in the side of his head, police counted four guns: a 9-mm semiautomatic carbine, two sawed-off shotguns, and a handgun (Obmascik, 1999). Exactly 1 month later, a 15-year-old high school sophomore injured six students in Conyers, Georgia with a .22 caliber rifle. After the assault, the student dropped to his knees, pulled out a .22 caliber revolver, and placed it in his mouth. Before he could shoot, a school administrator talked the teenage gunman into dropping the weapon. Concerned parents, teachers, administrators, and policymakers wondered if violence presented on the media contributes to such behavior.

RISING CONCERNS ABOUT MEDIA VIOLENCE

The main concern about the relationship between media violence and aggressive behavior boils down to one fundamental issue—people encounter an enormous amount of violence in the media. Americans spend about 3,300 hours annually with media, which is about 42 hours each week. About 70% of this time is spent viewing television, cable, and videotapes and the remaining 30% using newspapers, magazines, books, and other media (U.S. Statistical Abstracts, 1996, cited in Potter, 1998). With so much time engaged with television and so much violence presented, the public, scholars, and media practitioners seem justified in worrying about the effect of contemporary films and television programs on the nation's youth.

Laying the blame for school violence squarely with the media, radio commentator Paul Harvey noted that the television set is on in most homes for about 7 hours a day. The programs, he asserted, are packed with sex and violence that is "unfit for adult consumption. We allow (or even encourage) our children to enter into virtual worlds in which, to win the game, one must kill as many opponents as possible in the most sadistic way possible" (Harvey, 1999). Scholars quickly joined the chorus challenging the media to take a proactive role in providing more positive role models. Many assert that *glorifying* acts of violence such as the school shootings encourages potentially unstable youths to commit murder. Furthermore, they suggest that the media's obsession with bizarre news creates the erroneous impression that the society is comprised primarily of malcontents, criminals, and misfits, as an op-ed piece in the *Boston Herald* indicates (see Box 7.1).

BOX 7.1. Op-Ed: A Culture That's Ripe to Sustain Evil

May 11, 1999, *Boston Herald*, p. 25

By Jack Levin, director of the Brudnick Center on Violence and Conflict, and James Alan Fox, dean of the College of Criminal Justice, both at Northeastern University, Boston, MA. Used with permission.

In an attempt to explain the recent school massacres in Jonesboro, West Paducah, Pearl, and Littleton, many commentators have implicated the prevalence of violence in television, films, and video games. Not only has the First Lady made this her latest soapbox issue, but the White House hosted a summit focusing on the effects of entertainment on youth violence. Right or wrong, they still may have missed a far more important point: Americans have created a popular culture in which evil is celebrated.

The most popular of the morality plays of yesteryear have gone the way of *Leave it to Beaver*—and with them America's heroes. Only the bad guys remain to serve as role models for our children. Everywhere you look in popular culture, you find villains.

Professional wrestling provides an apt metaphor for viewing such changes. Until recently, the typical wrestling match consisted of the powerful and virtuous good guys (dressed in white tights adorned with Stars and Stripes) who almost always beat the physically and morally inferior bad guys (dressed in menacing black costumes). But professional wrestling of the 1990s has instead become dominated by darkness and brutality—opponents are set on fire, hit with a barbed-wire baseball bat, or dumped into a garbage bin and carried away on a stretcher. The traditional good guy has been written out of the script.

Talk shows of the 1980s—Oprah, Donahue, and the like—similarly featured good against evil, the abusive or womanizing husband vs. his victimized wife, the child who terrorized his classmates. Audience members would typically boo and hiss the villain and support the victims. But Jerry Springer's youthful audience now cheers wildly as equally sleazy guests pound one another with their fists as the cameras roll. Springer is now more popular than Oprah—especially with eighth graders.

Prime-time TV programs have traditionally included a variety of contests such as westerns and police dramas in which the guys with the white hats ultimately defeated the forces of evil. Today, such shows are more likely to focus on the complexities of morality rather than its virtues. Chuck Norris'

(Continues)

Walker, Texas Ranger is one of the few programs to retain a morality-play aspect, and it is routinely attacked by critics who regard it as the most violent show on television. They too have missed the point.

We used to put our heroes on pedestals, but those days are long gone. Today's children grow up collecting trading cards that bear the images of mass murderers rather than baseball players.

On their bedroom walls, youngsters hang calendars featuring Ted Bundy and the Hillside Strangler. Instead of chronicling the good deeds of super heroes, cartoons and comics today depict the seedier side of life. *Batman and Robin* have been supplanted by *Beavis and Butt-Head* as well as *South Park*; the conquests of Superman have been replaced by a comic-book version of Jeffrey Dahmer. Children can also locate killer Web sites, wear killer T-shirts, and join killer fan clubs. They listen to the lyrics of Marilyn Manson, who inspires them to try Satanism, Gothic fashion, and mass murder.

Why have we abandoned hero worship? The answer is clear: Our traditional exemplars have let us down; our idols have feet of clay. Over the last 30 years, there have been repeated scandals at the highest levels of government, industry, and entertainment—Chappaquiddick, Watergate, Abscam, Irangate, Whitewater, Filegate, S&L, Monicagate, and campaign financing. Even worse, former heroes have been accused of myriad activities. Cases in point: Hulk Hogan (steroids), Pete Rose (illegal gambling), Mark McGwire (a diet supplement), Mike Tyson (rape), Hugh Grant (cavorting with a prostitute), Michael Jackson (child molestation), Pee Wee Herman (indecent exposure), Chris Farley (drug abuse), Michael Milken (insider trading), Bob Packwood (sexual harassment), O. J. Simpson (murder), and Bill Clinton (womanizing and sexual assault).

The latest Americans celebrated for their evil ways are the two Littleton teenage shooters. Although most youngsters have rightly identified with the victims' pain, too many children instead identify with the power of the perpetrators. What is more, Eric Harris and Dylan Klebold became instant celebrities when they had their photos plastered across the covers of magazines and newspapers, coast to coast, inspiring a series of copycats seeking their own 15 minutes of infamy.

Celebrating evil has turned morality inside out, making heroes into villains and villains into heroes. We no longer trust our traditional role models because they have too often let us down. Notorious criminals, on the other hand, may not have the virtues we would like our children to emulate, but at least they will never disappoint us.

FRIGHTENING FILMS

The evidence to support the proposition that television, movies, and other media are to blame for aggression and even murder appears to be overwhelming. As early as 1915, the ranks in the Ku Klux Klan swelled and lynching statistics shot up following the release of the film, *The Birth of a Nation*. The release of *A Clockwork Orange* in 1971 was followed by several rapes in England accompanied by the rapists' renditions of *Singin' in the Rain.* The late film director Stanley Kubrick subsequently had the film permanently removed from British circulation. Numerous other examples of copycat behavior attest to the power of the media to inspire aggression and murder (see Box 7.2).

BOX 7.2. Examples of Incidents in Theatrical Film That Spawned Copycat Behavior

- In 1974, two armed men entered a stereo electronics store in Ogden, Utah, shortly before closing time and forced three young employees into the basement. They forced the victims to drink Drano and sealed their mouths with duct tape. Because the Drano failed to kill quickly enough, they shot each victim in the head. They did the same thing to two parents of employees who came to the store to find out why their children had not arrived at home. Three of the victims died and another one was left in a vegetative state. The fifth managed to force the duct tape off with his tongue, but not before the Drano burned his esophagus. A witness testified that the killers had gotten the idea from watching the 1971 Clint Eastwood film, *Magnum Force* (Thomas, 1999).
- *The Deer Hunter* precipitated a rash of fatal Russian roulette duels.
- A fierce love of *First Blood* sent a deranged Michael Ryan tearing through his English village commando-style, killing randomly.
- Inspired by a scene from the movie *Taxi Driver*, John Hinckley, Jr., attempted to assassinate former President Ronald Reagan. It was later learned that he hoped to impress Jodie Foster who had appeared in the movie.
- The 1992 *RoboCop* killer on Long Island, who sliced one of his six victims from throat to stomach, told police, "I did exactly what I seen in the movie" (Leiby, 1995, p. G1).
- Just days after its premiere, the Wesley Snipes film *Money Train*, which was based in part on real incidents, inspired token-booth thieves to incinerate the clerk inside. Two armed men squirted gasoline into a subway token booth and set it ablaze, causing an explosion and nearly killing the clerk (Leiby, 1995).
- High school football players were maimed and killed lying down on busy highways after viewing *The Program*.
- *Child's Play* and its first two straight-to-tape sequels hold the record for the number of victims who perished. Two-year-old Jamie Bulger was stoned to death by a pair of 10-year-old Chucky fans in Liverpool. Sixteen-year-old Suzanne Capper was burned alive in Manchester by Chucky fans who played lines of the movies' dialogue to her as she was being tortured. Thirty-five Tasmanian vacationers were slaughtered by Martin Bryant, a mental patient who was obsessed with Chucky (M. Atkinson, 1999).

In the 1990s, however, the rash of violent incidents and the ruthlessness of these acts by youths captured the attention of scholars, the public, and policymakers. On March 5, 1995, for example, Sarah Edmondson, the 18-year-old daughter of one of Oklahoma's most prominent political families, and her 17-year-old boyfriend, Ben Darras, spent considerable time in her family's cabin with a video copy of *Natural Born Killers*, a Smith & Wesson .38, and a reported 17 tablets of the hallucinogen, LSD. It remains unclear how many times they watched the film and whether the use of drugs contributed to the events that would unfold over the next 2 days. The teenagers took a southern road trip first shooting and killing Bill Savage, a Hernando, Louisiana, cotton-gin manager. The following day, the pair shot convenience store clerk Patsy Byers, leaving her a quadriplegic. She later died of cancer. The youths had originally intended to go to a Grateful Dead concert in Memphis, but got the date wrong. Edmondson received a 35-year prison sentence and Darras received life.

In 1997, three Kentucky girls were left dead following the prayer-group shooting spree of 14-year-old Michael Carneal. The executions came after Carneal witnessed a dream sequence of Leonardo DiCaprio shooting his classmates in *The Basketball Diaries*. In April 1999, the parents of the three victims filed a $130 million lawsuit against at least 25 parties, including the five film companies that produced and distributed the film. The family of Patsy Byers filed a civil suit against Edmondson, Darras, Edmondson's parents, *Natural Bon Killers* director Oliver Stone, and Time Warner, maintaining that the film's creators "knew . . . or should have known" that violence would result from its being shown (M. Atkinson, 1999, p. 58).

Whether the courts ultimately hold media corporations responsible for the aggression that occurs after viewing violent material remains unclear. Millions of people around the globe have seen *The Basketball Diaries* and *Natural Born Killers* without committing acts of aggression afterward. Nonetheless, social scientists agree that special caution must be taken where child development is concerned. It is especially important to understand how television contributes to the development of ideas, attitudes, and beliefs in children because the early years are instrumental in the socialization process that lasts a lifetime. As Van Evra (1998) explained:

> Their attitudes, beliefs, and ideas about the world—as well as physical, cognitive and social skills—are taking form, and they absorb information from everywhere. Because of the considerable number of hours children spend viewing television, however, television becomes a disproportionately large potential informational and attitudinal source. (p. xi)

The debate has grown to the point that former presidents, entertainers, and academics have called on the Hollywood studios that produce both films and television programs to demonstrate a measure of restraint.

TELEVISION NEWS: IF IT BLEEDS, IT LEADS . . .

The drift toward sensationalism in network and local television news can be traced to the early 1980s. Until then, the major broadcast networks and local stations had little competition for the news audience. Only three outlets existed in most broadcast markets. However, as CNN and other new cable networks began to siphon off viewers, networks executives pondered new ways to stem audience erosion. They quickly found creative new ways to boost the ratings by presenting reports and interviews featuring dramatic and sensational content. Bottom-line considerations also spawned the proliferation of news magazine shows that can be produced cheaply with the on-hand staff. It took little time for network executives to discover that programs featuring exposes and celebrities attract audiences (Rust, 1999).

News events such as the arrest and trial of O. J. Simpson in 1994, Susan Smith's murder of her two sons, Lorena Bobbitt's attack on her husband, and the attack on skater Nancy Kerrigan by the husband of her rival, Tonya Harding, all had the elements needed to capture and maintain the attention of the audience. Court TV and E! provided ongoing coverage of some of these events. Television and radio talk shows along with syndicated programs like *Inside Edition* and a *Current Affair* did as well. Local stations soon discovered that tabloid news laced with sex and violence increases news ratings. Murder and mayhem now reign supreme as the centerpiece of many local television newscasts.[1]

Given the focus on violence on local, network television, and cable news, it is not surprising that TV news frightens many elementary school children. Young viewers who watch a significant amount of television tend to overestimate the violence and crime around them. In her 1998 book, *Mommy I'm Scared: How TV and Movies Frighten Children and What We Can Do to Protect Them*, Joanne Cantor (who also worked on the NTVS project to be reviewed shortly) recommended that children should not be

---

[1]Ironically, a study released in January 1999 suggests that the whistles and bells of tabloid TV are not the only road to success for local television. The study—funded by the Pew Charitable Trusts and conducted by the Project for Excellence in Journalism, a group affiliated with the Columbia University Graduate School of Journalism—studied newscasts at 61 stations in 21 cities. It concluded that quality news broadcasts were more likely to succeed than fail in the ratings. However, tabloid-oriented broadcasts also do well, indicating that the stations that suffer are those confused about which direction to take.

exposed to scary TV dramas, cartoons, news programs, and feature films. These media images may produce intense fear, and the resulting psychological harm may be permanent. Differences in age and gender may also mitigate the effects. Cantor contended that television stories involving child victims are particularly frightening and urged parents to prevent children under the age of 8 from watching television news.

A survey of 300 parents of children ranging from kindergarten through sixth grade indicated that children have trouble distinguishing fantasy from reality because they are at such an impressionable age (Cantor & Nathanson, 1996). A survey of 125 children conducted by Barbara J. Wilson (cited in Elias, 1998; Smith & Wilson, 1995) also revealed that more than half of the children could describe a television news clip that had scared them. Natural disasters such as floods, fires, and earthquakes triggered the worst terror in young kids. Third through sixth graders were most frightened by crime reports. The more television news they watched, the higher they thought the local murder rate was and the further their estimates were from the truth. For older children, Cantor recommended viewing family-friendly stations, with parents placing stories in a more positive context.

CHILDREN PROCESSING MEDIA

Attention

As with adults, information processing in children involves attention, comprehension, and retention. Children as young as 2 years old often pay attention to television because they want to understand it. If they fail to comprehend television, attention may drift to other activities or stimuli. As Van Evra (1998) explained, "attention is guided actively by the child's assessment of the comprehensibility of the content, attempts to comprehend content, situational variables including other viewers, and other activities" (p. 4).

Age is an important variable in determining whether children are more likely to pay attention to television. Young children are more prone to pay attention to salient features of messages such as animation, unusual voices, or upbeat music than are older children (D. R. Anderson & Levin, 1976). As children grow older, they begin to rely both on message salience and scripts, which aid in comprehending the content. As such, the common belief that children are passive recipients of media content may be incorrect. Children, like adults, appear to employ processing strategies that are quite active and relatively complex (D. R. Anderson & Smith, 1984). Finally, gender is another important variable in children related to attention. Boys tend to focus more attention to the visual features of violence than do girls (Alvarez, Huston, Wright, & Kerkman, 1988).

Comprehension

Older children are typically better than younger children at comprehending media messages. Other variables including motivation for viewing, experience with various media, socioeconomic status (SES), and innate skills are also important predictors of the child's ability to interpret and comprehend media content. Children younger than 3 find it difficult to distinguish between reality and fictional programs. They also have difficulty distinguishing real from fictional characters. However, by the age of 4 or 5, children develop skills at interpreting what is real. Therefore, in younger children, images that are scary may induce fear. For older children, familiar plots (i.e., scripts) that signal danger may induce more fear. For example, Cantor and Sparks (1984) reported that 40% of the parents of preschool-age children spontaneously said the series "The Incredible Hulk" produced fright reactions in their children. The series involved a normal hero who undergoes physical changes to become a hideous green-faced monster with superhuman powers. He used these powers for benevolent purposes.

Grotesque forms may also produce fear in older children. However, as older children become more attuned to the scripts and texts, comprehension leads to fears that danger may lurk. The television movie, *The Day After*, did not produce fear in younger children. The film depicted the results of a nuclear war that produced shortages of food, radiation sickness, and eventually the end of global civilization. Relatively few visuals depicted the graphic results of the war. Instead, the plight of the survivors was conveyed primarily through dialogue. Older children viewing the program demonstrated more fear because they perceptually understood the implications of the story line and recognized that such an event was possible. As with attention, comprehension appears to be influenced by the prior experience and knowledge that the child brings to the viewing situation (Wright & Huston, 1981).

Retention

What children retain from watching television is important because these memories influence how they interpret future media messages. As noted in chapter 6, message content and structure determines whether a message stimulates attention and comprehension, which ultimately leads to retention. The amount of mental effort that is allocated to processing media messages also affects how well they are retained. Children appear to remember visual information best when audio information supports the main points. Prior knowledge or a framework on which to assimilate new information is also important. Five- to 8-year-old children with advanced story schema skills (i.e., those that possessed a repertoire of scripts for media messages) demonstrated less processing effort, greater memory for the main themes, and more attention than did children with less developed story schemas (Meadowcroft & Reeves, 1989). The ability of a child to interpret content is inextricably linked with the ability to retrieve it. As such, the content encountered is important both in terms of how a child learns about the world and how future information is processed.

EFFECTS OF VIEWING AGGRESSING

Interest in curbing violence in the media intensified as it became increasingly clear that violence presented on television can have a negative effect on individuals and society. The three most commonly noted effects of viewing televised violence are (Huesmann & Eron, 1986; Paik & Comstock, 1994): (a) learning aggressive behavior and attitudes, (b) desensitization to aggression and violent behavior, and (c) cultivating an increased fear of violence because the media contribute to beliefs that the world is more violent than it is in actuality.

Although the link between media violence and aggressive behavior is becoming more explicit, the media environment must be analyzed in conjunction with a host of other variables. Biological and psychological factors, as well as broader social and cultural influences, may affect individual behavior. The relationship between viewing violence and subsequent aggressive actions depends both on the nature of the depiction shown and the composition of the audience.

To complicate the issue, the same portrayal of violence may have a different effect on different audience members. Higher viewing levels may lead to more aggressive behavior. Yet more aggressive children habitually and frequently choose violent television programs (Eron, 1982; Huesmann, 1986). In other words, aggressive people may selectively expose themselves to violent programming (Zillmann & Bryant, 1985). Finally, the same incidents portrayed on television or in films may produce fear in some children and aggression in others.

Peer influences, family role models, SES, educational level, and the availability of weapons each influences the likelihood of a particular reaction to viewing violence on television. These variables may also mitigate what children learn from watching television and films.

LEARNING AGGRESSIVE BEHAVIOR AND ATTITUDES

Social Learning Theory

At the most basic level, social learning theory (also called *modeling*) suggests that we learn how to behave by imitating the actions of others

(Bandura, 1977). The media in general, but especially television, play a critical role in teaching children how to act. Social learning begins when a child pays attention to media messages. He or she must then think about (i.e., rehearse) the behaviors witnessed. The child also must possess the cognitive ability and motivation to perform the behavior (Harris, 1999).

Laboratory studies have demonstrated that both adults and children may acquire novel behaviors by observing the actions of other people (Bandura, Ross, & Ross, 1961). These studies typically show adults or children behaving in an aggressive manner. The behavior is then either rewarded or punished. Those individuals who watch someone receive a reward are more likely to imitate the aggressive behavior demonstrated. Field studies tend to provide support for social learning theory as well. A now classic longitudinal study tracked the influence of televised violence on criminal behavior. Huesmann, Eron, Lefkowitz, and Walder (1986) followed viewing patterns and aggressive behavior in a group of research participants over two decades. In the study, data on aggression and television viewing were collected on subjects when they were 8, 18, and 30. In boys, early viewing of aggression correlated highly with aggressive tendencies later in life, increasing the possibility that they would ultimately become involved in crime. Furthermore, the results were uniform irrespective of social class, intellectual skills, or variables related to family and parents (Huesmann, 1986).

Although social learning theory may explain where children learn about certain behaviors, it does not provide an entirely satisfactory explanation as to why they imitate actions they see on television or in films. Few children jump from a skyscraper because they witnessed such an act on television. Nevertheless, it is not uncommon for children to mimic the aggressive behaviors of the Teenage Mutant Ninja Turtles or the battles of Luke Skywalker or Han Solo. Thus, modeling appears to be more related to some behaviors than others.

Scripts and Priming Theory

Complementing social learning theory is the idea that children develop scripts that guide their behavior. Repeated exposure to programming in which fights resolve conflict may cause a child to assume that aggression is appropriate behavior. Therefore, environmental stimuli may cause a child to activate the script for conflict resolution that may include violence. As Van Evra (1998) explained, "TV viewing affects behavior by activating certain scripts in the viewer, such that the behaviors seen on television are associated in the viewers' minds with other thoughts, events or conditions" (p. 134). Consequently, programming that features antisocial behavior may produce aggression. Conversely, positive prosocial behavior may teach children appropriate scripts.

Related to the idea of accessing scripts is priming. *Priming* is the process by which media attend to certain issues while excluding others. Certain concepts eventually become linked. Repeated coverage of scandals in the Clinton White House had the effect of developing a schema for the president that included less than flattering descriptors (such as *adulterer*). As with scripts, priming effects theory takes into account the likelihood that messages alone do not produce immediate aggression on the part of the child. When something is witnessed on television or in other media, ideas are activated that bring forth associated ideas that were stored in schemas in memory. Aggressive behavior presented in the media may cause children to summon similar violent memories (L. Berkowitz, 1984). The theory relies on general principles of semantic associative networks discussed in chapter 6.

Using scripts and priming both denote a two-way interaction between children and the media. That is, although media violence may contribute to aggression, it must interact with factors that encourage children to act violently. The right combination of these factors and heavy diets of televised violence will produce reciprocal effects. The more that children see aggression, the more enjoyable it becomes and the more they choose to watch. The five factors most related to aggressive behavior in children are (Huesmann, 1986):

1. the intellectual achievement level of the child,
2. popularity of the child,
3. the extent to which a child identifies with television characters,
4. the extent to which a child believes that television violence is real, and
5. the amount that a child fantasizes about media violence.

Children with lower levels of academic achievement tend to be more aggressive, watch more violent programming, and believe the portrayals more accurately reflect real life (Huesmann & Eron, 1986). Aggression acts as an intervening variable that may explain alienation of the child from teachers, peers, and family members. Poor academic achievement may be related to watching violent programming in two fundamental ways. Excessive television viewing may interfere with intellectual growth because children who find learning difficult fail to excel at school. These children may then choose instead to watch more television (Lefkowitz, Eron, Walder, & Huesmann, 1977). In addition, not only do aggressive children become more unpopular, but unpopular children may also become more aggressive. These unpopular children turn more to television than interpersonal interaction and, therefore, see more televised violence (Huesmann & Eron, 1986).

The similarities and differences between the actors and real-life role models are also important. Furthermore, environmental factors at home and in school may contribute to the ways in which children model behaviors seen on television and in film. School communities contribute significantly to the development of healthy prosocial behaviors. Having in place a safe and responsive foundation helps children and enables school communities to provide more efficient and effective services to students who need more support (see Box 7.3).

Box 7.3. Factors Contributing to a Safe School Environment

Well-functioning schools foster learning, safety, and socially appropriate behaviors. They have a strong academic focus, support students in achieving high standards, foster positive relationships between school staff and students, and promote meaningful parental and community involvement. Most prevention programs in effective schools address multiple factors and recognize that safety and order are related to children's social, emotional, and academic development.

Effective prevention, intervention, and crisis response strategies operate best in school communities that:

1. *Focus on academic achievement.* Effective schools convey the attitude that all children can achieve academically and behave appropriately while appreciating individual differences. Adequate resources and programs help ensure that expectations are met. Expectations are communicated clearly, with the understanding that meeting such expectations is a responsibility of the student, the school, and the home. Students who do not receive the support they need are less likely to behave in socially desirable ways.

2. *Involve families in meaningful ways.* Students whose families are involved in their growth in and outside of school are more likely to experience school success and less likely to become involved in antisocial activities. School communities must make parents feel welcome in school, address barriers to their participation, and keep families positively engaged in their children's education. Effective schools also support families in expressing concerns about their children, and they support families in getting the help they need to address behaviors that cause concern.

3. *Develop links to the community.* Everyone must be committed to improving schools. Schools that have close ties to families, support services, community police, the faith-based community, and the community at large can benefit from many valuable resources. When these links are weak, the risk of school violence is heightened and the opportunity to serve children who are at risk for violence or who may be affected by it is decreased.

4. *Emphasize positive relationships among students and staff.* Research shows that a positive relationship with an adult who is available to provide support when needed is one of the most critical factors in preventing stu-

---

(Continues)

dent violence. Students often look to adults in the school community for guidance, support, and direction. Some children need help overcoming feelings of isolation and support in developing connections to others. Effective schools make sure that opportunities exist for adults to spend quality, personal time with children. Effective schools also foster positive student interpersonal relations—they encourage students to help each other and to feel comfortable assisting others in getting help when needed.

5. *Discuss safety issues openly.* Children come to school with many different perceptions—and misconceptions—about death, violence, and the use of weapons. Schools can reduce the risk of violence by teaching children about the dangers of firearms, as well as appropriate strategies for dealing with feelings, expressing anger in appropriate ways, and resolving conflicts. Schools also should teach children that they are responsible for their actions, and that the choices they make have consequences for which they will be held accountable.

6. *Treat students with equal respect.* A major source of conflict in many schools is the perceived or real problem of bias and unfair treatment of students because of ethnicity, gender, race, social class, religion, disability, nationality, sexual orientation, physical appearance, or some other factor—by both staff and peers. Students who have been treated unfairly may become scapegoats and/or targets of violence. In some cases, victims may react in aggressive ways. Effective schools communicate to students and the greater community that all children are valued and respected. There is a deliberate and systematic effort (e.g., displaying children's artwork, posting academic work prominently throughout the building, respecting students' diversity) to establish a climate that demonstrates care and a sense of community.

7. *Create ways for students to share their concerns.* It has been found that peers are often the most likely group to know in advance about potential school violence. Schools must create ways for students to safely report such troubling behaviors that may lead to dangerous situations. Students who report potential school violence must be protected. It is important for schools to support and foster positive relationships between students and adults so students will feel safe providing information about a potentially dangerous situation.

8. *Help children feel safe expressing their feelings.* It is very important that children feel safe when expressing their needs, fears, and anxieties to school staff. When they do not have access to caring adults, feelings of isolation, rejection, and disappointment are more likely to occur, increasing the probability of acting-out behaviors.

9. *Have in place a system for referring children who are suspected of being abused or neglected.* The referral system must be appropriate and reflect federal and state guidelines.

10. *Offer extended day programs for children.* School-based before- and after-school programs can be effective in reducing violence. Effective programs are well supervised and provide children with support and a range of options, such as counseling, tutoring, mentoring, cultural arts, community service, clubs, access to computers, and help with homework.

(Continues)

11. *Promote good citizenship and character.* In addition to their academic mission, schools must help students become good citizens. First, schools stand for the civic values set forth in our Constitution and Bill of Rights (patriotism; freedom of religion, speech, and press; equal protection/nondiscrimination; and due process/fairness). Schools also reinforce and promote the shared values of their local communities, such as honesty, kindness, responsibility, and respect for others. Schools should acknowledge that parents are the primary moral educators of their children and work in partnership with them.

12. *Identify problems and assess progress toward solutions.* Schools must openly and objectively examine circumstances that are potentially dangerous for students and staff and situations where members of the school community feel threatened or intimidated. Safe schools continually assess progress by identifying problems and collecting information regarding progress toward solutions. Moreover, effective schools share this information with students, families, and the community at large.

13. *Support students in making the transition to adult life and the workplace.* Youths need assistance in planning their future and in developing skills that will result in success. For example, schools can provide students with community service opportunities, work-study programs, and apprenticeships that help connect them to caring adults in the community. When established early, these relationships foster in youth a sense of hope and security for the future.

Watching television may also generate aggressive scripts that are encoded into a child's memory. Many aggressive or violent scenarios presented in action or dramatic programs recur repeatedly. Less realistic depictions of violence probably do not generate the same attention levels as depictions that appear realistic. Realistic depictions seem more relevant to the viewer. As a result, these more believable depictions may cause the child to rehearse or think about them. This process ultimately leads to the retrieval of related scripts from memory. They may act together to reinforce the proposition that violence portrayed is representative of real life, which may ultimately produce aggressive behavior on the part of the child (Huesmann & Eron, 1986; Huesmann, Lagerspetz, & Eron, 1984).

DESENSITIZATION TO AGGRESSION AND VIOLENT BEHAVIOR

For years researchers have also expressed concerns that, over time, television violence may habituate and desensitize people to aggression and violence (Drabman & Thomas, 1975). The repeated and continued exposure to violence in the mass media may less the development of sympathy or concern for the victims of the violent actions presented. Heavy viewers are more likely to enjoy violence and see it as justified. They tend to react less emotionally to violence than do lighter viewers (Van der Voort, 1986).

Even early studies focusing on the short-term effects of violence showed that heavy viewers were less prone to respond to violence physiologically. Arousal decreases as viewers watch more violent programs. Furthermore, both children and adults were susceptible to this effect (Cline, Croft, & Courrier, 1973). Desensitization may occur because the novelty wears off when violent acts are routinely presented in the media (Griffiths & Shuckford, 1989).

A persistent concern is that reduced emotional attachment to victims presented in the media may lead people to respond more slowly when real-life violence takes place (Van Evra, 1998). Furthermore, much of the research demonstrates that callousness may occur after prolonged exposure to depictions of women being victimized. Linz, Donnerstein, and Penrod (1984) studied college men who viewed portrayals of women being victimized over a 5-day period. By the end of the study, the men found the material less degrading than they did at the outset. The subjects also said they found the material less depressing and enjoyed it more by the end of the study. The findings generalize to victims of rape presented in a reenactment of a trial. The fundamental concern is that the callousness that may arise with respect to media portrayals of victimization may carry over to real-life situations. Researchers have also begun to question whether music videos and other newer programming genres contribute to the desensitization process.

CULTIVATING FEAR

Cultivation theory examines the extent to which repeated media exposure gradually shapes perceptions of social reality over time. The theory holds that media—especially television because it is so pervasive and used so heavily—may influence how people perceive reality (Gerbner & Gross, 1976; Gerbner, Gross, Morgan, & Signorielli, 1986). People who rely heavily on media and lack direct exposure to real-world experiences begin to accept the depictions presented as accurate and reflective of the society. Cultivation theory postulates that people perceive that crime and violence are considerably more prevalent than in reality because television programs and newscasts allocate so much time to such topics (O'Keefe, 1984; Perse, 1990a, 1990b).

Initially developed by George Gerbner, cultivation theory posits that when direct experience with one's environment is in harmony with mediated messages, messages tend to reinforce and even amplify each other. This phenomenon is known as *resonance* (Gerbner, Gross, Morgan & Signorielli, 1980; Morgan, & Signorielli, 1990). However, if an individual has little or no personal experience on which to formulate conceptualizations of reality, media messages may dominate. If these media messages are distorted, they may ultimately lead to incomplete or incorrect cognitive representations of one's environment. Because most people cannot experience everything that takes place, they rely on the media for information and interpretation of news and events. Media information ultimately influences their ideas, opinions, attitudes, and beliefs (Graber, 1980). Heavy users of television appear to be the most susceptible to cultivation effects (Signorielli, 1990).

The process of being influenced by media messages is called *mainstreaming*. Heavy users of media may develop shared meanings because of extensive exposure to similar messages over a period of time. In other words, groups of people may develop similar attitudes, opinions, and beliefs because they use media in excessive, instead of developing perceptions through discussions with other people or personally observing various aspects of the social, economic, and political order.

Cultivation research is usually conducted by comparing heavy and light viewers of television using statistical correlation techniques. Some experimental cultivation research was conducted. For example, Bryant, Carveth, and Brown (1981) exposed adults to 6 weeks of programming in which unjust acts and violence were punished or unpunished. Those who witnessed violent and aggressive behaviors that received no punishment were more pessimistic about the consequences of violence in the real world than those who saw these aggressive behaviors punished. Finally, heavy viewers generally describe the world as more similar to the one they witness on television, whereas lighter viewers characterize it more as it actually exists. People who watch programs containing significant amounts of violence report that the world is more dangerous than it is in reality (Signorielli, 1990).

CRITICISMS OF CULTIVATION THEORY

Critics have expressed methodological and theoretical concerns about cultivation theory. First, correlational data do not reveal the direction of causation. Although heavy viewers may develop certain perceptions of the world, these very perceptions may guide their program choices and viewing habits in the first place. Moreover, heavy and light viewers may differ on other dimensions such as education, and SES. The amount of viewing may actually serve as a proxy for another variable or combination of variables.

Potter (1991b) argued that the cultivation process contains a number of components that operate independently of each other. The effects may be a consequence of how viewers perceive and interpret program content. This may be particularly true if viewers perceive the program as being more realistic (Potter, 1986). The frequency with which a popular protagonist appears in a program may have far more influence than dozens of less visible characters (Greenberg, 1988). Furthermore, the cultivation effects may not be cumulative as Gerbner and his associates asserted. Exposure to violent television programming may increase the likelihood that more pessimistic thoughts are recalled. As Comstock and Paik (1991) explained, "Frequency of exposure in this instance may not be a measure of the history of viewing but the likelihood of recent exposure to violence or distressing events in entertainment, news or other programming" (pp. 185–186).

The contemporary media environment may also lessen the cultivation effect because it provides audiences with more options. One may now watch the History Channel, ESPN or A&E instead of broadcast networks that routinely fill primetime with violent programs (Perse, Ferguson, & McLeod, 1994). Response bias may influence the findings of cultivation studies because the approach assumes that television messages are basically similar to each other (Potter, 1993; Rubin, Perse, & Taylor, 1988).

To deal with some of its limitations, cultivation theorists reinterpreted the findings to highlight the implications of the active audience. In this case, the content of television is secondary to what the audience members do with messages after they encounter them. The fact that people consciously or unconsciously attend to certain programs and genres, and actively process the information in the context of stored knowledge, becomes the focus. As such, cultivation theory remains important as a backdrop in the study of what different people do with different kinds of media programming despite the inherent theoretical and methodological issues.

HARD DATA: THE NATIONAL TELEVISION VIOLENCE STUDIES

Although debates on the effects of television violence have raged, new data have illuminated the incidence of aggression on television. Funded by the National Cable Television Association, the National Television Violence Studies (NTVS) were begun in 1994 as a 3-year effort to assess violence on television and cable (see Box 7.4).

The sampling frame for the content analysis was drawn from 23 broadcast stations and cable networks between the hours of 6 A.M. and 11 P.M. Approximately 60% of all entertainment programs presented included violence in some form, as did 38% of all reality programs such as news. Ninety percent of all movies analyzed contained violence, and 18% of all programs studied contained nine or more violent acts. Experiments on media effects tended to suggest that, when media violence is rewarded, it is more likely to stimulate aggression. When aggression and violence are punished, aggressive behavior may be reduced.

BOX 7.4. The National Television Violence Studies (NTVS)

The National Television Violence Studies analyzed media over 3 years beginning in 1994. More than 300 people worked on the project, which involved videotaping nearly 10,000 hours of television programming. More than 1,600 people also participated in five separate experiments. The results of the content analysis represent the most comprehensive sample of the television and cable programming ever collected.

The National Television Violence Studies involved the collaborative efforts of media researchers at four universities, an oversight council of representatives from national policy organizations, and project administration and coordination. Researchers at the University of California–Santa Barbara studied violence in entertainment programming such as drama, comedy, movies, children's shows, and music videos. Researchers at the University of Texas at Austin examined violence in reality-based shows such as tabloid news, talk shows, police shows, and documentaries. Researchers at the University of Wisconsin–Madison considered violence ratings and labels or advisories used on television, including their impact on the viewing decisions of parents and children. Researchers at the University of North Carolina–Chapel Hill examined the effectiveness of antiviolence PSAs.

The project also involves the efforts of an oversight council charged with: (a) safeguarding the integrity and independence of the study, (b) providing advice and counsel to the researchers, (c) ensuring the scientific validity of the study, and (d) identifying implications from the findings.

The council was composed of representatives from 17 national organizations interested in the effects of television on individuals and society. It included individuals from the fields of education, medicine, law, violence prevention, psychology, sociology, and communication. One third of the council members were also drawn from the entertainment industry. The administration and coordination of the study has been conducted by the Center for Communication and Social Policy at the University of California–Santa Barbara. The project yielded three volumes of data on the content and effects of television programming.

In National Television Violence Study 3 (1998), content coders kept careful track of the consequences portrayed. Rewards and punishment for violent behavior were coded following each violent scene and at the end of the program. The study reported:

In the majority of violent scenes (54%), aggression is neither rewarded nor punished when it occurs. A much smaller proportion of scenes present violence as being explicitly punished (20%) or rewarded (17%), and even fewer depict violence as both rewarded and punished (9%). Violence that goes unpunished poses the greatest risk for viewers in terms of learning aggressive attitudes and behaviors. Taken together, our findings indicate that nearly three fourths of violent scenes on television (71%) portray no punishments for violence within the immediate context of when it occurs. This robust pattern holds across all types of genres, including children's programs. The pattern also holds across the various types of channels. (p. 87)

The National Television Violence Studies also investigated the effect of content ratings on television programs. Few of the ratings appear to make any significant difference in adolescents' interest in watching a particular show. However, older children say they are more interested in watching programs rated PG-13 than ones rated PG. Furthermore, content analysis revealed that these two labels do not differ in terms of the amount of violence presented. The PG-13 warning label is intended primarily to alert viewers that the shows may contain sex and adult language. Experiments conducted on the use of the warning *parental discretion advised* indicate that they may dissuade children from choosing to watch a program when the decision is made jointly with a parent or an older child. The influence of the label, however, is negated if the child alone makes the viewing choice.

The research also considered the effect of antiviolence public service announcements (PSAs) on children. The PSAs were relatively ineffective at attracting the attention of or engaging young viewers. The youths reported that many of the 100 PSAs analyzed contained sources and appeals that were noncredible. Furthermore, the content analyses of regular programs indicated that only 4% of programs that contain violence include an antiviolence message of any sort.

TARGETING CHILDREN WITH ADVERTISING

Other concerns about the media's effect on children have also been studied. Children are often the targets of intense advertising campaigns. Most television commercials are 30 seconds long, and children are exposed to an average of 25 per hour. A child viewing television for 4 to 5 hours a day may be exposed to more than 100 commercials a day, about 45,000 a year, or nearly 8 hours of televised advertising per week (Himmelstein, 1984). Kunkel (1992) observed that the majority of these advertisements promote toys and breakfast cereals with sugary snacks pushing the percentage to 74%. Healthy foods represented only about 3% of the advertising to which children were exposed.

The extent to which children are influenced by television advertising is unclear because age and developmental factors may mitigate the impact. Advertising designed to appeal to children often includes production techniques that attract and maintain attention. These may include quick edits, music, jingles, slogans, visual effects, and animation. Maturity level of the child may interact with attention factors that may in turn lead to remembering advertising content. Younger children are more attracted to animals, animation, and other attention-getting techniques and have difficulty distinguishing between programs and advertisements. Older, more cognitively advanced children are better able to distinguish advertising from program content and make reasoned assessments of the claims made. Irrespective of age, effective children's advertising relies on recognition rather than retrieval of information from memory (Singer & Singer, 1983).

Advertising may influence the interaction between parents and children because these appeals cause children to pressure their parents to purchase the advertised products. Much of the children's advertising is not intended to directly persuade them to ask for a product. Rather, it is intended to create an awareness of the product and link it with something good or desirable (Cheney, 1983). Advertising is geared more toward persuading children by using emotional appeals and encouraging them to believe products will make them feel happy or content. As such, children's advertisements rarely rely on rational arguments or comparisons between competing products (Nelson, 1987).

Many product categories produce advertising directed toward children. Large media companies promote products simultaneously in books, films, video games, and toys to name but a few. Cross-marketing between these products may include not only media and toys. Action figures from the film *Toy Story 2* adorned McDonald's Happy Meals during the Thanksgiving and Christmas holidays in 1999. One of the most ambitious cross-marketing campaigns involved the collaboration between Burger King and Nintendo to promote the Pokémon phenomenon (see Box 7.5).

Educators, parents, and social scientists have long expressed concerns that advertising targeting children may produce negative effects—ranging from cynicism to overconsumption. This advertising is designed to manipulate the emotions of the vulnerable young viewers. However, it seems unlikely that efforts to cultivate these young consumers will subside anytime soon. Parents and educators should teach children how advertising works and explain the motivations of the producers. In so doing, children may learn how to interpret and use advertising messages most effectively.

PROSOCIAL CHILDREN'S PROGRAMMING

Parents can also use the media to teach children prosocial behavior. Television can teach children positive attitudes and act as a catalyst for learning. In the 1960s, interest developed in educational children's programming

---

BOX 7.5. Do You Want Some Pokémons With Your Burger?

Beginning in early November 1999 and running throughout the holiday season, Pokémon fans were able to satisfy their hunger and craving for the tiny monsters by purchasing meals at more than 8,000 Burger King restaurants in the United States. The 8-week promotion enabled children to collect 57 different toys during a 56-day period. The toys, each of which are packed in a Poké Ball inserted in a kids' meal, included 1 of 151 trading cards. The promotion represented a partnership between Burger King and Nintendo of America, Inc. It was also timed to coincide with the November 10, 1999, release of Pokémon's first animated feature, WB Kids Presents *Pokémon: The First Movie* (the title foreshadowing the prospect of more Pokémon films in the future).

The promotion also offered consumers the option of purchasing one of six collectible 23K gold-plated trading cards for $1.99 with the purchase of any value meal. The cards came packaged in a mechanized Poké Ball and included a certificate of authenticity. Burger King restaurants around the country scheduled trading nights on Tuesdays enabling children to trade their Pokémon collectibles. The promotion and the trading nights were supported by significant national television, radio, print, and billboard advertising.

The 57 toys given away included squirters, bean bags, keychains, launchers, light-ups, talking plush toys, and rev-tops. The trading cards, which are randomly packed with the toys, were created exclusively for Burger King. Nintendo-licensed Pokémon characters were printed on the front and back of the trading cards and featured 1 of 10 scenes from the first Pokémon film.

The Pokémon promotion also featured a site on the Web (www.burgerking.com), which enabled children to track their progress in collecting all the toys. The Pokémon phenomenon in America began in September 1998 with the release of the original Blue and Red Game Boy games and debut of the television series. More than 7 million Pokémon-related video games have been sold to date.

The Burger King Corporation is a part of Diageo, the international food and drinks company, that includes such brands as Pillsbury, Häagen Dazs, and Guinness. Nintendo Co., Ltd., of Kyoto, Japan, has sold more than 1 billion video games worldwide, having created such industry icons as Mario and Donkey Kong.

---

that would provide positive role models, teach socially positive attitudes and behaviors, and be commercial free. In 1967, responding to the recommendations of the prestigious Carnegie Commission study group, Congress created the Corporation for Public Broadcasting (CPB). In 1969 and 1970, the CPB joined with public radio and television stations. This association led to the formation of the noncommercial National Public Radio (NPR) and the Public Broadcasting Service (PBS). Children's programming improved dramatically during this time with the formation of the Children's Television Workshop (CTW) in 1968.

One of the first and most important projects undertaken by the CTW was the production of *Sesame Street*. This children's program, which has transcended generations, has been adopted by broadcasting systems around the world. The intent of the program was to provide a preschool foundation to foster an interest in reading and learning. Puppets and animation were produced and developed to appeal specifically to disadvantaged children in multicultural and urban settings. The show quickly gained favor among all social strata with regular characters like Big Bird and the Cookie Monster.

Sesame Street employed many of the same devices used by commercial programmers to capture the attention of children. The show contains a lively mix of animation and puppets that sing, dance, read, and play games. In maintaining parallel structure to commercial broadcasting, *Sesame Street* is *sponsored* by entities such as the letter "M" or the number "3." The program always placed a premium on providing a balanced interracial, intercultural, ethnic, and gender mix. Stereotyping is avoided by placing emphasis on characters of different races, gender, or socioeconomic status.

Research on the effects of *Sesame Street* indicate that viewing improves vocabulary and early reading skills. It fosters positive social skills and develops healthy attitudes including evidence of nonracist beliefs or behaviors (D. R. Anderson, 1998; Rice, Huston, Truglio, & Wright, 1990). Furthermore, recent longitudinal research indicates that preschool children who watch *Sesame Street* often score higher school grades in English, math, and the sciences (Huston & Wright, 1998). Greenberg (1982) reported that minority children who watched *Sesame Street* demonstrated an enhanced sense of self-confidence and cultural pride and better interpersonal skills. The show also elevated the attitudes of White children toward children of other races (Christenson & Roberts, 1983).

In 1971, CTW introduced *The Electric Factory* to help improve reading skills in older children. It employed many of the same educational techniques and strategies that were developed in *Sesame Street*. The show never gained the critical praise of *Sesame Street* and was eventually canceled in 1986. *Barney* (the large purple dinosaur) also adopted a multicultural format that encourages cooperation and sharing. Other additions to the education lineup on PBS include *The Puzzle Place, Reading Rainbow, Dragon Tales* and *Mr. Rogers*. These, along with *Sesame Street*, remain prime staples of the PBS daytime lineup.

CONCLUSION

Television is an important part of children's lives. As much of the content that is presented attracts and engages the attention of children. Children also retain much of what they hear and see on television. Research demonstrates that children do imitate behaviors they witness on television, including violence and aggression. However, aggressive incidents presented through the media may summon similar aggressive scripts from memory. The cumulative effect may be that aberrant behavior seems more normal to children.

Children demonstrate violent tendencies as a result of repeated exposure to aggressive behavior. If a child grows accustomed to seeing other people victimized, they may lose the instinct to sympathize or empathize. A growing concern is that this effect may carry over to real-life situations. Some believe that seeing constant victimization in the media may cause people to become indifferent or sedentary when similar events occur in one's community.

Media aggression is also theorized to create a sense of unnecessary fear among heavy television users. Because the television screens are filled with murder and mayhem, one may come to believe that the real world is a scary place. Although critics assert that this oversimplifies the role of media in contemporary society, evidence from the National Television Violence Studies encourages us to consider this proposition in a broader context. The studies reveal that when aggression on television is punished, it is less likely to be imitated by children. However, in more than 70% of the instances of televised violence analyzed, aggression went unpunished.

Children have always been the targets of advertising campaigns for products such as toys, snacks, and breakfast cereals. Recently advertisers recognized that cross-marketing strategies involving diverse products may generate interest among children. One recent trend involves theme-based toys, films, books, and videotapes. To promote these products, advertisers enter into arrangements with firms such as fast-food restaurants. Effective product promotion may lead to the remarkable success of products such as Nintendo's Pokémon. Parents and teachers should help children understand the nature of advertising and how to interpret the claims made within advertising.

Finally, certain types of media and television programs may have a beneficial effect on how children grow and develop. Studies reveal that children can and do learn prosocial attitudes, beliefs, and behaviors from programs like *Sesame Street*. These programs, which encourage racial harmony, a positive outlook, and the mission of educators and parents, can provide a positive foundation for learning throughout life.

8 The Radio and Television Talk Show Audience

SUMMARY

- Radio and television talk shows *satisfy* certain personal needs and gratifications.
- Talk shows enable people to keep their pulse on social issues.
- Talk shows enable people to hear about the attitudes, beliefs, and opinions of other people.
- Talk shows foster *parasocial relationships* between the members of the audience and the hosts and, in some cases, between guests and listeners or viewers.
- Regulatory changes in broadcasting enable talk shows to become *interactive*.
- Programmers use different types of talk shows to attract different types of *audience segments*.
- People report that they now rely on talk shows for information.
- Talk shows have been *criticized* for setting the media agenda, focusing on salacious topics, and cultivating the impression that society is faced with widespread distress.
- Talk shows have been criticized for undermining social, economic, and governmental institutions.
- Talk shows have been criticized for teaching antisocial behavior such as resolving conflict through fighting.
- Talk shows have been *praised* for stimulating social dialogues.
- Talk shows enable people to feel better about their own circumstances by witnessing the trials and tribulations of others.
- Most people recognize that *antisocial behaviors* presented on television are departures from the norm.
- People appear to recognize that talk shows presenting antisocial behavior as *exemplars* do not lead to the construction of social scripts.

THE NATURE OF TALK SHOWS

In this chapter, we consider the growing importance of the syndicated radio and television talk shows and consider why they are so popular. We also analyze the ways in which they may contribute to constructions of social reality among audience members. The remarkable increase in this programming genre and the ratings that talk shows produce suggest that people derive considerable gratification from listening to them on the radio or viewing them on television.

Talk shows are not new, as host Rosie O'Donnell explained:

> No other family was as obsessed with TV in my neighborhood as mine was. We were allowed to watch TV 24 hours a day. And, we did. My favorite shows were "Merv Griffin" and "Mike Douglas." I would literally run home from school every day and switch them on. I hope we can bring back that kind of show to television. (http://www.rosieo. warnerbros.com).

O'Donnell may have shared much in common with contemporary children who spend afternoons on the couch with Oprah Winfrey or, alternatively, Jerry Springer.

Talk shows are as varied as their hosts, ranging from the Sunday morning variety such as *Meet the Press,* which is intended to analyze political news, to the *Jerry Springer Show,* which routinely features fist fights, outbursts, and melees among family members, friends, and lovers. Although serious broadcast network economic or news talk shows like *Wall Street Week* on PBS or ABCs' *This Week* recognize the need to entertain to maintain their audience, their primary function is to inform. By contrast, individual stations enter into contracts with program producers to acquire talk shows such as *Montel Williams* and *Rosie O'Donnell,* which are shown during nonnetwork programming time slots. Broadcast stations like to run syndicated programs because they can be extremely profitable. This is because stations sell all or most of the advertising time slots within the program to local advertisers.

Journalists, educators, and citizens have profoundly different views on the effects of talk radio on the American political system. Some believe that these programs unnecessarily stir up political issues, denigrate politicians, and question the integrity of governmental institutions. They arouse emotions and may tilt the outcome of elections by creating public cynicism. As a result, these programs may potentially pose a significant danger to the stability of American economic and political culture. Others contend that talk radio programs are simply part of a stable of new program genres that engage the audience and bring about social debates and political discourse. These programs serve a therapeutic function by sparking new dialogues among citizens that contribute to the marketplace of ideas.

The number of television talk shows grew dramatically during the past few years. Shows like *Oprah* and *The Rosie O'Donnell Show* were praised as presenting enlightened discussion and interesting guests. Others, like "Jerry Springer" and "Jennie Jones," were criticized for introducing topics that result in profanity and fist fights between guests. In this chapter, we focus primarily on entertainment-oriented syndicated radio and television talk shows such as *The Rush Limbaugh Show, The Jerry Springer Show,* and *Oprah*. The appetite of audience members for these varied programs has grown steadily over the years and will undoubtedly continue to grow for some time to come. We now consider why audience members find these programs so entertaining and informative.

THE USES AND GRATIFICATIONS MODEL

The uses and gratifications model endeavors to explain the psychological benefits that accrue to people when they use media. People use media to be entertained; to escape from daily pressures; for companionship; to keep track of world, national, and local events; and for personal objectives such as reinforcement of values or reassurance (McQuail, Blumler, & Brown, 1972; Palmgreen, Wenner & Rosengren, 1985; Rubin, 1994). Katz, Blumler, and Gurevitch (1974) asserted that the model focuses on the

1. social and psychological origins of
2. needs, which generate
3. expectations of
4. the mass media or other sources, which lead to
5. differential patterns of media exposure (or engagement in other activities), resulting in
6. need gratifications, and
7. other consequences, perhaps mostly unintended ones. (p. 20)

In a significant refinement of the uses and gratifications model, Palmgreen et al. (1985) outlined the basic assumptions of the approach:

1. People use media in a goal-oriented fashion and are fairly active in the selection process.
2. People use media to satisfy certain needs or desires that may range from companionship to helping them find information.
3. Social and psychological factors such as beliefs, attitudes, predispositions, and environment drive the ways in which people use media.

4. Media compete with other forms of communication for the attention of the audience. In so doing, some media serve a parasocial function displacing interpersonal contact with other people. The issue in this regard is not that media are evil or good. Rather, the assumption suggests a need to understand the dynamic that takes place when people become engaged with media.

5. People tend to hold the upper hand in their relationship with media programming. As Klapper (1960) argued, effects of media are typically quite minimal. Under certain circumstances, however, media messages have the potential of altering the social, economic, and political fabric of society. Although this is not necessarily bad, it is important for people to understand the potential impact of interacting with media (Rosengren, 1974; Rubin & Windahl, 1986).

Together the assumptions stress that people willingly interact with media. People select from competing media offerings to satisfy their current needs. Because we are all different, beliefs, attitudes, predispositions, innate intelligence, and a host of other variables guide our media-seeking behavior. The underlying significance of the uses and gratifications model is that it encourages researchers to investigate what motivates audience members to use media by identifying the benefits derived from its use.

The uses and gratifications model is useful in explaining the dramatic increase in radio and television talk shows over the years. Many of these programs are informative or entertaining. Some provide reassurance that the personal circumstances of an individual are not as bad as they may appear. Some reinforce attitudes and beliefs. However, critics express concern that talk shows may cultivate unhealthy attitudes, opinions, or beliefs.

TALK RADIO COMES OF AGE

Talk radio has undergone a period of remarkable growth since 1960, when only KABC in Los Angeles and KMOX in St. Louis presented talk formats. During the next several decades, several important events took place that stimulated the rapid proliferation of talk radio. First, the radio industry went through significant changes in the 1970s and 1980s. The advent, development, and growth of FM radio with high-quality stereophonic capabilities posed significant problems for AM stations because they could not effectively compete with their technologically superior counterparts on the FM dial. As audiences continued to drift toward FM stations, AM stations began to offer talk formats because such programming did not require stereophonic sound (Stark, 1995). From an economic standpoint, talk radio was also attractive because a single host could fill hours of air time. Furthermore, the advent of cheap satellite transmission technology in the 1980s helped the number of all-talk or news/talk radio stations climb from 200 to more than 800 in a decade ("Everybody's Talkin," 1995; Jost, 1995).

Significant regulatory changes occurred during the 1980s and 1990s that made talk radio the most popular format in the country by the end of the 1990s. Although the early talk shows in the 1960s dabbled in political discussions, they avoided politically charged and divisive issues. Stations wished to avoid the wrath of advertisers and did not want to run afoul of the Fairness Doctrine, which required them to present opposing viewpoints from those that had been presented on a station (see Head, Sterling, & Schofield, 1994, for a discussion of the Fairness Doctrine). In 1987, however, the Fairness Doctrine was repealed. The elimination of these rules encouraged the development of radio programs that presented their hosts' partisan positions.

Several other events in the late 1980s and early 1990s propelled the proliferation of political radio talk shows. The formation of the National Association of Talk Show hosts in 1988 gave a voice to the developing programming genre. News topics surfaced that provided plenty of *bait* to lure listeners to the programs. These hot topics included a decision by Congress to cancel a pay raise for itself in 1989, claims made by Gennifer Flowers that she had an affair with Bill Clinton during his quest for the Democratic nomination in 1992, a bid for the White House by Ross Perot, the debate over gays in the military in early 1993, the Whitewater affair, the 1994 national health care debate, the Oklahoma City bombing, the Monica Lewinsky affair, and the impeachment proceedings of President Bill Clinton (Bolce, De Maio, & Muzzio, 1996; Page & Tannenbaum, 1996).

The Telecommunications Reform Act of 1996 also advanced the rise of radio talk shows. The Act enabled a company to acquire up to eight stations in a single market, doubling the previous limit. As a result, a handful of large companies spent the second half of the 1990s acquiring mom-and-pop stations across the country. In 1994, for example, Chancellor Broadcasting owned only a couple of radio stations in Sacramento, California. Now known as Chancellor Media, it was the largest owner of radio stations in the United States in 1998 as a result of a $4.1 billion merger with Capstar. The merger meant that the company owned 463 stations or about 4% of the nation's radio outlets. Companies such as Chancellor Media may negotiate package deals on syndicated programming for many stations at a time. Instead of growing at a rate of one or two stations at a time, the producers of *Rush Limbaugh* or *Dr. Laura Schlesinger* may negotiate licensing deals with corporations that own scores or even hundreds of stations.

THE RUSH LIMBAUGH PHENOMENON

In the early 1980s, "the radio oracle known today as Rush Limbaugh was just another journeyman disc jockey, spinning records under the name Jeff Christie" (Paige, Danitz, Hickey, & Russell, 1998, p. 9). In 1988, New York's WABC–AM hired the conservative talk show host. He became an immediate phenomenon. Within a decade, talk shows was the most popular radio format, with Limbaugh attracting more than 19.5 million listeners each day on more than 650 radio station in the United States between the hours of noon and 3:00 P.M. EDT[1]

The program produces approximately $27 million in ad sales annually, and a newsletter brings in $13 million for an annual overall profit of about $25 million ("Wheeling & Dealing," 1998). Limbaugh forgoes his salary in exchange for a 50% cut of show profits and the right to endorse products on air. He received a $30 million one-time payoff in 1997 when Jacor Communications bought EFM Media for $80 million. Eight other national programs claim more than 60% of the talk-show audience, and 7 out of the top 10 hosts are conservatives (Paige, Danitz, Hickey, & Russell, 1998).

Blumler and Gurevitch (1995) characterized Limbaugh and other conservative *talkmeisters* as "a new breed of politically influential *nonpoliticians* who employ power without political responsibility" (p. 213). Because listeners of political talk radio are more likely than nonlisteners to be conservative Republicans, talk radio may influence the outcome of elections as well as public policy debates (Cappella, Turow, & Jamieson, 1996; Hollander, 1996).

During the rise of Limbaugh, talk radio became popular on some FM stations. By 1998, shock jock Howard Stern's radio program was heard on about 60 FM stations in the United States and Canada during the early morning hours. Stern makes close to $20 million annually from radio, cable, and broadcast television. Unlike Limbaugh, who delights in roasting Democrats and liberals, Stern specializes in presenting the bizarre. His programs have featured a former professional stripper giving Stern a lap dance; an overweight, surgically scarred woman disrobing in a desperate bid to win a Frankenstein Makeover; several women undressing from the waist up in a competition to win a set of breast implants; and "a misguided 15-year-old male straining to set some sort of record for flatulent emissions" (Kelleher & Blonska, 1998, p. 27). Video excerpts from the morning program are presented on cable's E! Entertainment Television at 11:00 and 11:30 P.M. on Sunday through Friday nights.

---

[1]The audience for Rush Limbaugh actually declined between 1996, when it stood at 21 million, and 1999. Heath (1998) explained that the decline is more a function of added competition from new media such as the Internet and other talk radio formats.

In summary, the radio environment changed dramatically during the past 15 years. The FCC is now less prone to respond to criticism by listeners because deregulation of the industry enabled program hosts to introduce politically charged topics and test the boundaries of good taste. The name of the game is to find new ways to attract the attention of the audience. Although the messages may differ and on-air personalities may change, the main strategy behind the talk radio is to get the audience involved with the program. In the case of talk show hosts like Limbaugh, this is done by tossing out hot topics and red herrings, lampooning liberals and Democrats, and inviting the audience to call the host. Howard Stern uses an alternative tactic such as engaging in discussion and presenting behavior so far out of the norm that it cries out for attention.

WHO IS LISTENING TO WHAT CHANNEL WITH WHAT EFFECT?

Between 1983 and 1998, the number of all-talk radio stations or news-and-talk stations went from only 53 to more than 1,330 or about 13.5% of all stations in the United States, making talk radio the most popular format (Paige, Danitz, Hickey, & Russell, 1998). Two thirds of news/talk listeners are White, one third have college degrees, 58% earn $50,000 annually, more than half of the AM talk-radio audience are over 50, and 41% are 65 or older (Heath, 1998).

In the 1990s, news/talk began to target segmented audiences by presenting specialized programs aimed at women and younger audiences. As the audience for talk political talk/radio grew, scholars and media critics alike began to wonder how these new programs with their flamboyant hosts and unique attention-getting strategies were contributing to the formation of opinions, attitudes, and beliefs of audience members with respect to social, cultural, economic, and political institutions (Katz, 1991; Page & Tannenbaum, 1996). Citizens groups such as the American Families Association of Tupelo, Mississippi, became outraged with certain programs and talk show hosts such as Howard Stern. In response to what the organization considered objectionable programming, it began positing lists of stations carrying the program along with the sponsors that support it on its Web site.

Research on the effects of talk radio has produced inconclusive and even conflicting results. Some scholars suggest that political talk radio plays an agenda-setting function by getting people to consider certain issues (Traugott et al., & Young, 1996). Others assert that listening to talk radio encourages citizens to contact public officials (Pan & Kosicki, 1997) and engage in other kinds of political participation (Hofstetter & Gianos, 1997). Still other researchers contend that political talk radio is clearly negative toward most institutions with public figures serving as the main "targets of abuse" (J. L. Katz, 1991, p. 42). This causes citizens to lose confidence in their leaders and become negative toward governmental institutions in general.

Some analyses suggest that the listeners of talk radio are more politically alienated, inattentive to public affairs, socially isolated, and more cynical than nonlisteners. They tend to take extreme sides on policy issues and be more suspicious of elites than nonlisteners (Avery & Ellis, 1979; Crittenden, 1971; J. L. Katz, 1991; Levin, 1987). In a 1991 survey of San Diego talk radio listeners, a different picture emerged. Listeners paid more attention to politics and participated more in political activities (including voting, campaign work, community action, and contacting public officials) than nonlisteners. The search for information was offered as the major reason people use talk radio (Hofstetter et al., 1994). Others dispute the contention that political talk radio produces a sense of deepening alienation between citizens and political institutions (Herbst, 1995; Hollander, 1996; Roberts, 1991).

Most negative commentary about radio and television talk shows implicitly or explicitly raises the issue of the cultivation of ideas, attitudes, or beliefs as a consequence of exposure to media messages. Political talk radio shows, which feature hosts with clear political leanings or those that attract guests or callers with similar dispositions, may have a significant influence on how people come to perceive the world, nation, and community in which they live.

Talk show hosts are accused of creating the impression that society is faced with widespread distress (Levin, 1987). Based on a nationwide study, The Times Mirror Center for The People and The Press reported that, "American public opinion is being distorted and exaggerated by the voices that dominate the airwaves of talk radio" (Kohut, Zukin, & Bowman, 1993, p. 1). The study indicated that 84% of the listeners are motivated to tune into talk radio for surveillance and keep up with major issues. Eighty-five percent reported that they used talk shows to find out how other people feel about issues. Nearly half of talk listeners reported that they were interested in hearing people with views in opposition to their own. The Times Mirror study also found talk show audiences to be more conservative, more Republican, more anti-Congress, and more critical of President Bill Clinton than nonlisteners. This study and the research by Hofstetter and his associates suggest that the talk radio constituency pays attention to politics. These listeners are more likely to participate in public meetings, write letters to their officials, and vote.

It nevertheless remains unclear whether talk radio influences attitudes enough to alter voting patterns when listeners are confronted with partisan or biased commentary on political leaders and governmental actions or policies. The results of a content analyses conducted by Pfau, Moy,

Radler, and Bridgeman (1998) echo the findings of the Times Mirror study. The analysis reveals that political talk radio's depictions of the office of the presidency, news media, and public schools were consistently negative. The results reiterate that popular political talk radio personalities are decidedly gloomy in their depictions of democratic institutions (J. L. Katz, 1991; Levin, 1987; Rehm, 1996). These depictions are associated with unfavorable perceptions among heavier users of this communication source, as the Times Mirror study suggested (Kohut, Zukin, & Bowman, 1993).

A study in 1996 revealed that the amount of talk radio use corresponded to negative evaluations of President Clinton and that it reinforced political opinions (Owen, 1997). Data from a national probability sample indicate that call-in talk shows on TV and radio are important venues for expressing and influencing public opinion on political issues (Pan & Kosicki, 1997). A *New York Times* exit poll conducted during the 1994 midterm congressional elections revealed that nearly half of all voters occasionally listened to political talk radio, with the most frequent listeners voting for Republican candidates by a three to one margin (Egan, 1995).

One study of political talk shows during the 1996 presidential primary season reported that talk shows could have a significant influence in the so-called "distant phase" of a presidential primary (Pfau, Kendall, Reichert, & Hellweg, 1997). During the final week of the New Hampshire primary campaign, researchers surveyed 315 prospective voters in four states whose primaries followed New Hampshire's by 1, 2, 4, and 5 weeks. The researchers wanted to find out if reliance on political talk radio contributed to the formation of perceptions of candidates during the primary campaigns. People who listened to a significant amount of talk radio had more favorable perceptions of Bob Dole and Steve Forbes. Talk radio seemed more important than traditional media such as newspapers and television, which appeared to exert relatively little influence on beliefs, attitudes, and opinions during the course of the Republican presidential primary campaigns.

The explanation for the apparent influence of political talk radio on Republican voters may be a function of two factors working together. First, citizens continue to rely less each year on traditional media such a newspapers and television (Fallows, 1996). As noted in chapter 3, newspaper readership has been declining for quite some time. However, a more recent phenomenon is the erosion of the television network news audience (D. Potter & Gantz, 1999). A survey conducted for the Pew Foundation Center for the People and the Press (1996) revealed that the proportion of people who said they watched television news in any form during the previous day declined precipitously from 74% as recently as 1994 to just 59% in 1996. This is especially important with respect to Republicans because research suggests that, compared with Democrats or independents, Republican voters are much more distrustful of traditional media news (Pfau et al., 1999).

Pfau, Moy, Radler, and Bridgeman (1998) pointed out that understanding the influence of political talk/radio on listeners may require a sensitivity to evaluating this genre with attention to both content and structural variables. Although the program content is highly negative toward political institutions, the hosts invite and encourage participation of like-minded listeners. Therefore, listeners may not even recognize that the tone of these programs can reinforce and even cultivate new negative attitudes toward these institutions.

It is also possible that talk radio listeners are different from other media users. Talk radio listeners may not fit conceptually into traditional analytical categories used to define other groups or collectives such as race and ethnicity, occupation, region, class, religion, generation, or gender. Consequently, researchers may wish to consider users of talk radio in the way they study African Americans, Christian fundamentalists, union members, farmers, southerners, the poor, senior citizens, and other groups that have historically demonstrated distinct voting patterns. Some have even argued that the most salient and theoretically meaningful characteristic of talk voters is the medium and the type of programming to which people listen (Bolce, De Maio, & Muzzio, 1996).

SEGMENTING THE RADIO AUDIENCE

As news/talk radio expands beyond the confines of political discussions, niche programming in radio has proliferated. Just as radio stations differentiate themselves by presenting various formats, news/talk programs now attempt to segment the audience that in the past was dominated by men. As many as 24 recognized categories exist within talk radio, including shows devoted exclusively to religion, business, personal finance, interpersonal and family issues, cigars, cars, health and fitness, urban talk, as well as specialized Hispanic and African-American programs (Heath, 1998; Paige et al., 1998).

Two of the largest names in talk radio, Rush Limbaugh and Howard Stern, found competition in the 1990s from Dr. Laura Schlessinger. Her show skyrocketed to become the second most popular program in 1998 attracting 14.5 million listeners (Heath, 1998). Dr. Laura, as she is known by her listeners, was the first major talk show personality to attract a mostly female audience. The audience for Limbaugh, for example, was 61% male, with 72% over the age of 45 in 1998. During the same period, Howard Stern drew an audience that was 72% male, with three quarters between the ages of 25 and 54. By contrast, the audience for Dr. Laura was

54% female and drew most heavily on the 35- to 44-year-old age group (Heath, 1998).

Dr. Laura is described by *Psychology Today* as a "mythological creature who is equal parts therapist, rabbi, and drill sergeant" (Dr. Laura Wants, 1998, p. 28). Her listeners praise her efforts to revive public discourse on character. She also writes a syndicated newspaper column and is the author of three best-selling books, including one entitled *10 Stupid Things Men Do to Mess up Their Lives*. Schlessinger chides, cajoles, and sometimes condemns her callers whose actions fail to meet her puritanical standards. In an ironic twist in November 1998, Schlessinger was the beneficiary of mixed blessings when her ratings soared after nude photographs of her taken 20 years earlier were posted on the Internet (see Box 8.1).

BOX 8.1. Warts and All . . .

Warts and all . . .

Nude-pix flap hasn't changed the way fans view Dr. Laura Schlessinger: Public often forgives naked ambition

    by April Adamson, Philadelphia Daily News Staff Writer

Thursday, November 12, 1998, p. 5.
Copyright (c) 1998, Philadelphia Newspapers Inc.

Sophia had fired her babysitter for stealing.
Chris disowned her 17-year-old daughter for losing her virginity.
But they weren't really sure they made the right decisions—and only the mother of all talk radio could offer them moral guidance.
Suddenly Dr. Laura Schlessinger was on the line, slinging solid advice, and her followers were star-struck, gushing praise for this matriarch of morality. "Hi, Dr. Laura. You are the roots and I am your tree. I love you," offered one adoring fanatic yesterday on WWDB-FM (96.5), before beseeching Dr. Laura to dispense her wisdom.
Listening to this back and forth, it is hard to imagine that a dozen nude and sometimes crude photos of this 1990s June Cleaver are posted all over the Internet. And it is hard to imagine the scandal exploded only 2 weeks ago. But somehow, Dr. Laura Schlessinger has managed to win this battle of the bawdy, maintaining and increasing her following—with her ratings up as much as 15%, some radio industry writers estimate—since the scandal exploded 2 weeks ago.
Dr. Laura's seamy, sexy shots—taken when she was a sprightly 20-something separated from her husband and having a fling with a talkradio pioneer—show the conservative, stand-by-your-man, prolife talk show queen

(Continues)

in various stages of undress. Industry observers say Schlessinger hasn't just weathered the embarrassment of having the photos on the Web at Clublove, the online sex provider that first brought you honeymoon photos of "Baywatch" babe Pamela Anderson and her rocker husband Tommy Lee consummating their nuptials in sand and surf, she has actually emerged victorious. Perhaps listeners have a few nude pictures of themselves floating about and can empathize with Dr. Laura's youthful indiscretion. Local camera stores confirm such playful poses are not a rarity—they appear once or twice a day amid regular film.

The controversy began when IEG bought the 20-year-old photos of Schlessinger for $50,000, according to those familiar with the contract, and posted them on the Web on October 22. Last week, Dr. Laura lost a court case in California, where her show originates, to keep the photos off the IEG site. IEG claimed it paid for the pictures and therefore owned the copyrights. A judge agreed. Experts say Dr. Laura's ratings have soared thanks to die-hard fans who have forgiven her and new fans who listen to see how she explains the pics. Even folks who have never heard of her are checking out the show—after checking out the steamy site.

Although Arbitron does not issue weekly ratings for syndicated shows, experts estimate Schlessinger's listenership has increased 15% in the past 2 weeks. "People outside the talk radio universe who heard about this wild radio psychologist are tuning in," said Michael Harrison, editor of Talkers, a talk radio industry magazine based in Massachusetts. Harrison said surveys of radio stations across the country show an increased volume of phone calls and interest in the show. Schlessinger's radio show operations manager, Keven Bellows, claims faxes of support have been flooding in, urging Schlessinger not to "let the bastards get you down." "I think she's weathered this beautifully," said Tom Taylor, editor of the MStreet Daily, a talk radio industry newsletter based in Nashville. "I think Laura's taken it in stride and handled it with great aplomb and moved on."

On her show last Tuesday, Dr. Laura publicly apologized for the "embarrassment," claiming she was 28, separated from her husband, and acting as her "own moral authority. The inadequacy of that way of life is painfully obvious today," Schlessinger said. Industry watchers called her apology masterful and smart. "If I were a spin doctor," said Harrison, "that's what I would have had her say. She's become an incredibly interesting attraction."

Dr. Laura—who has a doctorate in physiology and license in marriage and family therapy—has made a cult of conservative talk radio advice. Her column appears in the Daily News on Thursdays and WWDB carries her syndicated talk show. She has also written several books always advising her followers to act using a moral compass, not simply their feelings. She urges couples to remain married for the sake of their children and chastises them for straying to other lovers. So when the nude pictures went public, critics labeled Schlessinger a hypocrite.

In the past few weeks, WWDB claims it has not seen an increase in calls or letters in response to the scandal. Nationally, many listeners have been fascinated by the scandal, experts say. Dozens of porn pirates have down-

(Continues)

loaded the saucy Dr. Laura photos from Clublove. Now Web sites here and in Canada are displaying the pictures for free.

Internet Entertainment Group president Seth Warshavsky says that, although 7 million Web surfers hit clublove.com on a normal day, photos of Dr. Laura are attracting 14 million viewers daily this week. IEG says it bought the photos from Bill Ballance, the Los Angeles radio legend and Schlessinger's former mentor and boyfriend. Ballance allegedly took the photos himself in the mid-1970s, capturing Schlesinger topless, totally nude, and in striking sultry poses. Ballance, who lives in San Diego County, did not return several calls placed to his house this week seeking comment.

The IEG Web site quotes Ballance, now 80, as saying the two were hot and heavy—she a young, waify brunette who moved to California and wanted to leave her husband, he a smitten radio icon who loved her bedside manner. "Whenever I look at the photos I am now reminded of this very attractive woman who was an absolute demon in bed," the IEG site quotes Ballance as saying. "I know that if I had married her I would have been dead 20 years ago, death by exhaustion."

Sports talk is also one of the many ways talk radio is adapting to an increasingly congested talk show environment. Stations are now offering a wide range of content and looking for hosts who draw in new listeners. Talk radio programs have historically done best among older Americans. This is changing however, as stations like KLSX in Los Angeles aggressively target 18- to 34-year-olds with talk on the FM dial. Stations are now attempting to attract a young crowd by studying what they want and then providing it. Topics may range from advice on relationships and saving money to dealing with difficult bosses. Youths find hearing about these topics more interesting than listening to discussions about Washington scandals or attacks on political institutions.

Special interest programming should continue as radio stations focus on ever narrower audience segments. United Station Radio Networks added entertainment and Christian talk to its line-up in 1997. Psychic Friends Radio Network launched a nightly radio talk show spin-off of its television infomercials. The Sci-Fi Channel expanded to radio with *Sightings*, its popular program about the paranormal. Another Sci-Fi series hosted by Art Bell is the most popular radio show that specializes in unexplained events. Just as Dr. Laura offers quick fix solutions for personal problems and morality plays, new varieties of niche radio programs with differing themes will undoubtedly continue to emerge for years to come.

WHO IS WATCHING WHAT CHANNEL WITH WHAT EFFECT?

In 1985, only Phil Donahue, Oprah Winfrey, and Sally Jessy Raphael had television talk shows. A decade later, an estimated 10 million viewers select from nearly 20 daily daytime syndicated talk shows (Alter, 1995).

About 6 in 10 viewers of daytime TV talk are women and about half are over the age of 45. Low-income African Americans and the unemployed are also heavier viewers. Sixty percent have completed less than 1 year of college, and 45% are unemployed (Heath, 1998).

The first participatory television talk show was hosted by Phil Donahue and debuted in 1967 on WLWD-TV in Dayton, Ohio. The show became a national phenomenon collecting 20 Emmy's during its 29-year run, which yielded more than 7,000 shows. Guests included global leaders ranging from Nelson Mandela to Jesse Jackson, who appeared 29 times. In May 1996, however, Donahue taped his last program because viewers were tuning him out in favor of younger hosts and juicier topics. Donahue broke many television taboos. His was the first program to feature openly gay men. Yet Donahue never allowed it to get raunchy as did some of his daytime rivals (Gliatto & Longley, 1996).

Although Donahue may be remembered nostalgically for his thoughtful interviewing style and selection of socially relevant topics, his program did contain its own brand of stunts to attract ratings. On occasion, shows included visits from strippers and one featured Donahue hosting the show in a dress and high heel shoes to discuss men who like to wear women's clothing. Compared with the growing breed of talk shows that emerged in the late 1980s and 1990s, Donahue was tame. Celebrating 1 year on the air in 1988, Geraldo Rivera hosted a show on neo-Nazi skinheads in which a fight erupted and he was the beneficiary of a broken nose thanks to a flying chair. So began the new era of televised *confrontainment* (K. Powers, 1998).

New television talk shows continue to proliferate producing dubious results and featuring less than credible guests. One man who claimed to be an impotent husband on Sally Jessy Raphael appeared later as an unmarried virgin on Geraldo (McNeil, 1991). What may have been a low ebb for TV talk programs occurred in March 1995. A guest on the Jenny Jones show murdered another guest following the taping of the show. John Schmitz shot Scott Amedure with a 12-gauge shot gun after being lured to the show with a promise that he would be introduced to someone who had a secret crush on him. Schmitz said that he had received assurances that the admirer would not be a male, although producers contend that they told him the person might be either male or female. In the aftermath of the disaster, Jenny Jones made the talk show rounds herself to explain that she had no regrets about shows in which guests are set up. She said she would air programs of that type again in the future (Vatz & Weinberg, 1998; see Box 8.2).

Producers of talk shows have also begun to discover the previously untapped children's audience. For example, Nickelodeon produces occasional television talk shows about controversial subjects that are geared toward children. Once such program dealt with the scandal surrounding

---

Box 8.2. Jenny Jones Show Ordered to Pay $25 Million

On May 7, 1999, a Pontiac, Michigan, jury awarded the family of slain Scott Amedure $25 million in a wrongful-death lawsuit brought against *The Jenny Jones Show*, Warner Brothers, and Telepictures. The jury deliberated for more than 6 hours over 2 days before deciding that the show was at least partly responsible for Amedure's death.

The Amedure family and its attorney hailed the award as a victory against what it called irresponsible television shows. However, media representatives believe the verdict poses a threat to the First Amendment. "This will have a profoundly chilling effect not only on talk shows but on all media," said Warner Brothers' senior lawyer, Zazi Pope. Floyd Abrams, a prominent First Amendment lawyer, said the verdict was unwarranted. "Whether we have a Jenny Jones Show or a Jerry Springer Show is a matter of public taste," Abrams said. "I think that the public is entitled to watch these shows if it wishes and that these shows are protected" by the Constitution's First Amendment (Bradsher, 1999, p. 10).

At the time of the killing, programs like *The Jenny Jones Show*, along with others hosted by personalities such Rikki Lake, Montel Williams, and Jerry Springer, were among the most profitable shows on television. Talk shows such as these earned as much as $50 million to $60 million a year in profits. They frequently relied on ambushing guests with people they were not expecting to see. Topics were raised that guests had not been told were going to be discussed. Since the Amedure killing, the shows have fallen off sharply in popularity and advertisers have begun to shy from them. Except for *The Jerry Springer Show*, which continues to rely heavily on confrontational topics leading to fist fights virtually every day, the subject matter has been toned down on many of the shows.

---

the relationship between Bill Clinton and Monica Lewinsky and the impeachment trial that followed (see Box 8.3)

VIDEOMALAISE AND CRITICISM OF TELEVISION TALK SHOWS

As early as 1975, M. Robinson (1975) coined the term *videomalaise*, which means that the media's tone instills doubt and hostility, resulting in a deepening cynicism. National media news reports became increasingly hostile toward major political institutions in the wake of Vietnam and Watergate (Weaver, 1972). Television news reporting began to stress "what's wrong with institutions" (M. Robinson, 1976, 1977). University of Virginia Professor Larry Sabato (1991) characterized the post-1974 era of journalism as "harsh, regressive, and intrusive" (p. 26) because it fixates on the foibles, follies, and failings of public figures and institutions. In the post-Fairness Doctrine era, it should come as little surprise that talk shows developed the same hard edge as their journalism counterparts.

**Box 8.3. Everything Kids Ever Wanted to Know About Sex,
But Were Afraid to Ask**

Children had a hard time escaping ubiquitous coverage of the investigation surrounding the Clinton/Lewinsky affair. According to a phone survey of 300 children between the ages 8 and 14 conducted by Viacom's Nickelodeon, the children's cable TV network, 60% of the respondents on an unaided basis were able to cite the Clinton/Lewinsky saga as a major news story. Of those, 9 in 10 said they learned of the issue watching television news, with another 48% saying they had read about it in newspapers. According to Nickelodeon, the survey was designed to foster discussion about the affair between parents and children.

On September 28, 1998, journalists Linda Ellerbee and NBC's Katie Couric, along with lawyer Reid Weingarten, hosted a primetime program on Nickelodeon based on the survey. Ten children between the ages of 10 and 14 were recruited to discuss the affair and its implications for government and society. "The mission" explained Ellerbee, "in these specials is to help kids make sense of the news they're hearing, not to tell them what to think, but to let kids know it's O.K. to have questions about these things and O.K. to discuss them, and to let parents see that kids do have questions and are thinking seriously about this" (Mifflin, 1998, p. 5).

One of the children said Congress should not have posted the whole Starr report on the Internet because "kids use that as their backyard." The children asked what the terms *perjury* and *censure* meant and what would happen if Clinton "stopped being president." One child demonstrated wisdom beyond his years in posing this question: "Couldn't we give him a time-out?" (i.e., remove him from office for a week or two so he has a chance to reflect on his misdeeds). Indeed, parents, educators, and the media must explain complicated issues to their children.

Sociology Professor Vicki Abt, at Penn State University's Abington/Ogantz campus near Philadelphia, believes that trash talk television harms those who are most psychologically vulnerable (Abt, 1994; Abt & Mustazza, 1997). Speculation about psychological harm to viewers generally focuses on the degree to which shows are capable of manipulating emotions by employing tactics and introducing topics that encourage anger and other strong emotions (Keller, 1993). One talk show producer explained that confrontation is the most important element in booking guests for a program (J. Gamson, 1995, 1998).

The charges against television talk shows generally suggest that talk shows make the abnormal seem normal. They desensitize viewers to human suffering and tend to cause viewers to trivialize complex social issues (Davis & Mares, 1998). Although intuitively these assertions seem reasonable, they are based primarily on supposition. Television talk show critics contend that presenting bizarre or antisocial behavior may distort viewers' perceptions of society. They assume that audience members fail to recognize that bizarre behaviors and deviant actions of guests represent a departure from normal behavior. It further assumes that, because the guests are often portrayed as normal people, audience members may perceive bizarre behavior to be normal. As a result, viewers may model the characters, activities, and behaviors portrayed on television talk shows. Critics of these shows say the problem is especially acute when children are exposed to them.

A THEORY OF SOCIAL COMPARISON

Why do viewers choose to watch programs that promote disharmony between guests? One explanation may be that people need or want to make comparisons between their attitudes and opinions and those of other people. Social comparison theory suggests that people look to empirical data such as salary, lifestyle, test scores, or grades to develop a self-identity and a sense of self-worth (see Brown, 1986; Goethals & Zanna, 1979; Isenberg, 1986; Wheeler, 1991, for reviews of social comparison theory). When such data are not available, they compare their circumstances to the situations of others (Goethals, 1986). By comparing one's own life against the lives of the talk show guests, one may derive a better sense of self-worth. This may reinforce a sense of social well-being and enable people to see themselves in a more positive light.

Zillmann and Bryant (1986) explained that

> Seeing misfortunes befall others and seeing them suffering from it thus may make viewers cognizant and appreciative of how good they have it. And as such positive feelings accrue to seeing tragedy strike, *in reality or in fiction*, tragedy becomes appealing despite the negative affect that is initially associated with it. (p. 317)

Festinger investigated the processes associated with social comparison in 1954, observing that people make comparisons between themselves and others when they are uncertain about their abilities and opinions. People compare themselves to others to determine norms in society, to lift their spirits, to justify their self-worth, to validate ideas and opinions, and to assess skills and abilities relative to other people (Suls & Wills, 1991). In addition, social comparisons may be used as a means of self-evaluation, self-enhancement, or self-improvement (Wood, 1989; Wood & Taylor, 1991).

People seem to find it useful to evaluate themselves in the context of others to assess where they stand in the social order. In some situations, self-evaluation may guide self-improvement by using examples they encounter as role models. If one is motivated to move socially upward, then one may emulate behaviors of those who have achieved higher social status. Furthermore, self-enhancement may occur when people make downward comparisons to others in a less than ideal social situation. Certainly talk shows featuring individuals with serious personal problems, involved in dysfunctional relationships, possessing social abnormalities, or those who are simply down on their luck may serve to elevate the spirits of the viewers watching. Indeed, the concluding lyrics of a satirical country and western song about talk shows performed by talk show host Jerry Springer capture the sense of social comparison nicely (performed on NBC's *Tonight Show*, October 23, 1998):

> But if that's your world,
> or part of it,
> where madam's are sometimes sir's!
> You'll quit complaining,
> things could be worse,
> Those calamities could be yours.

IN DEFENSE OF TRASH TELEVISION

One may wonder whether witnessing the travesties of others is a healthy or beneficial pastime. Emerson University Professor Jane Shattuc believed the programs "offer vicarious connections to other people, and the outrageousness of it is entertaining" (cited in Heath, 1998, p. 52). She contended that even the least-educated and most economically disadvantaged understand that "trash-talk shows are mostly theatrical overkill and camp." As such, "Americans for the most part are critical of these shows, and they're media savvy enough to know when they're being had."

A study about television talk shows conducted in the 1990s by Greenberg, Sherry, Busselle, Hnilo, and Smith (1997) arrived at a similar conclusion. Television talk shows may be less harmful than some fear because people recognize that the behavior demonstrated is aberrant. Although the sample of shows studied was collected in 1994 and 1995, before talk shows became as inflammatory as they did in later years, the authors theorized, as did Shattuc, that people recognize that the portrayals, scenarios, and aggression presented do not represent the behaviors, ideas, and attitudes reflected by most members of society.

Greenberg and his colleagues (1997) considered the possibility that talk shows may teach people certain attitudes and beliefs as well as antisocial behavior. The researchers considered whether talk shows will cultivate perceptions and cause people to exaggerate the frequency of antisocial behavior or the incidence of dysfunctional relationships that exist in contemporary society. This proposition was rejected because talk shows occupy a relatively small percentage of the total amount of broadcast time. Because television viewers encounter a wide range of programming, they can put talk shows in perspective. As Greenberg et al. (1997) explained, "the topics, behaviors and role models on television talk shows are constrained largely to this one genre and are not replicated elsewhere on the medium. What you find on these shows are largely idiosyncratic TV experiences" (p. 424).

As an alternative to cultivation theory, the researchers explained,

> the topics and role models are cast, to the extent possible, as 'one-off' relationships, highlighted because of their bizarre and/or unique characteristics. It is more probable that viewers will find cause to distance themselves from these guests perceiving that they themselves are better off by comparison, rather than to identify with the participants and problems. As such, social comparison serves a therapeutic function and the behaviors demonstrated will not necessarily be imitated by viewers. (Greenberg et al., 1997, p. 424)

Greenberg and his associates suggested that the viewing experience associated with talk shows is related to the exemplar view of social categorization (see Smith & Medin, 1981, for a review). Viewers are capable of recognizing that the dysfunctional relationships, aberrant behaviors, and deviant characters presented are a departure from the norm. In other words, people do not average information encountered in the Ricki Lake show with information contained on ABC's *World News Tonight* to develop cognitive representations of the real world. An individual is presumed to remember separate instances or exemplars once encountered, "rather than some average prototype abstracted from experience. One has several exemplars for a category and, in this view, people categorize a thing by seeing whether it resembles a lot of remembered exemplars from a single category" (Fiske & Taylor, 1991, p. 112).

Programs featuring bizarre behaviors, dysfunctional relationships, or other topics may test the limits of good taste, but people do not believe that these shows represent the norm. Hence, although a viewer may receive an emotional lift by witnessing the trials and tribulations of others acted out on television, in most cases, he or she recognizes that even if the physical encounters and vile language are genuine, they certainly do not represent an appropriate means by which to resolve conflict.

The contemporary media-rich environment provides significant opportunity for commentary and criticism of the programming presented by broadcast and cable networks. Even Jerry Springer, during a 1998 interview with Jay Leno, dismissed his own program as nothing more than a "silly little show."

CONCLUSION

Both radio and television talk shows are enormously popular. In a deregulated marketplace with competition from cable and satellite broadcasting on the rise, many of these shows routinely strive to attract audiences through shock appeals. Although the long-term impact of such programming may not be well understood, audiences appear to recognize that—like professional wrestling or roller derby—they represent little more than comic relief from the day-to-day stresses of contemporary society.

The future trend in talk radio is toward the growth of niche programming. Like Dr. Laura Schlessinger with her advice format and the advent of other genres, new types of segmented programs will continue to appear. The best available research, contrary to popular opinion, suggests that, although people may become highly engaged with news talk radio program, they do not have the ability to significantly shift attitudes, opinions, and behavior. With respect to political talk shows, people seem to seek out programming that either reinforces beliefs, as is the case with Rush Limbaugh, tend to shock them, as does Howard Stern, or provide information in an entertaining fashion, as does Dr. Laura.

Television talk became a prized commodity as the 1990s closed. In 1998, Oprah Winfrey signed a contract to host her daily syndicated talk show for 3 more years. Under the terms of the contract, which keeps her with the show in production through 2002, King World paid Winfrey's Harpo Productions advance fees of $75 million immediately after the signing and another $75 million by June 1999. In mid-October 1998, Jerry Springer garnered a rating of 6.3, representing slightly more than 6 million viewing households to finish ahead of Oprah who had a rating of 5.5 and about 5.5 million viewers. A single rating point represents 994,000 households.

No shortage of opinion exists when it comes to the behaviors of both hosts and guests on broadcast and cable television talk shows (see Box 8.4), but people do not live in a vacuum when it comes to watching television talk shows. They appear quite capable of sorting out reality from fiction. It seems likely that even the most devoted Jerry Springer or Ricki Lake viewers probably recognize the programs for what they are, in the words of Springer—nothing more than "silly little" shows. Nevertheless, researchers should continue to investigate whether repeated exposure to bizarre behavior or extreme opinions may affect listeners and viewers of talk shows over time. As noted earlier in this volume, media effects are often subtle and difficult to detect. For this reason, the talk show phenomenon continues to offer fertile ground for serious scholarly inquiry.

BOX 8.4. Review of the Talk Show, *Politically Incorrect*

Excerpted from: Not political incorrect, just tasteless
By Andy Humm
Social Policy, Fall 1997, p. 53.

From C-Span to CNN to Sunday morning network news analysis shows, there is a ton of political talk on television, but do we ever learn anything or hear anything new? Afraid of true left and right perspectives—from whence might actually flow a few ideas—nervous news producers tend to book conservative Republicans and moderate Democrats who argue over nuances in the muddled middle. ABC-TV's late-night show, *Politically Incorrect* with Bill Maher—imported from cable TV's Comedy Central—purports to be a cure for what ails political discourse. It fails miserably as both political discourse and comedy.

A big problem is that the show tries to make light of deadly serious subjects. The very day after 39 cultists took their lives in Rancho Santa Fe, Bill Maher was making tasteless jokes about them. Another time, he presided over a jokefest about the death penalty, pitting Ann Richards—a witty person who nevertheless executed many Texans as governor—against nihilist comedian Dennis Miller to her right and former *M*A*S*H* star Mike Farrell to her left. Conductor Zubin Mehta was also in the mix, but he looked as if he did not know why he was there and did not venture to try out any death penalty "jokes" during the segment. Bravo, maestro.

Not only is this show far from uncensored, it is basically useless. The exchanges on *Politically Incorrect* do not add to current political debates, they debase and cheapen them with cynical and childish "humor." Good comedians are good social commentators, helping us to understand the human condition better. They entertain us with insight. They help us see by drawing us in and then zapping us in a way that lets us laugh at ourselves and our society.

Maher's vulgarity, rudeness, and offensiveness are a poor substitute for the sharp, biting political talk that TV so desperately needs. Putting together such a show would take old-fashioned American hard work—something in short supply on this program, which takes on big, unsubtle targets that it can't miss or trivial topics that it shoots with an elephant gun.

9 The Internet Audience

SUMMARY

- The Internet was created to assist research scientists.
- The public embraced the Internet and the World Wide Web (WWW) as an important source of *information* and *entertainment*.
- People use the Internet to derive many of the same *gratifications* of older media such as newspapers and television.
- The Internet provides users with a sense of *community*.
- *Virtual communities* with defined social protocols formed in cyberspace.
- These communities and societies foster *parasocial interactions* among Internet users.
- People socialize in cyberspace using *MUDs, chatrooms, and electronic distribution lists*.
- As the Internet evolves, it remains unclear whether cyber communities will *enhance civic engagement*.
- As the Internet evolves, it remains unclear whether cyber communities will *facilitate social interactions* among people.
- Internet use threatens to *erode time* that was previously allocated to human interaction.
- *Reduced human interaction* is linked to feelings of loneliness and despair.
- Evidence suggests that certain features of the Internet are *addictive* to certain people.
- Large media corporations have taken a keen interest in monitoring the Internet because it provides *access* to a market for their goods, products, and services.
- *Audience measurement firms* now monitor homepage traffic suggesting that the Internet is rapidly developing as a mechanism of commerce.

THE INTERNET AS MEDIA

Media institutions produce and structure messages to attract audiences. These messages engage audience members and stimulate them to think about messages in certain ways. As media companies encourage citizens to interact with media, media scholars should consider the growing importance of the Internet and the WWW as media entities to discern the ways in which people are learning to employ this important new technology.

The Internet evolved over the past 25 years from a network designed by the U.S. Department of Defense to aid the scientific community and engineers in research and to assist the academic community in scholarly pursuits. Although continuing to serve these constituencies by acting as an enormous database and facilitating collaborations among scholars, the Internet developed into a significant commercial entity. The Internet is described as "an enormous computer network in which any existing network can participate. It encompasses satellites, cable fiber and telephone lines, and it seems to have grown exponentially. Now, everyone from students to commercial enterprises" use the Internet to access vast amounts of information on other computer systems around the world (Calem, 1992, p. 11). The WWW is the computer network that enables people to easily move among computers that store information. It is also considered the multimedia dimension of the Internet that contains homepages, e-commerce sites, and a wide range of graphic and textual material.

Few homes were equipped with a personal computer just 15 years ago. At that time, most personal computers were used by scientists and engineers, and by businesses to conduct office work (Venkatesh & Vitalari, 1992.) However, adoption of the personal computer occurred rapidly. By 1998, an estimated 40% of all American households owned at least one (Kraut, Patterson, Lundmark, Kiesler, Mukopadhyay, & Schleris, 1998) and nearly 62 million U.S. residents had Internet access (Kokmen, 1998), representing approximately 30% of the U.S. population 16 years or older (Maguire, 1998).

Research about it has grown nearly as rapidly as the Internet itself. Much of the research focused on what may be achieved with the Internet in the future and how it is expected to develop (e.g., Jones, 1997, 1998; Kiesler, 1997). Some scholars investigated how the WWW must adapt to become more user-friendly, especially to citizens with special linguistic needs or language disorders (Singh, Gedeon, & Rho, 1988). Others focused on the increasing importance of the WWW and other forms of Internet communication and discourse in political campaigns (Warnick, 1998). Researchers analyzed the Internet, using the political economy approach, to evaluate the evolving National Information Infrastructure

(NII) and the growing concentration of ownership and control over the NII (Bettig, 1997). Scholars even investigated whether a web page created by Indian immigrants may speak simultaneously to an interpretive community of ingroup as well as outgroup members (Mitra, 1997). Perhaps the most provocative research on the Internet probes the ways in which people interact psychologically with it and the WWW.

GRATIFICATIONS FROM THE INTERNET

People use the Internet to receive the same type of gratifications they receive from older media such as newspapers and television. The Internet provides users with a sense of companionship by enabling them to join virtual communities. It affords them the opportunity to engage in virtual online adventures and games. The virtual shopping mall enables customers to go on shopping sprees 24 hours a day. Because the Internet provides such varied offerings, it quickly became a major competitor for the time and attention of the consumer. In addition, the Internet has become a *place* that is used in a myriad of ways to produce a variety of gratifications.

People discovered that the Internet is an important source of news and information. According to a survey conducted in 1999 by MSNBC online, the Internet was in a statistical dead heat with cable television and radio and is used slightly more often than magazines for the acquisition of information. Michael Silberman, executive editor of MSNBC.com, reported that on a typical day his Web site attracts a larger audience than CNN television. People also use the Internet simply for entertainment. Although the report did not imply that the Internet was a more important source of information than conventional media, it did suggest that adoption for the purpose of information gain is occurring at a remarkable rate.

Internet technology enables people to travel to fantasy worlds such as Multi-User Dungeons (MUDs) and visit homepages maintained by museums, communities, and professional sports teams. People can engage in conversations with others at distant points around the globe through chatrooms. As with other traditional media, the Internet and the WWW offer an excellent opportunity to avoid mundane chores or homework.

One fundamental difference between the Internet and older media is the degree to which a user must become actively engaged to achieve maximum benefits. One must navigate the WWW using search engines and key words to acquire information or visit various locations. Furthermore, one can assess the quality of information contained within homepages and the accuracy of discussion in chatrooms or information posted on virtual lists. Internet users must invest the time to consider the opinions, attitudes, and beliefs of other people to benefit from online discussions.

One must exert the effort to develop an online persona if one hopes to be accepted as a player in a MUD. In short, the benefits obtained from using the Internet appear to be closely aligned with the amount of effort that one exerts to utilize it.

Large media companies have taken a keen interest in the Internet for a variety of reasons. First, the Internet offers access to consumers and promises to provide an economical distribution system for media products such as books, music, and, ultimately, video. Second, the remarkable rate of adoption of the Internet surpassed all earlier predictions. Media programmers and companies invested heavily in the Internet and the WWW, and both are destined to be important sources for marketing, information, and entertainment for years to come.

USING THE INTERNET TO SATISFY COMMUNICATION NEEDS

People use the Internet to satisfy a wide range of communication gratifications, including staying in touch with family and friends, exchanging ideas, collaborating on a journal article with colleagues at other universities, obtaining a road map before taking a trip, or finding out what other people think about Rogaine. In many respects, the Internet and the WWW satisfy the same needs as older technologies such as the telephone or television. As with television or the telephone, the Internet is capable of satisfying multiple needs simultaneously. Just as "World News Tonight" with Peter Jennings may inform and entertain, users of the Internet acquire new information while they drift between homepages for relaxation and entertainment.

The Internet is unique as a new technology because it continues to evolve. Older technologies like radio and television have changed little over the years. The development of frequency modulation (FM) afforded radio programmers the opportunity to introduce stereo and present a high-quality signal, which in turn paved the way for the advent of talk radio on AM stations. Similarly, the advent of color improved the quality of the programming on television and enhanced the viewing experience. However, the basic ways in which people use these mediums have changed little over the years. By contrast, the Internet and the WWW continue to change as people develop new and innovative uses.

The so-called *information superhighway* now runs to libraries and schools. The Internet is now a center for commerce as the virtual shopping mall continues to expand. Some wonder if the Internet will eventually supplant the telephone as a facilitator of mediated interpersonal communication. In short, the popularity of the Internet and the WWW indicate that both may become a primary means by which people interact with other people. These new uses will determine what gratifications are derived from the Internet.

PARASOCIAL RELATIONSHIPS, THE MEDIA,
AND THE INTERNET

Media often try to enable the audience to feel connected to the protagonists presented. Novelists strive to make readers feel connected to the hero or heroine. Television and film scriptwriters and directors present unattractive actors in shadowy circumstances using unflattering lighting and camera angles to portray them as the villains. These writers recognize that effective story telling requires actively engaging the audience in the plot.

Many of the same principles hold with news programs in which newscasters attempt to convey a sense of integrity, competence, credibility, friendliness, and warmth to the audience. News stories contained within newscasts often contain unflattering video of the suspects sporting prison attire while being hustled into a courtroom or the back seat of a police car. Although the shackled convict may be a disturbing image to audience members, the even demeanor of the newscaster provides reassurance that things in general are under control and that the social and legal order remain intact.

Be it a newscast or theatrical drama, audience members enjoy feelings of kinship with protagonists. This explains why people often call Peter Jennings, Oprah Winfrey, or Rush Limbaugh by their first names when chance encounters occur. It is not surprising that many viewers felt a sense of intense loss when Bobby Simone, played by actor Jimmy Smits, finally succumbed to complications from a heart transplant in the November 24, 1998, episode of "NYPD Blue." When audience members share a sense of loss, distrust, or joy with television or film actors, they are engaging in parasocial relationships. These relationships or bonds that develop between actors and the audience take on many of the characteristics of interpersonal relationships and serve as an excellent predictor of viewing behavior. Although parasocial relationships may determine the degree to which an audience remains engaged with a plot, there is no reason to believe that such relationships serve as a suitable substitute for human interpersonal contact. Relationships between people are based on two-way interaction in which certain responsibilities and obligations are assumed.

Just as viewers enter into relationships with performers like Oprah Winfrey, newscasters such as Peter Jennings, and fictional characters such as Bobby Simone, Internet users enter into relationships with online *friends*. Many users report that the Internet is an especially useful tool for obtaining information because it is a fairly easy way to interact with other people and solicit online advice, companionship, and support. Furthermore, the Internet is increasingly becoming an arena for people to seek out interpersonal communication, reduce stress, and alleviate boredom. It is common for regular members of chatrooms to ask whether another member "has been by recently."

People participating in chatrooms commonly discuss issues and events that produce collective joy, sadness, or anxiety. Sympathy for a chatroom member may occur when an individual shares information about an upsetting or disturbing situation such as failing a course in college or the collapse of a marriage. Conversely, the spirits of an entire chatroom appear to be elevated when one participant reports on a promotion at work, a proposal of marriage, or the birth of a child. Members of chatrooms seek out and provide advice on topics ranging from AIDS to romance to Wall Street investing. The Internet seems to encourage interpersonal interaction because so many Internet applications facilitate the sharing of information and the opportunity for people to become engaged with others.

The quality of these online interactions among people does not generally represent the kind of human contact that occurs when people discuss issues face to face or even on the telephone. Human relationships typically develop over time. Interpersonal conversations are punctuated by vocal intonation, facial expressions, or physical contact. An understanding exists between members engaged in interpersonal communication that a relationship will continue in the future. This relationship is understood to be far stronger than the relationship that may exist between an audience member and a television actor, radio personality, or news anchor. Few online encounters result in long-term relationships with genuine bonds between people. Although the Internet appears to be a highly social and interpersonal *place*, the interaction that occurs may best be explained in the context of mass rather than interpersonal communication theory.

INTERNET SOCIETY: LISTS, MUDs, MOOs, CHATROOMS, AND USENET

Internet-based communication takes the form of electronic mail, distribution lists (i.e., listserves), multi-user dungeons (MUDs; also called multi-user object domains [MOOs]), chatrooms, and Usenet. These applications create virtual communities in which people exchange ideas, debate issues, participate in virtual games, and find information. The first virtual communities were formed to enable employees within companies to communicate and work collaboratively on company documents (Sproull & Kiesler, 1991). Employees conducted electronic brainstorming sessions with individuals or groups of employees to solve problems or develop plans. As commercial online services became available and personal computers became more popular, people began to form groups for entertainment, assistance, and advice.

Electronic lists developed as a logical outgrowth of electronic mail. Instead of discussing issues with one other person, listserves distribute posted messages to each member of the interest group. Usenet is a collection of Internet discussion groups, each devoted to particular topics, in which people post messages to obtain information or advice or share experiences. Usenet, like electronic lists, enable people with common interests to post information and discuss issues with other people.

People discuss issues on lists that are distributed to a group when a member posts a message. These discussion groups began on the Internet in 1979 and grew from modest beginnings to the largest and most comprehensive of any of the online communities. More than 20 million participants post and read more than 7 million monthly messages in more than 35,000 discussion groups. People discuss and share advice on topics as diverse and specific as baseball, the stock market, and health concerns. Some lists act as election soap boxes (see Box 9.1).

MUDs or MOOs are basically software programs that enable multiple users to interact with each other in a shared space. Entering a MUD is an entirely social experience in which people interact with each other in a virtual community. The users, often called *players*, converse in this virtual gathering place, which has a set social protocol. The players may move between *rooms* in the MUD by way of passages and exits. The entire *MUDDING* experience is text-based and devoid of the fancy graphics and other eye-catching elements that adorn many homepages or chatrooms (Curtis, 1997). MUDs have strict social codes of conduct that govern behavior in these virtual gathering places.

Chatrooms, listserves, and other discussion forums are typically organized by topics such as sports, sex and romance, current events, music, religion, or the stock market. These cyber communities are far less structured than MUDs; visitors are usually welcome to drift in and out of discussions as they wish. As long as decorum and civility are observed, chatrooms and electronic lists welcome the input of newcomers. Listserves, chatrooms, and MUDs appear to satisfy many of the same kinds of needs and gratifications that the media establishment served in the past such as providing users with information and entertainment.

SOCIALIZING IN CYBERSPACE

The Internet—with its electronic mail, listserves, Usenet, MUDs and chatrooms—appears to be a very social place in which interpersonal communication flourishes (Kraut, Mukopadhyay, Szczypula, Kiesler, & Scherlis, 1998). In this respect, the Internet seems to take on more of the characteristics of telephone than television because it encourages interaction among individuals. Conversations among people on the Internet

BOX 9.1. The Internet as an Electronic Soap Box

The American conception of the marketplace of ideas places a premium on enlightened debate about political and social issues. The Internet and the WWW afford citizens the opportunity to exchange ideas and opinions. These technologies serve as an electronic soapbox in which information disseminated through traditional media such as newspapers and television may be evaluated and debated.

For example, following President Clinton's apology for the Lewinsky affair and the subsequent release of the report by Special Prosecutor Kenneth Starr, discussions and interaction among citizens worldwide commenced. Tony Palmeri, Chair, Department of Communication at the University of Wisconsin—Oshkosh, told subscribers of the *Communication Research and Theory Network* (CRTNET News), an Internet discussion list devoted to discussions of communication issues, that:

> Like Linda Tripp's speech outside the federal courthouse a few weeks previously, Mr. Clinton's August 17th effort was a kind of secular televangelism. The Christian televangelist, especially when confronted with cash flow problems, banks on his connection to the Almighty. Thus he becomes "Holier Than Thou," urging assent on the basis of a piety given to him straight from THE SOURCE.

On the same discussion list, Bob Vartabedian of West Texas A&M University wrote: "In my opinion, this speech is even more apologetically troubling when examined as a written [versus spoken] manuscript. As I examine the written text of this speech, I sense three main categories that emerge: (1) enhancing ethos, (2) accepting blame, and (3) shifting blame."

Although citizens discussed the scandal online, coverage and analysis of events continued on television, radio, and in newspapers. On the Friday afternoon when the Starr Report, was released, the media focused on the most lurid and salacious aspects of the Starr report, hinting that impeachment or resignation were all but inevitable. To spice up the evening newscasts, members of the national news corps scoured Congress to find members who would go on camera to advocate impeachment proceedings. A correspondent for National Public Radio during "All Things Considered" took Clinton to task characterizing his behavior as *infantile*. A British newscaster warned that the Clinton Presidency was "hanging by a thread."

Over the weekend, instant public opinion polls were conducted. On Monday, September 14, the *Washington Post* reported: "A majority of Americans now believe President Clinton probably broke the law and should be censured but not forced from office for lying about his sexual relationship with former White House intern Monica S. Lewinsky." At the same time, the poll found that "most Americans continue to praise Clinton's stewardship of the nation's economy and the overall job he is doing as president—even as they increasingly question his personal behavior and express growing doubts about his long-term ability to lead" (Morin & Dean, 1998, p. A1).

By Monday, the international media were considering the matter in a somewhat different light. *The Financial Times* of London explained:

(Continues)

For all the gratuitously lurid detail about Mr. Clinton's tryst with Monica Lewinsky, the most surprising thing about the Starr report is how unsurprising it is. Flip over the graphic sex and there is nothing we did not already know. Where is the smoking gun? Where, as the president's defenders have already asked, is the Whitewater affair, Travelgate, Filegate and the rest? The special prosecutor's $40 million, four-year investigation has produced little more than a tawdry soap opera. As for the calculated prurience of the script, it tells us as much about Mr. Starr as it does about the president. None of this exonerates Mr. Clinton. It is hard to empathize with a man so deliberately careless of the truth, particularly since his present predicament is self-inflicted. ("Flawed but not out." 1998, p. 20).

Discussion of the scandal persisted throughout the next several weeks. On a discussion list for journalism educators <JOURNETL@AMERICAN.EDU>, list member Eric Fenster considered the legality of the investigation, writing: "ABOUT LAW: Clinton aside, Kenneth Starr's threat is to America's legal foundations. 1) Grand jury testimony—taken without the legal protections of confrontation of witnesses or cross-examination and thus meant to be kept secret to assure the eventual fair trial of any accused—will be made public, indirectly at least, via the report to Congress." In response, Charles J. Reid expressed his discontent with the investigation in a different fashion: "My cursory reading the of Starr Report enables me to conclude that Judge Starr appears to be an unfulfilled virgin, still confounded by the mysteries of sex, so confounded, in fact, that the report appears to me to be prima facie evidence that he is a pervert."

Thus, the Internet can serve the important function of providing citizens with an opportunity to exchange ideas and opinions with citizens worldwide.

seem to mirror real life, with strangers in MUDs or chatrooms greeting each other with questions like: "Have you been here before?" "Have we met?" or "Long time no see." Players in MUDs often consult lists to determine whether friends are in the room. In both MUDs and chatrooms, users are free to leave the main room and occupy other rooms if they wish to get away from the crowd or discuss issues in private. MUD users frequently present themselves as characters created around a fantasy medieval landscape containing dragons, princesses, and peasants. They also may simply exist as an open space awaiting other players who will then decide on a theme (Turkle, 1997).

Human interaction in virtual rooms is not confined to talking. It is not uncommon for a user to enter a room describing gestures such as waving, smiling, or hugging. As in electronic mail, users display smiles [:-)] to express pleasure and frowns [:-(] to express anger or sadness. An Internet shorthand language has also evolved. A user may reply to a post, for example, indicating that a comment posted by another user caused her to *LOL* (laugh out loud). As with any room full of people, numerous discussions may occur simultaneously. In a chatroom or MUD, one may become engaged in several discussions simultaneously and assume several identities at once. The discussion within virtual rooms is governed by a protocol that was established by a common consensus over time or by the administrator of the server.

As in real life, celebrations and special events occur within virtual communities. Users may schedule a time to celebrate the wedding or birthday of a member of the group. Players in MUDs play games like chess, backgammon, and Monopoly to relax. The rooms often develop into a quasisociety over time in which certain members assume the demeanor of opinion leader, inhouse comic, social critic, or town fool. Some people spend enormous amounts of time in virtual rooms but the lure is not technology or computers. As Curtis (1997) explained, "people are not addicted to computers, but to communication; the global scope of the Internet MUDs implies not only a great variety in potential conversants, but also 24-hour access" (p. 137).

The owner of the server housing the virtual room has a special role in the virtual community. He or she (known as a *Wizard* or, in some cases, a *God*), is occasionally called on to arbitrate disputes among members. Just as a person would call the police or file a lawsuit in most social orders, he or she may call on a Wizard to intervene. The typical punishment for misbehaving in a MUD consists of ostracizing, humiliating, or expelling the offending player. Wizards are players with special administrative authority much like system administrators in real-world computing systems. They attempt to mediate disputes that have arisen among players by attempting to engage players in calm and rational discussions. When this fails to work, a Wizard might punish an offending player by *toading* or changing the name and description of the player, often to something repulsive like a wart toad. A Wizard may also deny offenders access to the MUD in the future or subject the player to various types of public humiliation to discourage future deviant behavior. Wizards appear to represent a wide range of personalities with varying degrees of power (see Box 9.2).

Electronic lists and Usenet do not offer the same kind of real-time experience as do chatrooms and MUDs. However, they do offer on-going discussions that may involve many participants. Like chatrooms, Usenet news or discussion groups are organized around specific topics and themes and certain social rules apply. In one Usenet discussion group, it may be entirely appropriate to rant and rave about whether Babe Ruth, Roger Maris, Sammy Sosa, or Mark McGwire is the most talented batter of all time. More somber discussion would be expected in a Usenet group about cancer or spouse abuse. Some discussion groups are moderated, and posting must first be approved by the supervisor before they are listed.

Usenet discussion groups are classified hierarchically by subject. Messages are posted to these newsgroups. These articles are then broadcast to other interconnected computer systems. Usenet is available on a wide va-

BOX 9.2. Reflections of the LambdaMOO "Wizard."

MUD players typically spend their connected time socializing with each other, exploring the various rooms and other objects in the database, and adding new objects of their own design. They vary widely in the amount of time they spend connected on each visit, ranging from only a minute to several hours; some players stay connected (and almost always idle) for days at a time, only occasionally actively participating.

Wizards, in general, have a different experience of mudding than other players. Because of their palpable and extensive extra power over other players, and because of their special role in MUD society, they are frequently treated differently by other players. Most players on LambdaMOO, for example, on first encountering my Wizard player, treat me with almost exaggerated deference and respect. I am frequently called "sir" and players apologize for wasting my time. A significant minority, however, appear to go to great lengths to prove that they are not impressed by my office or power, speaking to me bluntly and making demands that I assist them with their problems using the system, sometimes to the point of rudeness.

Because of other demands on my time, I am almost always connected to the MUD but idle, located in a special room I built (my "den") that players require permission to enter. This room is useful, for example, as a place in which to hold sensitive conversations without fear of interruption. This constant presence and unapproachability, however, has had significant and unanticipated side effects. I am told by players who get more circulation than I do that I am widely perceived as a kind of mythic figure, a mysterious Wizard in his magical tower. Rumor and hearsay have spread word of my supposed opinions on matters of MUD policy. One effect is that players are often afraid to contact me for fear of capricious retaliation at their presumption.

Although I find this situation disturbing and wish that I had more time to spend out walking among the "mortal" members of the LambdaMOO community, I am told that player fears of wizardry caprice are justified on certain other MUDs. It is certainly easy to believe stories that I hear of MUD Wizards who demand deference and severely punish those who transgress; there is a certain ego boost to those who wield even simple administrative power in virtual worlds, and it would be remarkable indeed if no one had ever started a MUD for that reason alone. In fact, one player sent me a copy of an article, written by a former MUD Wizard, based on Machiavelli's *The Prince*; it details a wide variety of more-or-less creative ways for wizards to make ordinary MUD players miserable. If this wizard actually used these techniques, as he claims, then some players' desires to avoid Wizards are understandable.

From: *Culture of the Internet* edited by Sara Kiesler (1997).Lawrence Erlbaum Associates. Used with permission.

riety of computer systems and networks, but the bulk of modern traffic is transported over the Internet. Like e-mail lists, Usenet newsgroups cover a hodgepodge of interests. Rather than clogging up an e-mail box, newsgroups post messages that can be accessed by any interested Internet user. Although older messages expire on local Usenet news servers, some services, such as DejaNews, archive the old postings.

TWO THEORIES: THE VIRTUAL SOCIETY OR THE VIRTUAL DESERT?

Research on the interaction between people by way of the Internet is limited, but two hypotheses have been advanced. Some observers believe that Internet use reduces social interaction as people isolate themselves at computer terminals, surf homepages and databases, or communicate with anonymous strangers (e.g., Stoll, 1995; Turkle, 1996). Conversely, others suggest that the Internet reduces distance making people and places around the world more accessible. Members of the latter camp contend that the Internet facilitates communication and the sharing of ideas among people with common interests. It enables the infirm and elderly to stay connected with friends, relatives, and other members of society (e.g., J. E. Katz & Aspden, 1997).

Those who assert that the Internet facilitates communication note that it affords people the opportunity to access instant information on thousands of topics. Users compare notes with others in Usenet discussion groups or through other electronic forums. In so doing, the Internet helps people gain knowledge and become informed consumers. Furthermore, it fosters interpersonal relationships by enabling people to economically send electronic mail messages, thereby staying in touch with friends and family members. These messages may operate like postal letters that often include news, jokes, recipes, or photographs. In addition, visiting MUDs, chatrooms, and Usenet locales permits people to affiliate with others, receive social support, and possibly make friends. In this way, the Internet facilitates associations with friends, family, and others with common interests.

Some Internet researchers contend that online communities (and especially MUDs) provide evidence that appears to debunk some of the more provocative claims that MUDs are addictive (Schiano, 1997). Evidence is lacking to support the proposition that the social structure will fragment as more and more people discover and utilize MUDs or other virtual spaces. As with any technology, citizens must learn to use this new tool to enhance interpersonal one-on-one interaction and facilitate the planning of larger social gatherings. Schiano (1997) asserted that research reveals some similarities between the ways in which people conduct themselves in real life and in the LambdaMOO MUD she studied. Thus, virtual communities are not inherently unhealthy. People must simply recognize that the Internet—like any media entity or programming genre—competes for the attention of the audience. As with other media, the issue is teaching people to use the technology with care and sobriety.

Other researchers hint that a critical issue with respect to the Internet involves encouraging people to think about how they use it. Kraut et. al., (1998) explained that if the Internet is used like a telephone rather than a television, it may contribute to civic and social engagement and enhance interpersonal communication. People use it to socialize, plan events, and obtain information from other people. Although virtual communities may exist within MUDs or chatrooms, the development of strong interpersonal ties are rare. True interpersonal relationships are associated with "frequent contact, deep feelings of affection and obligation, and application to a broad content domain, whereas weak ties are relationships with superficial and easily broken bonds, infrequent contact and narrow focus" (Kraut et al, 1998, p. 1019). Although it is clear that information and entertainment drive Internet usage, it remains unclear whether the system will help people maintain strong interpersonal bonds, which will ultimately contribute to interaction and social and civic engagement.

COMPARING THE INTERNET TO TELEVISION AND TELEPHONE ADOPTION

Television exploded onto the American scene with set penetration rising from a mere handful of viewers in 1948 to 90% in 1960 (Head, Sterling, & Schofield, 1994). Since then, civic participation has continually declined (Putnam, 1995). Although other factors including the increasing mobility of citizens and women entering the workforce may account for some of this, many believe that television is primarily responsible for the decline in civic engagement. This is because when people stay home watching television, they spend less time with community affairs and events. They also participate less in social activities. The consequence of this disengagement is higher crime and less efficiency in government. When citizens take stock in their communities and join civic organizations, politicians respond and work harder to elevate the quality of life in the community. Once people interact with other people, they become both physically and psychologically healthier (Cohen & Wills, 1985).

Excessive television viewing is also associated with a lack of social interaction (Brody, 1990; Jackson-Beeck & Robinson, 1981; Maccoby, 1951; S. B. Neuman, 1991). People who spend too much time watching television engage in less physical activity and are less mentally and physically healthy (R. E. Andersen, Crespo, Bartlett, Cheskin, & Pratt, 1998; Sidney,

Sternfeld, Haskell, Jacobs, Chesney, & Hulley, 1998). Significant amounts of television viewing is also related to feelings of unhappiness and boredom (Kubey & Csikszentmihalyi, 1990). Lonely people tend to watch more television (Canary & Spitzberg, 1993), although some use it to reduce loneliness (Rook & Peplau, 1982; Rubinstein & Shaver, 1982). The main point, however, is not that watching television is inherently harmful or destructive. Rather, spending too much time watching television detracts from civic participation and interferes with interpersonal and social interaction (Fischer, 1992). With sets in American households turned on for more than 7 hours a day and the average person consuming nearly 3.5 hours daily (Nielsen Media Research, 1995), it seems likely that people have less time for healthy human interaction than they did in the past.

As the Internet, like television, becomes a household technology, significant changes are expected in the ways in which government, media, and education contribute to its development. On the positive side, it may help schools and universities establish educational outreach and distance education programs. Interactive databases like *UMI ProQuest Direct* and the *Lexis-Nexis Academic Universe* distribute full text copies of articles that appear in scholarly and legal journals as well as magazines, newspapers, and transcripts of network television and radio newscasts. These services enable scholars, lawyers, and students to quickly and efficiently access the most recent knowledge or information about thousands of topics. Town hall meetings may be held in cyberspace enabling citizens to visit with the mayor or city council members. Such a scenario implies that continued investment by government and the corporate sector will serve the society and citizens very well.

However, like watching television, using home computers and the Internet are sedentary activities that do not necessarily promote interpersonal interaction. Although using home computers and the Internet may enhance skills and help people feel self-confident about their technological abilities (Lundmark, Kiesler, Kraut, Scherlis, & Mukopadhyay, 1998), users operate in a kind of social vacuum because they spend so much time alone. Game playing in MUDs, chatting, or discussing issues on Usenet cannot be considered a substitute for human conversations and interpersonal contact. Some research suggests that home computing is displacing television watching as 18- to 35-year-olds scaled back their television viewing to spend more time online (Kohut, 1994; Technology Forecast, 1997). Time that was once spent engaged in family interaction continues to decline (Vitalari, Venkatesh, & Gronhaug, 1985).

Telephones facilitate two-way interpersonal communication that ultimately benefits both the individual and society. If the Internet develops as a technology that stresses interpersonal interaction, then, it too should encourage the development of better citizens and a healthier society. However, the Internet may contribute to civic and social disengagement if it retards social interaction and civic participation. Therefore, understanding and teaching the advantages and liabilities of the Internet to new users may play an important role in how future generations judge the contributions that the Internet has made, or failed to make, in helping cultivate a civic-minded and socially involved citizenry.

SOCIAL AFFILIATION, PSYCHOLOGICAL WELL-BEING, AND INTERNET USE

The jury remains out on how interacting with the Internet will ultimately affect people psychologically. However, one important well-funded research project known as HomeNet deserves attention (Kraut et al., 1998). In the study, the researchers examined the social and psychological impact of the Internet on 169 people in 73 households during their first 1 to 2 years online. The participants were from diverse neighborhoods in Pittsburgh, Pennsylvania, who previously demonstrated a significant interest in civic affairs.

Although the homogeneity of the sample renders the results nongeneralizable to the overall population, the researchers reported that

a surprisingly consistent picture of the consequences of using the Internet [emerged]. Greater use of the Internet was associated with small, but statistically significant declines in social involvement as measured by communication within the family and the size of people's local social networks, and with increases in loneliness, a psychological state associated with social involvement. Greater use of the Internet was also associated with increases in depression. Other effects on the size of the distant social circle, social support, and stress did not reach standard significance levels but were consistently negative. (p. 1028)

The explanation for these findings appears obvious. As people spend more time using computers, they spend less time engaged in human interaction. The fundamental flaw in this thinking is that the Internet is inherently social because people use it to keep up with friends and family on e-mail or make new acquaintances or develop friendships in MUDs or chatrooms. However, distinctions should be made between using electronic forums to keep up with friends or family members and developing relationships with people in MUDs or chatrooms. Using e-mail as a tool to remain connected to friends and family represents the strength of the technology because it facilitates interpersonal linkages and relationships.

Conversely, spending time in MUDs or chatrooms represents communication between people with weak ties. Using the Internet enables people to interact with many other people on a daily basis. However, these interactions are not substitutes for relationships that lead to the solidification of strong ties (Krackhardt, 1994). The HomeNet study revealed that online acquaintances rarely developed into friendships with strong bonds. The findings parallel the results of national survey data revealing that only 22% of respondents who used the Internet for 2 or more years ever made a new friend (J. E. Katz & Aspden, 1997).

Friendships established online—even those maintained over a period of time—lack many attributes of interpersonal communication such as vocal intonation, facial gestures, and touch. Software developers should consider ways to make the computing experience more interpersonal as the evolution of the Internet continues. The most important issue, however, involves training users to understand the benefits, strengths, and liabilities of the Internet. Although the Internet and the WWW may serve a valuable function both now and in the future, children should be taught that, as with television, recreational use should be moderated. If it erodes time normally devoted to human interactions with strong ties, like those with parents, teachers, and friends, it may over time contribute to feelings of isolation, depression, and despair.

ADDICTION TO THE INTERNET

Jupiter Communications, a New York-based research firm, reported that more than 116 million Americans will have access to the Internet by the year 2002 (Greene, 1998). Most will appreciate the benefits of the medium, but a few will not be able to control their online time. Some mental health professionals believe that between 5 and 10% of all Internet users have the potential to become addicted. James Fearing, president of the National Counseling Intervention Services in Minneapolis, believes that Internet addiction will become a significant issue in the next few years (Armour, 1998). Preliminary online data from the Internet Usage Survey show that of the majority of users surveyed (563 users with a mean age of 34 years) reported instances in which the Internet interfered with various aspects of their lives. The most commonly noted problem involved time management (Brenner, 1997). However, a subgroup of these users described multiple usage-related problems, including several similar to those found in alcohol or gambling addictions.

Considering this, it is not surprising that there is a certain mistrust of computers. A survey by the Department of Trade and Industry in the United Kingdom indicated that more than 60% of the population expressed concerns about overreliance on computers (Cooper, 1998). Parents who buy computers for their children have similar worries about overreliance, overuse, inappropriate contacts, and easy access to adult material. Anthony Wolf, a Massachusetts child psychologist, urges parents to supervise and monitor Internet usage by their children (K. Thomas, 1998). Because younger people tend to experience the greatest problems with Internet addiction disorder, parents fears may be well founded.

The first book to chronicle Internet addictions, *Caught in the Net* by psychologist Kimberly Young, reveals that logging off causes some users to experience feelings of moodiness, irritability, and depression. These individuals forego sleep, risk job opportunities, and lie to family members to stay connected. Young (1996) reported on a 43-year-old female homemaker who appeared to be addicted to using the Internet. Although the woman had a stable home life, with no prior history of addiction or other psychiatric problems, she used the Internet to the detriment of her family and social relationships. Young chronicled instances in which students, homemakers, and professionals fell into patterns of addictive Internet usage to the detriment of their own well-being by triggering problems at work or school or with family members (Young, 1998).

One subscriber to an Internet addiction support mailing list blames her husband's addiction to the Internet for the break up of their marriage. "It destroyed not only our marriage but my husband's personality, his values, his morals, his behavior, and his parenting." Another woman was fired when supervisors recognized her inability to curtail her use at the office. One young man details his obsession with Multi-User Dimension games, which had obvious consequences on his college career: "At my peak . . . I was playing sometimes 11 hours a day, sometimes 11 hours straight. I did poorly . . . because I would work for 20 minutes and then go MUD for two hours, come back, work for another 20 minutes, then MUD for four hours, then go to sleep" (Greene, 1998, p. 79). Other stories include a boy who risked climbing out of a third-story window to reattach a phone line his worried parents had cut in response to his overuse of the Internet. In another case, a man was beaten by his wife after he threw her modem out of a window (Greene, 1998).

Although Young's book drew criticism, many other psychologists and psychiatrists stand firmly behind her message. Ivan Goldberg, MD, a New York City psychiatrist, originally coined the term *internet addiction disorder* (IAD) as a joke—as a way of parodying new psychiatric conditions recognized by the American Psychiatric Association. However, colleagues said that his descriptions were accurate. Goldberg created an online support group, although he concedes that it is a lot like "having an AA meeting in a bar" (Goldsborough, 1997, p. 28).

University of Texas at Austin psychologist Kathy Scherer reported that some college students demonstrate addictive behavior. Her survey results reveal that 98% of dependent users said they stayed online longer than they wanted; a third reported problems in managing their social, academic, and work responsibilities that they attributed to overuse of the Internet; and half said they had tried to cut down but were unable to do so (Greene, 1998).

Maressa Hecht Ozarck, who lectures in psychiatry, founded a computer-addiction clinic at Harvard Medical School's McLean Hospital (Kiernan, 1998). Ozarck reported that addiction cuts across demographic lines and includes students, retirees, professionals, and housewives. Internet addicts seem to be people who seek refuge from loneliness, depression, and family conflicts through their computers (Stephen, 1998). Another study conducted at the University of Cincinnati revealed that serious psychiatric disturbances were common among those addicted to the Internet. Sufferers were *severely impaired* in their academic work (58%), in relationships (53%), financially (52%), and at jobs (51%; Stephen, 1998). Finally, a questionnaire posted on the ABCNEWS.com Web site by a Connecticut psychologist drew more than 17,000 responses. Nearly 1,000 respondents reported that they used the computer to escape their problems and felt anxious when they could not go online (Lawrence, 1999). The study revealed that an many as 11 million people may be addicted to the Internet (see Box 9.3).

BOX 9.3. A Web of Addiction

Internet proves a Web of addiction for 11 million worldwide; Study claims millions addicted to the Internet

By J. M. Lawrence, August 23, 1999, p. 1.

1999 Boston Herald Inc. Reprinted with permission.

The computer mouse might as well be a syringe full of heroin for an estimated 11 million worldwide who are addicted to porn, chat, and e-mail, according to the largest study yet of compulsive computer use. "There's a power here that's different than anything we've dealt with before," said West Hartford, Connecticut, psychologist David Greenfield, who conducted the study.

Released yesterday [August 22, 1999] in Boston during the annual meeting of the American Psychological Association, the study contends 5.7% of the world's 200 million Internet users may be hooked and their habit is wreaking havoc on work and relationships. The study was based on 17,251 responses to a questionnaire that Greenfield posted on the web site ABCNEWS.com.

The therapist drew the questions from a typical list used to diagnose gambling addiction. Nine hundred or 5.7% answered "yes" to five or more questions focusing on whether they used the computer to escape their problems and felt anxiety when they couldn't go online. "Marriages are being dis-

---

(Continues)

rupted, kids are getting into trouble, people are committing illegal acts, people are spending too much money," Greenfield said. "As someone who treats patients, I see it."

Another 10% of users met the definition of *abusers*. Their online time alters their moods, creates negative changes in their lives, and makes them neglect family obligations, the study found.

Participants in the study described feeling out of control, seduced by the hypnotic screen, and increasingly cut off from their families. Others talked of feeling rage at their Internet-loving partners. One woman discovered her fiancé was obsessed with computer porn. He promised to give it up, but a computer record of his surfing habits revealed his online haunts and his girlfriend sought revenge. "Our sex life was taking a back seat to this stuff," she told researchers.

"So I took a crescent wrench to the monitor and we no longer have this problem in the home."

Greenfield, who has referred to the Internet as "television on steroids," traces the medium's power to the instant intimacy users can feel with each other and their own lack of inhibitions thanks to anonymous communication. Addicts in the study spent their time online in these areas:

- Web surfing—78%.
- E-mailing—75%.
- Playing games—62%.
- Chatting—57%.
- Shopping—20%.

Those who met the criteria for addiction were more likely to get involved in cybersex and real-life meetings with their online lovers. Those who were not addicted engaged in much less sex talk, flirting, and masturbation.

The new study seems likely to bolster acceptance of compulsive Internet use as a legitimate psychological disorder. However, researchers noted the study contains flaws because it appeared on only one Web site and accompanied ABC's coverage on Internet addiction.

Therapists offering to treat online addiction are popping up, ironically, on the Internet. Kimberly Young, a psychologist at the Center for On-line Addiction in Bradford, Pennsylvania, said the study "adds a layer of legitimacy to the concern that Internet addiction is real." Young, who operates a Web site called *netaddiction.com*, charges $55 for a 50-minute online session designed to repair the damage wrought by cyberaffairs and porn addiction.

Internet addicts already are making the news with their destructive habits. Sandra Hacker, a Cincinnati mother of three, was recently charged with neglect after police found her surfing the Net while her children went hungry. Her apartment was littered with broken glass and human feces. She often spent 12 hours per day online, according to investigators.

(Continues)

In Cleveland in March, an angry husband who had been drinking cut the phone line on his home telephone to end his wife's online shopping binges. "It's worse than cigarettes and just as expensive as gambling," said one Internet user who responded to Greenfield's survey. The addict couldn't stop from making bids in online auctions. "I said to myself, 'I can quit anytime. I just need to slow down to one or two bids per day.'"

THE PROGRESSION OF INTERNET ADDICTION

Young studied 396 self-described *dependent* users of the Internet and 100 nondependent users using a short questionnaire that she devised. She posted the questionnaire on several Usenet groups in November 1994 and encouraged Internet users to answer it. She quickly received more than 40 responses from Internet users from Vermont to Oregon, as well as messages from Canada, England, Germany, and Hungary. As her study expanded, she found that dependent users averaged more than 38 hours per week online compared with nondependent users who spend fewer than 5 hours weekly online.

Americans seem most prone to develop the disorder because of the relative ease of getting plugged in. The proliferation of computers lowered their cost to under $1,000 for a basic model, and almost half of all American families own at least one. Internet service providers' offers enable users to surf the Web around the clock at a modest cost. Moreover, the American mind set commonly known as "keeping up with the Jones' " is also called the "contagion factor: because everyone else has an online computer and sends e-mails, you have to" (Stephen, 1998, p. 26). This, coupled with the availability of disposable incomes of the middle-class, "makes it de rigueur to communicate with each other via computer." This freedom that can be so helpful can also easily ruin lives (Stephen, 1998, p. 26).

As with alcohol, drug, or gambling addictions, which tend to progress, Internet addicts need more and more time to achieve satisfaction. Some people feel preoccupied thinking about previous online experiences or anticipating their next session. A few reported getting *the shakes* when logging off. Others use the Internet, much like alcoholics, to avoid problems or feelings of helplessness, guilt, anxiety, or depression. Many tried to control, cut back, or stop their use unsuccessfully (Young, 1999).

Training people to manage time works in some cases, but some suffer from multiple psychological problems. Young believes that the behaviors are worthy of their own classification in future revisions of the American Psychiatric Association's *Diagnostic and Statistical Manual of Mental Disorders* (Matson, 1998). Her definition of *Internet addiction* is broad-based and covers certain behaviors and impulse-control problems. She categorized five specific types of Internet addiction (Young, 1998):

1. cybersexual addiction to adult chatrooms or cyberporn;
2. cyberrelationship addiction to online friendships or affairs that replace real-life situations;
3. net compulsions to online gambling, auctions, or obsessive trading;
4. information overload to compulsive Web surfing or databases searches; and
5. computer addiction to game playing or programming.

A subtype of Internet addiction, *cybersexual addiction,* is now a hot topic on talk shows and advice columns. Approximately 70,000 sexually related Web sites are visited by an estimated 15% of all users. Young believed that the accessibility of these sites, along with the anonymity and privacy, contributed to a sense of being in control. The excitement associated with the ability to freely explore sexuality may become too much of a good thing for some people. Her early studies suggested that men are more likely to view cyberporn because it removes performance anxiety. By contrast, women are more likely to engage in erotic chat because it hides their physical appearance, and removes the social stigma that women should not enjoy sex. It also allows women a safe means for exploring their sexuality (Young, 1998). According to advice columns, addictive behavior and cyberaffairs that develop wreak havoc in marriages. Cybersex also interferes with job performance. A Stanford University survey found that roughly 20% use their office computers to visit sexually explicit Web sites (Hamilton, 1999).

As noted earlier, several mental health professionals see these behaviors, whether true addictions in the chemical dependency definitions or not, as serious problems. They offer help to those who believe they may have a problem with any type of Internet addiction. Young created a WWW self-help page that includes a short questionnaire. The questionnaire is designed to help people determine if they may be addicted to the Internet (http://netaddiction.com; see Box 9.4).

SEDUCING THE INTERNET AUDIENCE

The most compelling argument in favor of accelerating research on the psychological impact of Internet interaction is the degree to which business and industry is aggressively targeting the Internet audience. The Internet progressed quickly during the 1990s from a research tool to mass acceptance by the end of the decade. Early users of the Internet were found to have higher income and educational levels. However, a study by The Interactive Solutions Group (ISG) revealed that, by 1998, the 62 million Americans online were quite similar to their nonuser counterparts

---

BOX 9.4. Internet Addiction Test

To assess your level of addiction, answer the following questions using this scale:

   1 = Not at all

   2 = Rarely

   3 = Occasionally

   4 = Often

   5 = Always

1. How often do you find that you stay online longer than you intended?
   1   2   3   4   5
2. How often do you neglect household chores to spend more time online?
   1   2   3   4   5
3. How often do you prefer the excitement of the Internet to intimacy with your partner?
   1   2   3   4   5
4. How often do you form new relationships with fellow online users?
   1   2   3   4   5
5. How often do others in your life complain to you about the amount of time you spend online?
   1   2   3   4   5
6. How often do your grades or school work suffer because of the amount of time you spend online?
   1   2   3   4   5
7. How often do you check your e-mail before something else that you need to do?
   1   2   3   4   5
8. How often does your job performance or productivity suffer because of the Internet?
   1   2   3   4   5
9. How often do you become defensive or secretive when anyone asks you what you do online?
   1   2   3   4   5
10. How often do you block out disturbing thoughts about your life with soothing thoughts of the Internet?
   1   2   3   4   5
11. How often do you find yourself anticipating when you will go online again?
   1   2   3   4   5

(Continues)

12. How often do you fear that life without the Internet would be boring, empty, and joyless?

          1   2   3   4   5

13. How often do you snap, yell, or act annoyed if someone bothers you while you are online?

          1   2   3   4   5

14. How often do you lose sleep due to late-night log-ins?

          1   2   3   4   5

15. How often do you feel preoccupied with the Internet when off-line or fantasize about being online?

          1   2   3   4   5

16. How often do you find yourself saying "just a few more minutes" when online?

          1   2   3   4   5

17. How often do you try to cut down the amount of time you spend online and fail?

          1   2   3   4   5

18. How often do you try to hide how long you've been online?

          1   2   3   4   5

19. How often do you choose to spend more time online over going out with others?

          1   2   3   4   5

20. How often do you feel depressed, moody, or nervous when you are off-line, which goes away once you are back online?

          1   2   3   4   5

After you've answered all the questions, add the numbers you selected for each response to obtain a final score. The higher your score, the greater your level of addiction and the problems your Internet usage causes. Here is a general scale to help measure your score.

- 20–39 points: You are an average online user. You may surf the Web a bit too long at times, but you have control over your usage.

- 40–69 points: You are experiencing frequent problems because of the Internet. You should consider their full impact on your life.

- 70–100 points: Your Internet usage is causing significant problems in your life. You need to address them now.

Kimberly S. Young, Center for Online Addiction. Used by Permission.

with respect to buying habits, behaviors, and general attitudes concerning media usage.

The impact of this technological adoption by mainstream Americans may not be understood for years to come. By the beginning of 2000, the

Internet appeared to have turned an important corner. The revolutionary phase of the digital age ended as the WWW established itself as central a fixture in American culture as had the television set in the 1950s. Most technological advances pass through a brief period in which elite segments recognize their potential. Whereas the Internet was once used by the privileged few, the WWW of 2000 is dominated by suburban families and traditional businesses who used it for information, recreation, and commerce.

As the 20th century drew to a close, Internet firms recognized the economic potential of the medium. Understanding the principles of economies of scale, Netscape Communications merged with large America On-line to attract the still untapped audience. Concentration of ownership among Internet businesses continues as large players such as Yahoo, Disney, AOL Time Warner, and Microsoft dominate the industry. Venture capital financed new technological companies pushing the NASDAQ to record highs. PricewaterhouseCoopers reports that such funding exceeded $8.2 billion in 1998 compared with $5.4 billion in 1996 (Miller, 1998).

Much of the funding was geared toward marketing products on the Internet and developing the virtual mall, which now provides everything from books, CDs, and videotapes (http://www.amazon.com) to bridal registry (http://www.bridalregistry.com), which offers a one-stop shopping for wedding gifts. Wal-Mart, the world's largest retailer, unveiled its expanded site on January 1, 2000, offering thousands of products to online shoppers. In short, the race is underway to cultivate and develop the cybershoppers.

INTERNET RETAILING

Internet retailing made significant strides by the 1999 Christmas shopping season. Jeff Bezos, who helped create the electronic commerce by founding Amazon.com Inc., believes Internet sellers will ultimately capture 15% of the world's $5 trillion in annual sales. Internet shopping can be efficient and economical. Thousands of online retailers engage in intense competition cutting prices to the bone to attract new buyers. Consumers may avoid trips to congested malls and the inevitable traffic jams on the way. Many shoppers will gladly pay shipping fees to avoid unnerving visits to the mall.

However, even Bezos recognizes that the Internet is incapable of replacing retail stores and shopping malls. He asserts that cybershopping will never entirely replace shopping at the mall because "the physical world is the best medium ever invented, and betting against it has always proved wrong. To bet that people won't go into stores is to bet against human nature, which is always a bad bet. We are a gregarious species" (Goldman, 1999, p. C1).

Internet shopping cannot satisfy immediate consumer needs. Bezos, who was named *Time* magazine person of the year in 1999 for his foresight on e-commerce, believes political forces pushing for taxes on the new technology may retard or even quash e-commerce. He believes Amazon and other Internet companies should have been better prepared politically and should be doing more now to counter the threat of Internet taxation (Goldman, 1999). Finally, with all of its potential, many Internet retailers, including Amazon.com, have failed to make a profit yet. Although Internet retailers will undoubtedly see quarterly returns in the future, consumers still enjoy the experience of shopping in real-world shopping malls (see Box 9.5).

BOX 9.5. Profits allude Amazon.com

Amazon.com stock lost 28% of its value between December 20, 1999, when CEO was named *Time* magazine's man of the year, and January 6, 2000. The world's largest Internet retailer failed to generate the volume of sales it had anticipated during the fourth quarter of 1999, which includes the Christmas shopping season.

Amazon reported its sales more than doubled to about $650 million, from $253 million a year earlier, for the fourth quarter of 1999. However, the Internet retailer was still in the red because it was not able to sell off inventories acquired for Christmas sales. As a result, Amazon was forced to lower prices on overstocked merchandise. Shares in the Seattle-based retailer, which has lost more than $550 million since it began selling books in 1995, plunged $12.19 to $69.75 on Nasdaq on January 5, 1999, their lowest level in 2 months and biggest 1-day fall since the previous April.

Amazon has been a popular Wall Street stock in the Internet sector. It aggressively advertised during the holiday shopping season. Sales of electronics, toys, and other items, which Amazon began marketing in 1999, accounted for more than half of its fourth-quarter revenue. However, unlike books, unsold toys and electronic items cannot be returned to manufacturers. As a result, Amazon.com was forced to sell merchandise at or below cost in 2000. Charles Crane, chief market strategist at Key Asset Management, believes that a workable model for Internet retailing is still developing. "Selling below cost and hoping to make it up on volume is not the best way to run a business," Crane said (Amazon.com shares dive, 1999, p. C1). Amazon.com is unlikely to make a profit until 2001 or 2002.

MEASURING THE INTERNET AUDIENCE

The merging of Internet companies coincided with the movement of the Internet from an elite to a mass entity in which marketing and efforts were the central focus of much of the industry. Measuring Internet audiences, as is the case with television and radio, became important by 1999 because by that time the Internet played a major role in retailing. Media Metrix measures coverage of all digital media including more than 15,000 Web sites using a sample of more than 40,000 business and at-home Internet users. The company uses meters to measure the behavior of Internet users on minute-by-minute, page-by-page, and click-by-click bases. In other words, as more people use the Internet and the WWW, research on the users escalates. Today, the Media Metrix meters are tracking tens of thousands of people at their homes and businesses.

The data that Media Metrix and other measurement firms generate are sold to clients for planning, buying, and selling new media advertising. The information is used to develop advertising and marketing campaigns and to understand how consumers behave when deciding on purchases and investment strategies. The clients of these measurement firms include Microsoft, AOL, Intel, IBM, GM, Yahoo!, Netscape, Excite, CNN, Disney, and Amazon.com, as well as most major advertising agencies, financial institutions, and technological companies. The client companies combined represent an estimated 85% of the total dollars spent on Internet advertising, marketing, and e-commerce.

Nielsen Research, the television viewership measurement firm, joined with Internet-based NetRatings in 1998 to monitor who is surfing the WWW. Because the Internet provides firms with quick, easy, and efficient access to consumers, Web-based advertising campaigns are becoming complicated and expensive. Firms are becoming interested in discovering whether Web-based appeals will succeed in persuading Internet users to purchases products, goods, and services.

Measuring the audience is important because many experts predict the Internet will ultimately become an efficient advertising vehicle. Visitors to Web sites are often members of the specific audience segment that the firm identified as potential consumers. Whereas firms often infer a link between effective advertising campaigns in print or broadcast media, Web-based appeals produce immediate marketing results. For this reason, firms have a keen interest in developing and maintaining sites that are visually appealing and interesting, easy to use, and that create a sense of interaction between the consumer and the product or brand being sold.

Audience measurement firms also use traditional measurement strategies to identify users of the Internet and the WWW. Nielsen studies panels that represent a cross-section of Web users who, in turn, provide Net traffic feedback. Media Metrix, PC Data, Net Ratings, and Nielsen employ survey samples to follow Web usage in the United States. Other firms like MatchLogic, AdForce, and Engage Technologies primarily analyze Web traffic. They then draw conclusions about people who surf the Internet and pass this information onto their clients. In the end, all of these data are compiled and used to stimulate sales for products and produce an appetite for goods and services among members of the Internet audience.

CONCLUSION

The Internet and the WWW exploded into the media environment in the 1990s. The Internet originally developed as an electronic support system for research scientists. As it achieved widespread acceptance from the general population, it became an instrument that was used for information, entertainment, and commerce. Unlike other new technologies, such as radio and television, the Internet continues to change and evolve as users find innovative new applications. As a contender for the attention of the audience, it allows users to reinvent possible applications for the new technology.

As a provider of information and entertainment, the Internet appears to satisfy many of the same needs that were articulated in the uses and gratifications model from mass communication theory. Furthermore, it seems to fill a need for companionship and human interaction. People use MUDs and chatrooms to play games and exchange ideas with other Internet users. However, researchers have begun to question whether the overuse of these technologies and the development of virtual societies may lead to feelings of despair and loneliness. This concern is based on evidence suggesting that the seductive nature of the Internet and WWW erodes the amount of time that people invest in true human relationships. Evidence suggests that interacting in cyberspace may lead to addiction. Addiction to the Internet manifests itself, much like chemical addictions, in compulsive behaviors and symptoms of withdrawal when failing to spend expected amounts of time online. The great majority of users, however, find the Internet an entertaining and useful tool.

The Internet will clearly continue to develop as an important mainstream media source as business and industry continue to invest in its development. The advent of the virtual shopping mall, online banking, and stock trading, the services offered through the Internet, will influence buying habits and alter the ways in which we manage time. The increase in audience measurement firms provides evidence that industry sees the potential of the Internet as both a marketing tool and a source of entertainment for users.

The appeal of the Internet and the WWW will unquestionably have an impact on the future social order. As the Internet becomes more of a commercial entity in the already congested media environment, scholars, teachers, and students should consider how much time they spend interacting on the Internet and whether the time in cyberspace is being used constructively. Citizens should use the Internet constructively to enhance civic engagement and promote social interaction. Used properly, these new technologies may assist in making wise purchases and learning important information. As with any tool, using it efficiently, effectively, and responsibly can enhance the quality of one's life.

10 Learning to Use Media Constructively

SUMMARY

- Media corporations produce messages to attract the *attention* of audience members.
- Media messages are designed to target specific *audience segments*.
- People respond *cognitively* and *emotionally* to media messages.
- Interpreting media messages in the context of stored knowledge contributes to the *construction of social reality*.
- *Children* are especially vulnerable to the effects of media messages.
- Understanding how the media satisfy cognitive and emotional needs will help audience members *use them constructively*.
- Understanding how the Internet and World Wide Web satisfies cognitive and emotional needs will help audience members *use them constructively*.
- Audience members should work to create a *socially* and *politically constructive media system*.

USING MEDIA CONSTRUCTIVELY

People spend about 30 hours weekly watching television and another 12 engaged with other media such as radio, newspaper, or magazines. In addition, the Internet and the WWW have become major competitors for the time and attention of the audience. Audience members should consider the implications of using this much media. They should also understand the processes that take place when they use it.

Effects are most likely to occur when people use media heavily over a period of time, but they may also occur as a result of a single exposure to a message. In chapter 2 of this volume, we saw how *The China Syndrome,* followed by a nuclear accident at Three Mile Island in Pennsylvania, had the effect of galvanizing sentiment against nuclear power. Similarly, the film *Wag the Dog* contributed to public cynicism about government officials following the disclosures concerning Monica Lewinsky and President Clinton. Informed audience members should consider that the media frame entertainment and information. This framing can shape attitudes, opinions, and beliefs. Understanding these processes will enable to use the media more constructively.

MEDIA EFFECTS AND LITERACY

Media Corporations Produce Messages to Attract the Attention of Audience Members

Creative new methods of attracting the attention of the audience and engaging them are tested daily. Television programs routinely ask viewers to interact by expressing opinions about topics using the Internet and e-mail. Audience members can now play along with game show contestants on television. The advent of electronic books makes it possible for consumers to have instant access to the latest titles. The WWW now offers a multitude of online products and services. Media corporations will continue to aggressively vie for the attention of audiences using these interactive products and techniques. Literate consumers should learn how to evaluate these appeals to use the media constructively.

Media Messages are Designed to Target Specific Audience Segments

The idea of the mass audience has become antiquated. Instead, media organizations develop messages aimed at attracting segments of the overall audience. In such an environment, audience members find it easier to identify newspapers, television programs, and other media suited to their tastes. However, literate media consumers should recognize that these specialized messages might fail to provide the diversity needed to develop knowledge about important social issues. MTV, for example, helped President Bill Clinton and Vice President Gore to reach the youth vote in 1992 by inviting the candidates to appear on the *Rock the Vote* program. Nevertheless, audience members of such programs must understand that, in isolation, these programs cannot provide information needed to make informed decisions.

People Respond Cognitively and Emotionally to Media Messages

Persuasive communication campaigns use strategies designed to alter the behavior of the audience members by stimulating cognitions and emotions. An effective public service campaign may encourage people to avoid being the victim of crime. Effective advertising may generate an appetite for a product. Audience members should understand the principles of persuasive communication. In so doing, they are in a better position to analyze the claims contained within media messages.

News and public affairs information also stimulates cognitions and emotions. What audience members learn from the media is correlated with the predispositions of those who produce messages. Information presented through the news media is not entirely objective for a variety of reasons. Furthermore, editors decide which news items are covered and which are excluded. Information is gathered and distributed by individuals who are influenced by the culture of their news organization. Finally, reporters and editors operate from their own predispositions when they construct messages. These factors create messages that are interpretations of information by media professionals. Audience members should understand the processes that affect the news and information they receive.

Interpreting Media Messages in the Context of Stored Knowledge Contributes to the Construction of Social Reality

Conceptions of the world and social systems are based on total life experience. The media, along with family, friends, environmental factors, and innate intelligence, contribute to the active process of constructing social reality. Evaluating and interpreting information stimulates top–down processing. Knowledge stored in schemas guides the interpretation of new information. When people interpret media messages, they search for related or associated ideas or memories to construct reality. This process relies on the activation of schemas that assist in understanding and interpreting new information.

Many factors may influence the way in which schemas develop. Membership within various cultural, social, demographic, or psychographic groups may influence the development of schemas. The content and structure of media messages influence the development of schemas. Because each person possesses a unique set of schemas, audience members may interpret the same message differently.

Audience members should also understand the role of scripts in the process of constructing social reality. Media messages can teach people how to respond to certain situations that may arise, but scripts also perpetuate stereotypes about social group. Stereotyping may have a detrimental effect on attitudes and beliefs among audience members. The disproportionate use of minority groups members as perpetrators of crimes in film and on television may cause some to fear these groups. Audience members should recognize that the media are capable of shaping or reinforcing unhealthy attitudes, opinions, and beliefs by repeating stereo-typical scripts.

Children Are Especially Vulnerable to the Effects of Media Messages

Media surround children from the time they are born. Many of the pro-grams on television contain violent acts that go unpunished. Many factors may influence violence and aggression in children. However, research has shown that those who witness large amounts of violence on television tend to demonstrate more aggressive tendencies than do other children.

Young children have difficulty distinguishing between fictional and real characters presented on television. Behaviors witnessed by children on television may serve as a model for future behavior. As children age, they develop an understanding of plots and scripts. Repetition of these plots and scripts may cause children to assume that acts witnessed on television represent appropriate behaviors in the real world.

Repeated exposure to violent programming may also desensitize chil-dren to violence and aggression. This can translate into a lack of concern for actual victims of violence. Because most acts of television violence go unpunished, children may conclude that aggression and violence are suit-able methods for resolving conflict. Therefore, the media can have a pro-found effect on how children perceive the world. Media messages may teach behaviors that can last a lifetime.

Understanding How Talk Shows Satisfy Cognitive and Emotional Needs Will Help Audience Members Use Them Constructively

Radio and television talk shows satisfy human needs. The programs vi-cariously enable listeners and viewers to participate in discussions and de-bates on interesting or controversial subjects. Some people use these programs to learn about important social, political, or economic issues. Other people find comfort in hearing the attitudes and opinions of other like-minded individuals. As such, they reinforce attitudes and beliefs of the audience members. They also permit audience members to monitor perspectives that may be in opposition to their own. Such monitoring represents a form of surveillance that may be useful in discussions or de-bates in the future. Well-reasoned arguments on talk shows may also alter or reinforce opinions, attitudes, and beliefs.

People also use radio and television talk shows to satisfy emotional needs. Some people watch or listen to these programs to be reassured about their own attitudes, opinions, and beliefs. Other people use them to feel better about their own situations in comparison with others. Programs featuring oddballs, misfits, down-on-their-luck guests or individuals engaged in dysfunctional relationships may reassure viewers that their situations are, by comparison, not so bad. The interactive nature of these programs affords people the opportunity to use media to elevate their spirits and affirm convictions. Audience members should understand why they find certain programming genres enjoyable and interesting.

Understanding How the Internet and World Wide Web Satisfies Cognitive and Emotional Needs Will Help Audience Members Use Them Constructively

Media industries will continue to become more interactive. The most interactive of these, the Internet and the WWW, have become important sources of information, entertainment, and commerce. Information can be easily accessed from databases around the globe. The WWW offers the promise of providing the disadvantaged with better access to information systems.

Using the Internet or any media requires discipline. If online interactions replace strong ties among friends, family, and neighbors, users may perceive the world as a lonely place. To enhance the quality of their lives, audience members should find ways of using the Internet to stimulate human interaction and social interaction between people.

Audience Members Should Work to Create a Socially and Politically Constructive Media System

Citizens must recognize that they have ultimate control over their media environment. As former FCC Chairman Nicholas Johnson urged more than three decades ago, citizens must take an active role in the creation of an educational and socially constructive media system.

BUILDING BETTER MEDIA

At first glance, our media system appears to be remarkably diverse. The Telecommunications Act passed by Congress in 1996 was intended to spur competition, which would add to the multiplicity of voices in the marketplace. Instead of making it easier for companies to compete, the opposite has occurred. The megamergers that grew out of the Act produced a playing field with relatively few players. Many critics believe that so much power in the hands of so few people will inevitably retard the social and civic dialogues central to philosophy of the marketplace of ideas (Bagdikian, 1998, 2000; Mazzocco, 1994; McChesney, 1999).

In a concentrated media environment, some fear that quality journalism and program diversity may vanish. In his 1998 book, *Megamedia: How Giant Corporations Dominate Mass Media, Distort Competition and Endanger Democracy,* Dean Alger wrote that a dozen media conglomerates dominated the landscape (Alger, 1998). Just 2 years later, Alger suggested the number had declined to four (AOL/Time Warner, Disney/ABC, Viacom/CBS, and News Corporation the owner of Fox).

Critics fear that journalists in the new media environment will have little autonomy as corporations use media to boost corporate profits. A *Time* magazine cover in 1999 featured the Pokémon phenomenon and an article discussing the release of the Warner Brothers film, *Pokémon: The First Movie* (Barringer, 2000). It remains unclear whether the article was an example of corporate boosterism or a good excuse to write about an undeniable cultural phenomenon. Nevertheless, literate media consumers should recognize that large media conglomerates often find it tempting to create an audience for products and services through cross-promotion strategies.

HOW TO IMPLEMENT CHANGE

Audience members should recognize that they can influence the content produced by media organizations. To attract audiences, producers rely on tried-and-true formulas that contain sex, violence, action, and terror. Films like the *Basketball Diaries* and *Natural Born Killers*, which glorify violence, may have inspired senseless killing sprees. Producers of these films argue that their products enjoy First Amendment privileges and that they should not be held accountable when members of the audience imitate actions in films. Although it remains unclear whether the courts will ultimately agree, citizens should understand that violence and aggression can stimulate cognitions and emotions that lead to aggressive behavior or violence. Understanding these processes is especially important where children are concerned. Avoiding films or television programs featuring graphic sex and violence will send a message to the producers of these products.

The rash of school and workplace shootings during the past several years caused the attention not only of the public, but also of prominent politicians, performers, clergy, academics, and others. Some banded together to pressure television and film producers to employ a measure of self-restraint in the presentation of sex and violence. Former presidents and other luminaries signed the "Appeal to Hollywood" in an effort to reduce the amount of sex and violence presented through the media and especially in films (see Box 10.1). Citizen groups can have an impact on what media companies decide to produce and display.

BOX 10.1. The Appeal to Hollywood

The "Appeal to Hollywood" released by Empower America at a Capitol Hill press conference on July 21, 1999, and posted on the WWW carries signatures of more than 50 prominent Americans, including former Presidents Carter and Ford, Nobel Peace Prize winner Elie Wiesel, Generals Colin Powell and Norman Schwarzkopf, former Governor Mario Cuomo, former Senator Sam Nunn, C. Delores Tucker of the National Political Congress of Black Women, five U.S. senators, and leading clergy, academicians, business figures, and social activists. Well-known entertainers Steve Allen, Naomi Judd, Carol Lawrence, and Joan Van Ark also signed the abridged statement that follows:

> American parents today are deeply worried about their children's exposure to an increasingly toxic popular culture. Events in Littleton, Colorado, are only the most recent reminder that something is deeply amiss in our media age. Violence and explicit sexual content in television, films, music, and video games have escalated sharply in recent years. Children of all ages are now being exposed to a barrage of images and words that threaten not only to rob them of normal childhood innocence, but also to distort their view of reality and even undermine their character growth.

> Therefore we, the undersigned, call upon executives of the media industry—as well as CEOs of companies that advertise in the electronic media—to join with us, and with America's parents, in a new social compact aimed at renewing our culture and making our media environment more healthy for our society and safer for our children.

> We call upon industry leaders in all media—television, film, music, video, and electronic games—to band together to develop a new voluntary code of conduct, broadly modeled on the NAB code.

> The code we envision would (1) affirm in clear terms the industry's vital responsibilities for the health of our culture; (2) establish certain minimum standards for violent, sexual, and degrading material for each medium, below which producers can be expected not to go; (3) commit the industry to an overall reduction in the level of entertainment violence; (4) ban the practice of targeting of adult-oriented entertainment to youth markets; (5) provide for more accurate information to parents on media content while committing to the creation of "windows" or "safe havens" for family programming (including a revival of TV's "Family Hour"); and, finally, (6) pledge the industry to significantly greater creative efforts to develop good family-oriented entertainment.

From http://www.media-appeal.org

Citizen groups have also urged television producers to improve program quality. The Citizens for Better Television (CBT) believes that U. S. television broadcasters have an unsettled debt to be paid. The group contends that Congress gave $70 billion worth of public airwaves to broadcasters in 1996 when it mandated the conversion to digital television. In exchange, the group is urging the Federal Communications Commission

---

BOX 10.2. How to Improve Television

People for Better TV urges all Americans to get involved now. We are not just consumers of TV, we own the airwaves. TV stations get a license to use public property to make money; in return they are obligated to serve the public good. Only the public can say what the public good is. It has been over 60 years since the first guidelines were established; it is now time to write those guidelines again, and your thoughts are important.

• *Write a letter:* Using the People for Better TV Web site, write a letter to the Federal Communications Commission (FCC). Tell them what you want from TV in the future, and send a copy of your letter to Congress. You can do all this in just a few minutes on the Web site, or if you like we can send you sample letters and the information you need.
• *Visit your local stations:* You have a right to review the public records and program logs of your local television stations. Call your local station. Examine the TV program logs. Write to the FCC and tell them that you want TV that represents you.
• *Form a local group:* There are people in your state and neighborhood who also want to take action. Contact People for Better TV for help in getting your community organized. Call local leaders, including teachers and ministers. Invite your friends over to watch a video and talk about the impact of television.
• *Take a Stand:* We know most Americans are concerned about the impact of TV in the future. We have developed a set of recommendations we think will make TV better. You can find them on our Web site, or just ask and we will fax or mail them to you. And let us know what you think.
• *Become informed:* For educational resources, updates, and more information on taking action, contact People for Better TV.

From http://www.bettertv.org

(FCC) to create new guidelines for how broadcasters can best serve the public. According to the CBT, it is essential to "make the most of this moment before television makes the transition to digital and becomes an even more powerful force in American society." The group has provided guidelines on how citizens may help shape television of the future (see Box 10.2).

Individuals can also have a significant effect on the media content. Feedback in the form of a letter, e-mail, or phone call may persuade programmers to behave in a more responsible fashion. Media organizations such as radio and television stations and newspapers wish to maintain an image as good members of the community. For this reason, three types of feedback are especially important to media managers (Jamieson & Campbell, 1992):

1. Audience members should respond to inaccurate or deceptive claims. Newspapers and radio and television stations wish to maintain credibility within their communities. Media organizations that fail to maintain the trust of the public also run the risk of declines in circulation figures or ratings.

2. Audience members should respond to media programming that violates good taste and contemporary community standards. Broadcasters wish to avoid controversies that may arise from programming that contains gratuitous sex and violence. Initial complaints about the language and partial nudity contained in *NYPD Blue* prompted ABC to pressure program producers to clean up the show.

3. Audience members should respond to media programs that lack fairness and balance. They should also encourage producers of messages to listen to and report on opposing social, cultural, or political perspectives.

CONCLUSION

Despite the dangers associated with increased concentration of media ownership, citizens have the opportunity to use it constructively. The media offer many powerful and versatile tools and new interactive capabilities that can inform and entertain. Audience members should learn to evaluate the quality of messages produced by the media and understand how they influence the attitudes, opinions, and beliefs that shape perceptions of social reality.

Audience members should support quality programming. As we have seen, television programs like *Sesame Street* and *Mr. Rogers Neighborhood* succeeded in teaching generations of children the virtues of a positive approach to others and fostering a healthy outlook on life. Parents should monitor the viewing habits of their children and allow them to view programs that will teach positive attitudes and behaviors. Finally, parents should discuss program options with their children to help them learn to use media constructively.

Films, television, radio, and magazines continue to serve important entertainment and information functions. Enhanced versions of these media will inevitably merge with the digital world. USENET or online text services such Lexis-Nexis and UMI Proquest enable users to efficiently access information. Taking advantage of media tools can contribute to an enlightened and informed society.

The Internet and the WWW make it inexpensive and easy to maintain connections with family, friends, and other people. Used properly, the Internet and the WWW can save time, help inform and enlighten, serve as a shopping mall, and even enable people to find a diversion from the stresses of contemporary life.

Used constructively, media tools can enhance the quality of our lives in countless ways. Audience members should recognize that they can contribute to the development of a constructive media establishment. To do so, they should use media selectively to satisfy specific objectives, needs, and desires. Audience members should encourage media companies to offer more products that will contribute to their lives and the cultivation of an enlightened society.

References

Abt, V. (1994, Summer). The shameless world of Phil, Sally and Oprah: television talk shows and the deconstructing of society. *Journal of Popular Culture, 28*(1), 171–192.

Abt, V., & Mustazza, L. (1997). *Coming after Oprah: Cultural fallout in the age of the TV talk show.* Bowling Green, OH: Bowling Green State University Press.

Adamson, A. (1998, November 12). Warts and all . . . Nude-pix flap hasn't changed the way fans view Dr. Laura Schlessinger: Public often forgives naked ambition. *Philadelphia Daily News.*

Alexander, K. L. (1999, April 30). Local booksellers battle big chains. *USA Today,* p. 10B.

Alger, D. (1998). *Megamedia: How giant corporations dominate mass media, distort competition, and endanger democracy.* Lanham, MD: Rowman & Littlefield.

Aufderheide, P. (1993). *Media literacy: A report of the national leadership conference on media literacy.* Washington, DC: Aspen Institute.

Allen, C. (1997). Tackling the TV titans in their own backyard. ABC-TV, New York City. In M. D. Murray & D. G. Godfrey (Eds.), *Television in America: Local station history from across the nation.* Ames, IA: Iowa State University Press.

Allen, R. C. (1987). *Channels of discourse.* Chapel Hill: University of North Carolina.

Allport, G. W. (1954). *The nature of prejudice.* Reading, MA: Addison-Wesley.

Alter, J. (1995, November 6). Next: The revolt of the revolted. *Newsweek,* pp. 46–47.

Alvarez, M. M., Huston, A. C., Wright, J. C., & Kerkman, D. D. (1988). Gender differences in visual attention to television form and content. *Journal of Applied Developmental Psychology, 9,* 459–475.

Amazon.com shares dive on sales news. (1999, January 6). *The Los Angeles Times,* p. C1.

Andersen, R. E., Crespo, C. J., Bartlett, S. J., Cheskin, L. J., & Pratt, M. (1998). Relationship of physical activity and television watching with body weight and level of fatness among children. *Journal of the American Medical Association, 279,* 938–942.

Anderson, D. R. (1998). Education television is not an oxymoron. *The Annals of the American Academy of Political and Social Science, 557,* 24–38.

Anderson, D. R., & Burns, J. (1991). Paying attention to television. In J. Bryant & D. Zillmann (Eds.), *Responding to the screen: Reception and reaction processes* (pp. 3–26). Hillsdale, NJ: Lawrence Erlbaum Associates.

Anderson, D. R., & Levin, S. R. (1976). Young children's attention to "Sesame Street." *Child Development, 47,* 806–811.

Anderson, D. R., & Smith, R. (1984). Young children's TV viewing: the problem of cognitive continuity. In F. J. Morrison, C. Lord, & D. P. Keating (Eds.), *Applied developmental psychology* (Vol. 1, pp. 116–163). Orlando, FL: Academic Press.

Anderson, J. R. (1976). *Language, memory and thought.* Hillsdale, NJ: Lawrence Erlbaum Associates.

Anderson, J. R. (1983). *The architecture of cognition.* Cambridge, MA: Harvard University Press.

Anderson, J. R. (1990). *Cognitive psychology and its implications* (3rd ed.). New York: W. H. Freeman.

Anderson, J. R., & Bower, G. (1973). *Human associative memory.* Washington, DC: J. H. Winston.

Anderson, L. (1999, October 11). Interactive TV's new approach. *The Industry Standard,* 60–62.

Anthony, T. (1998, September 9). McGwire in a league of his own: Slugger launches home run No. 62 into history. *The Ottawa Citizen,* p. A1.

Applegate, J. L., & Sypher, H. E. (1988). A constructivist theory of communication and culture. In Y. Y. Kim & W. B. Gudykunst (Eds.), *Theories in interpersonal communication* (pp. 41–65). Newbury Park, CA: Sage.

Armour, C. (1998, April 21). Technically, it's an addiction: Some workers finding it hard to disconnect. *USA Today,* p. 4B.

Asch, S. E. (1946). Forming impressions of personality. *Journal of Abnormal and Social Psychology, 41,* 258–290.

Atkin, C. K., & Freimuth, V. (1989). A systems-based evaluation planning model for health communication campaigns in developing countries. In R. E. Rice & C. K. Atkin (Eds.), *Political communication campaigns* (2nd ed., pp. 15–38). Thousand Oaks, CA: Sage.

Atkinson, M. (1999, May 11). The movies made me do it. *The Village Voice, 44*(18), 58–59.

Atkinson, R. C., & Shiffrin, R. M. (1968a). Human memory: A proposed system and its control processes. In K. W. Spence & J. T. Spence (Eds.), *The Psychology of Learning and Motivation* (Vol. 2, pp. 89–195). New York: Academic Press.

Atkinson, R. C., & Shiffrin, R. M. (1968b). The control of short-term memory. *Scientific American, 225,* 82–90.

Aufderheide, P. (1993). *Media literacy: A report of the National Leadership Conference on Media Literacy.* Washington, DC: Aspen Institute.

Avery, R. K., & Ellis, D. G. (1979). Talk radio as an interpersonal phenomenon. In G. Gumpert & R. Catheart (Eds.), *Inter/Media: Interpersonal communications in a media world* (pp. 108–115). New York: Oxford University Press.

Baddeley, A. (1976). *The psychology of memory.* New York: Basic Books.

Baddeley, A. (1986). *Working memory.* New York: Oxford University Press.

Bagdikian, B. H. (1998). The realities of media concentration and control. *Television Quarterly, 29*(3), 22–27.

Bagdikian, B. H. (2000). *The media monopoly* (5th ed.). Boston: Beacon.

Baker, J. F. (1994, March 14). *Reinventing the book business.* New York: *Publishers Weekly.*

Ballard, P. B. (1913). Oblivience and reminiscence. *British Journal of Psychology Monograph Supplements, 1*(2).

Ball-Rokeach, S. J., & DeFleur, M. (1976). A dependency model of mass media effects. *Communication Research, 3*(3), 21.

Ball-Rokeach, S. J., & DeFleur, M. (1982). *Theories of mass communication.* New York: Longman.

Bandura, A. (1977). *Social learning theory.* Englewood Cliffs, NJ: Prentice-Hall.

Bandura, A., Ross, D., & Ross, S. A.. (1961). Transmission of aggression through imitation of aggressive models. *Journal of Abnormal and Social Psychology, 63,* 575–582.

Bandura, A., Ross, D., & Ross, S. A. (1963). Imitation of film-mediated aggressive models. *Journal of Abnormal and Social Psychology, 66,* 3–11.

Bandura, A., & Walters, R. H. (1963). *Social learning and personality development.* New York: Holt, Rinehart & Winston.

Barringer, F. (2000, January 11). Media megadeal: The journalists; Does Deal Signal Lessening of Media Independence? *New York Times,* p. C5.

Bartlett, F. C. (1932). *Remembering: A study in experimental and social psychology.* London: Cambridge University Press.

Basil, M. D. (1994). Multiple resource theory 1: Application to television viewing. *Communication Research, 21,* 177–207.

Bauer, R. (1964). The obstinate audience. *American Psychologist, 19,* 319–328.

Becker, L., & Whitney, C. D. (1980). Effects of media dependencies. *Communication Research, 7,* 95–120.

Berkowitz, D. (1996). Work roles and news selection in TV: Examining the business–journalism dialectic. *Journal of Broadcasting and Electronic Media, 37*(1), 67–81.

Berkowitz, D., Allen, C., & Beeson, D. (1996). Exploring newsroom views about consultants in local TV. The effect of work roles and socialization. *Journal of Broadcasting and Electronic Media, 40*(4), 447–459.

Berkowitz, L. (1984). Some effects of thoughts on anti- and prosocial influences of media events: A cognitive-neoassociation analysis. *Psychological Bulletin, 95*(3), 410–427.

Berlo, D. (1960). *The process of communication: An introduction to theory and practice.* San Francisco, CA: Rinehart.

Berlyne, D. E. (1970). Novelty, complexity, and hedonic value. *Perception and Psychophysics, 8,* 279–286.

Bettig, R. V. (1997). The enclosure of cyberspace. *Critical Studies in Mass Communication, 14*(2), 138–157.

Biocca, F. (1988). Opposing conceptions of the audience: The active and passive hemispheres of mass communication theory. In J. Anderson (Ed.), *Communication Yearbook 11* (pp. 51–80). Beverly Hills, CA: Sage.

Biocca, F. (1991). Viewers' mental models of political commercials: Towards a theory of the semantic processing of television. In F. Biocca (Ed.), *Television and political advertising: Psychological processes* (Vol. 1, pp. 27–89). Hillsdale, NJ: Lawrence Erlbaum Associates.

Bird, S. E., & Dardenne, R. W. (1988). Myth, chronicle, and story: Exploring the narrative qualities of news. In J. W. Cared (Ed.), *Media, myths and narrative: Television and the press* (pp. 67–86). Newbury Park, CA: Sage.

Blumer, H. (1946). Collective behavior. In A. M. Lee (Ed.), *Principles of sociology* (pp. 185–186). New York: Barnes & Noble.

Blumler, J. G., & Gurevitch, M. (1995). *The crisis of public communication*. London: Routledge.

Blumler, J. G., & Katz, E. (1974). *The uses of mass communication: Current perspectives on gratification research*. Beverly Hills: Sage.

Bobrow, D. G., & Norman, D. A. (1975). Some principles of memory schemata. In D. G. Bobrow & A. G. Collins (Eds.), *Representation and understanding: Studies in cognitive science* (pp. 131–150). New York: Academic Press.

Bolce, L., De Maio, G., & Muzzio, D. (1996). Dial-in democracy: Talk radio and the 1994 election. *Political Science Quarterly, 111*(3), 457–481

Bower, G. H. (1970). Organizational factors in memory. *Cognitive Psychology, 1,* 18–46.

Bower, G. H. (1972a). A selective review of organizational factors in memory. In E. Tulving & W. Donaldson (Eds.), *Organization of memory* (pp. 93–145). New York: Academic.

Bower, G. H. (1972b). Mental imagery and associative learning. In L. W. Gregg (Ed.), *Cognition in learning and memory* (pp. 51–88). New York: Wiley.

Bower, G. H. (1975). *Cognitive psychology: An introduction*. In W. K Estes (Ed.), *Handbook of learning and cognitive processes* (Vol. 1, pp. 25–80). Hillsdale, NJ: Lawrence Erlbaum Associates.

Bower, G. H., Black, J. B., & Turner, T. J. (1979). Scripts in memory for text. *Cognitive Psychology, 11,* 177–220.

Bower, G. H., & Springston, F. (1970). Pauses as recoding points in letter series. *Journal of Experimental Psychology, 83,* 421–430.

Bradsher, K. (1999, May 8). Talk show ordered to pay $25 million after killing. *New York Times,* p. A10.

Branford, J. D. (1979). *Human cognition, learning, understanding and remembering*. Belmont, CA: Wadsworth.

Breed, W. (1955). Social control in the newsroom: A functional analysis. *Social Forces, 33,* 326–355.

Brenner, V. (1997, June). Psychology of computer use: XLVII. Parameters of Internet use, abuse and addiction: The first 90 days of the Internet Usage Survey. *Psychological Reports, 80*(3, Pt. 1), 879–882.

Brewer, W. F., & Nakamura, G. V. (1984). The nature and functions of schemas. In R. S. Wyer, Jr., & T. K. Srull (Eds.), *Handbook of social cognition* (Vol. 1, pp. 119–160). Hillsdale, NJ: Lawrence Erlbaum Associates.

Brigham, J. C., & Giesbrecht, W. (1976). All in the family: Racial attitudes. *Journal of Communication, 26*(4), 69–74.

Broadbent, D. E. (1958). *Perception and communication.* London: Pergamon.

Brock, T. C., & Balloun, J. L. (1967). Behavioral receptivity to dissonant information. *Journal of Personality and Social Psychology, 6,* 413–428.

Brody, G. H. (1990, April). Effects of television viewing on family interactions: An observational study. *Family Relations, 29,* 216–220.

Brosius, H. B. (1993). The effects of emotional pictures on television news. *Communication Research, 20,* 105–124.

Brown, W., (1923). To what extent is memory measured by a single recall trial? *Journal of Experimental Psychology, 6,* 377–382.

Brown, J. (1958). Some tests of the decay theory of immediate memory. *Quarterly Journal of Experimental Psychology, 10,* 12–21.

Brown, J. D. (1986). Evaluations of self and others: Self-enhancement biases in social judgments. *Social Cognition, 4,* 353–376.

Bruner, J. S., & Tagiuri, R. (1954). The perception of people. In G. Lindzey (Ed.), *Handbook of social psychology* (Vol. 2, pp. 634–654). Reading, MA: Addison-Wesley.

Bryant, J., Carveth, R. A., & Brown, D. (1981). Television viewing and anxiety: An experimental examination. *Journal of Communication, 31*(1), 106–119.

Bryant, J., & Zillmann, D. (1991). *Responding to the screen: Reception and reaction processes.* Hillsdale, NJ: Lawrence Erlbaum Associates.

Bryant, J., & Zillmann, D. (1994). *Media effects: Advances in theory and research.* Hillsdale, NJ: Lawrence Erlbaum Associates.

Bryant, J., Zillmann, D., & Brown, D. (1983). Entertainment features in children's educational television: Effects on attention and information acquisition. In J. Bryant & D. R. Anderson (Eds.), *Children's understanding of television: Research on attention and comprehension* (pp. 221–240). New York: Academic Press.

Buchanan, B. (1991). *Electing a president: The Markle commission report on campaign '88.* Austin: University of Texas Press.

Buckley, W. F., Jr. (1998, October 12). The final minutes of Flight 111. *National Review, 50*(19), 67.

Burke, J. (1968). *Language as symbolic action: Essays on life, literature, and method.* Berkeley: University of California Press.

Burnkrant, R. E., & Sawyer, A. G. (1983). Effects of involvement and message content on information-processing intensity. In R. J. Harris (Ed.), *Information processing research in advertising* (pp. 43–64). Hillsdale, NJ: Lawrence Erlbaum Associates.

Butler, C. (1985, June). Consulting firms and stations forming a more potent partnership. *View,* pp. 22–24.

Cacioppo, J. T., & Petty, R. E. (1979). Effects of message repetition and position on cognitive response, recall and persuasion. *Journal of Personality and Social Psychology, 37,* 97–109.

Cacioppo, J. T., & Petty, R. E. (1982). A biosocial model of attitude change. In J. T. Cacioppo & R. E. Petty (Eds.), *Perspectives in cardiovascular psychophysiology* (pp. 151–188). New York: Guilford.

Calem, R. E. (1992, December 6). The network of all networks. *New York Times.*

Canary, D. J., & Spitzberg, B. H. (1993). Loneliness and media gratification. *Communication Research, 20,* 800–821.

Cantor, J. (1998). *Mommy I'm scared: How TV and movies frighten children and what we can do to protect them.* San Diego, CA: Harcourt Brace.

Cantor, J. (1991). Fright responses to mass media productions. In J. Bryant & D. Zillmann (Eds.), *Responding to the screen: Reception and reaction processes* (pp. 169–198). Hillsdale, NJ: Lawrence Erlbaum Associates.

Cantor, J., & Nathanson, A. (1996). Children's fright reactions to television news. *Journal of Communication, 46*(4), 139–152.

Cantor, J., & Sparks, G. (1984). Children's fear responses to mass media: Testing some Piagetian predictions. *Journal of Communication, 34*(2), 90–103.

Cappella, J. N., Turow, J., & Jamieson, K. H. (1996). *Call-in political talk radio: Background, content, audiences, portrayal in mainstream media* (Tech. Rep. No. 5). Philadelphia: University of Pennsylvania, Annenberg Public Policy Center.

Carmen, L. (1985). Television discourse processing: A schema theoretic approach. *Communication Education, 34*(2), 91–105.

Carr, R. (1998, August 21). Some skepticism but widespread support: A few members find the attacks' proximity to Clinton's Lewinsky speech suspicious. *The Orange County Register,* p. A18

Chaffee, S. H., & Schleuder, J. (1986). Measurement and effects of attention to news media. *Human Communication Research, 13,* 76–107.

Cheney, G. A. (1983). *Television in American society.* New York: F. Watts.

Christenson, P. G., & Roberts, D. F. (1983). The role of television in the formation of children's social attitudes. In M. J. A. Howe (Ed.), *Learning from television: Psychological and educational research* (pp. 79–99). London: Academic Press.

Clark, R. (1983). Reconsidering research on learning from the media. *Review of Educational Research, 66*(7), 445–449.

Cline, V. B., Croft, R. G., & Courrier, S. (1973). Desensitization of children to television violence. *Journal of Personality and Social Psychology, 27,* 360–365.

Cohen, C. E. (1981). Goals and schemas in person perception: Making sense out of the stream of behavior. In N. Cantor & J. Kihlstrom (Eds.), *Personality, cognition and social behavior* (pp. 45–68). Hillsdale, NJ: Lawrence Erlbaum Associates.

Cohen, S., & Wills, T. A. (1985). Stress, social support, and the buffering hypothesis. *Psychological Bulletin, 98,* 310–357.

Collins, W. A. (1983). Interpretation and inference in children's television viewing. In J. Bryant & D. R. Anderson (Eds.), *Children's understanding of television: Research on attention and comprehension* (pp. 125–150). New York: Academic Press.

Collins, W. A., & Loftus, E. (1975). A spreading activation theory of semantic processing. *Psychological Review, 82*(6), 407–428.

Comstock, G., & Paik, H. (1991). *Television and the American child.* New York: Academic Press.

Conan, N., & Montagne, R. (Reporters). (1998, August 25). *NPR Morning Edition* (NPR 10:00 am ET). Washington, DC: National Public Radio.

Converse, P. (1964). The nature of belief systems in mass publics. In D. Apter (Ed.), *Ideology and discontent* (pp. 206–261). New York: The Free Press.

Cooper, C. (1998, May 16). Jabs & jibes: Terminally addicted. *The Lancet 351*(9114), 1522–1532.

Craik, F. I. M., & Lockhart, R. S. (1972). Levels of processing: A framework for memory research. *Journal of Verbal Learning and Verbal Behavior, 11*, 671–676.

Crittenden, J. (1971). Democratic functions of the open mike radio forum. *Public Opinion Quarterly, 35*, 200–210.

Crocker, J., Fiske, S. T., & Taylor, S. E. (1984). Schematic bases of belief change. In J. R. Eiser (Ed.), *Attitudinal Judgment* (pp. 197–226). New York: Springer-Verlag.

Crockett, W. H. (1988). Schemas, affect and communication. In L. Donohew, H. E. Sypher, & E. Tory Higgins (Eds.), *Communication social cognition and affect* (pp. 33–52). Hillsdale, NJ: Lawrence Erlbaum Associates.

Curtis, P. (1997) MUDDING: Social phenomena in text-based virtual reality. In S. Kiesler (Ed.), *Culture of the Internet* (pp. 121–142). Mahwah, NJ: Lawrence Erlbaum Associates.

Daerr, E. (1998, May 1). FAA seeks fine of $2.25 million in Florida crash. *The Wall Street Journal* (Eastern edition).

Davis, S., & Mares, M. (1998). Effects of talk show viewing on adolescents. *Journal of Communication, 48*(3), 69–86.

Delia, J. G. (1976). The development of functional persuasive skills in childhood and early adolescence. *Child Development, 47*, 1008–1014.

Delia, J. G. (1977). Cognitive complexity, social perspective-taking, and functional persuasive skills in second- to ninth-grade children. *Human Communication Research, 3*, 128–134.

Delia, J. G., & O'Keefe, B. J. (1979). Constructivism: The development of communication in children. In E. Wartella (Ed.), *Children communicating: Media and development of thought, speech, understanding* (pp. 157–186). Newbury Park, CA: Sage.

Dooling, D. J., & Christiaansen, R. E. (1977). Episodic and semantic aspects of memory for prose. *Journal of Experimental Psychology: Human Learning and Memory, 3*, 428–436.

Downs, A. (1972). Up and down with ecology: The issue attention cycle. *Public Interest, 28*, 38–50.

Drabman, R. S., & Thomas, M. H. (1975). Does TV violence breed indifference? *Journal of Communication, 25*(4), 86–89.

Dr. Laura wants you to stop whining. (1988, February). *Psychology Today, 31*, 28–30.

Egan, T. (1995, January 1). Talk radio or hate radio. *New York Times*, p. A22.

Eich, J. M. (1982). A composite holographic associative recall model. *Psychological Review, 89,* 627–661.

Elias, M. (1998, August 18). Watching TV news can shake up kids. They see scarier world around them. *USA Today,* p 1D.

Entman, R. (1993). Framing: Toward clarification of a fractured paradigm. *Journal of Communication, 43*(4), 51–58.

Epstein, E. J. (1973). *News from nowhere.* New York: Random House.

Eron, L. D. (1982). Parent–child interaction, television violence, and aggression of children. *American Psychologist, 37,* 197–211.

Evans, W. (1990). The interpretive turn in media research. *Critical Studies in Mass Communication, 7*(2), 145–168.

Everybody's talkin' at us. (1995, May 22). *Business Week,* p. 105.

Ewen, S. (1996). *PR! A social history of spin.* New York: Basic Books.

Fallows, J. (1996). *Breaking the news: How the media undermine American democracy.* New York: Pantheon.

Fazio, R. H., & Williams, C. J. (1986). Attitude accessibility as a moderator of the attitude-perception and attitude-behavior relations: An investigation of the 1984 presidential election. *Journal of Personality and Social Psychology, 42,* 404–411.

Festinger, L. (1954). A theory of social comparison processes. *Human Relations, 7,* 117–140.

Festinger, L. (1957). *A theory of cognitive dissonance.* Palo Alto, CA: Stanford University Press.

Festinger, L. (1962). Cognitive dissonance. *Scientific American, 207,* 93.

Fischer, C. S. (1992). *America calling.* Berkeley, CA: University of California Press.

Fiske, S. T., & Dyer, L. M. (1985). Structure and development of social schemata: Evidence from positive and negative transfer effects. *Journal of Personality and Social Psychology, 48,* 839–852.

Fiske, S. T., Kinder, D. R., & Larter, W. M. (1983). The novice and the expert: Knowledge-based strategies in political cognition. *Journal of Experimental Social Psychology, 19,* 381–400.

Fiske, S. T., & Linville, P. T. (1980). What does the schema concept buy us? *Personality and Social Psychology Bulletin, 6,* 543–557.

Fiske, S. T., & Taylor, S. E. (1991). *Social cognition* (2nd ed.). New York: McGraw-Hill.

Flawed but not out: The impeachment case against Clinton is weak and resignation would only damage the position of the US presidency further. (1998, September 14). *Financial Times* (London), Comment and Analysis Section, p. 20.

Flay, B. R. (1981). On improving the chances of mass media health promotion programs causing meaningful changes in behavior. In M. Meyer (Ed.), *Health education by television and radio* (pp. 56–92). Munich: Saur.

Folkerts, J., Lacy, S., & Davenport, L. (1998). *The media in your life: An introduction to mass communication.* Boston, MA: Allyn & Bacon.

Freedman, J. L., & Sears, D., (1965). Selective exposure. In L. Berkowitz (Ed.), *Advances in experimental social psychology* (Vol. 2, pp. 58–98) New York: Academic Press.

Friedson, E. (1953). The relation of the social situation of contact to the media in mass communication. *Public Opinion Quarterly, 17,* 230–238.

Gamson, J. (1998). *Freaks talk back: Tabloid talk shows and sexual nonconformity.* Chicago, IL: The University of Chicago Press.

Gamson, J. (1995, Fall). Do ask, do tell: Freak talk on TV. *American Prospect, 23,* 44–50.

Gamson, W. A. (1988). The 1987 distinguished lecture: A constructionist approach to mass media and public opinion. *Symbolic Interaction, 11*(2), 161–174.

Gamson, W. A. (1989). News as framing: Comments on Graber. *American Behavioral Scientist, 33*(2), 157–161.

Gamson, W. A. (1992). *Talking politics.* Cambridge, England: Cambridge University Press.

Gamson, W. A., & Modigliani, A. (1989). Media discourse and public opinion on nuclear power: A constructionist approach. *American Journal of Sociology, 95*(1), 1–37.

Gans, H. (1979). *Deciding what's news.* New York: Pantheon.

Gardner, H. (1985). *The mind's new science.* New York: Basic Books.

Garrison, P. (1998, October). TWA 800 and EMI. *Flying, 125*(10), 111–113.

Gathercole, S. E., & Baddeley, A. D. (1993). *Working memory and language.* Hillsdale, NJ: Lawrence Erlbaum Associates.

Geiger, S., & Newhagen, J. (1993). Revealing the black box: Information processing and media effects. *Journal of Communication, 43*(4), 42–50.

Geiger, S., & Reeves, B. (1991). The effects of visual structure and content emphasis on the evaluation and memory for political candidates. In F. Biocca (Ed.), *Television and political advertising* (pp. 125–144), Hillsdale, NJ: Lawrence Erlbaum Associates.

Geiger, S., & Reeves, B. (1993a). The effects of scene change and semantic relatedness on attention to television. *Communication Research, 20,* 155–175.

Geiger, S., & Reeves, B. (1993b). We interrupt this program... Attention for television sequences. *Human Communication Research, 3,* 368–387.

Geller, E. S. (1989). Using television to promote safety belt use. In R. E. Rice & C. K. Atkin (Eds.), *Public communication campaigns* (2nd ed., pp. 201–203). Thousand Oaks, CA: Sage.

Gerbner, G., & Gross, L. P. (1976). Living with television: The violence profile. *Journal of Communication, 26*(2), 172–199.

Gerbner, G., Gross, L., Morgan, M., & Signorielli, N. (1980). The "mainstreaming" of America: Violence Profile No. 11. *Journal of Communication, 30*(3), 10–29.

Gerbner, G., Gross, L., Morgan, M., & Signorielli, N. (1986). Living with television: The dynamics of the cultivation process. In J. Bryant & D. Zillmann (Eds.), *Perspectives on media effects* (pp. 17–40). Hillsdale, NJ: Lawrence Erlbaum Associates.

Gitlin, T. (1980). *The whole world is watching: Mass media in the making and unmaking of the New Left.* Berkeley, CA: University of California Press.

Gliatto, T., & Longley, A. (1996, May 20). Donahue's last hurrah. *People Weekly, 45*(20), 54.

Goethals, G. R. (1986). Social comparison theory: Psychology from the lost and found. *Personality and Social Psychology Bulletin, 12*(3), 261–278.

Goethals, G. R., & Zanna, M. P. (1979). The role of social comparison in choice shifts. *Journal of Personality and Social Psychology, 37,* 1469–1476.

Goffman, E. (1974). *Frame analysis: An essay on the organization of experience.* New York: Harper & Row.

Goldman, A. (1999, December 24). Amazon chief sees limitations for Web commerce; Internet: But Jeff Bezos admits it's still a very big pie. He worries that the industry dallied in fighting threat of taxation. *Los Angeles Times,* Business Section, Part C1.

Goldsborough, R. (1997, November). When the Internet is your life. *CMA Magazine, 71*(9), 28.

Graber, D. (1980). *Mass media and American politics.* Washington, DC: Congressional Quarterly Press.

Graber, D. A. (1988). *Processing the News* (2nd ed.). New York: Longman.

Graber, D. A. (1990). Seeing is remembering: How visuals contribute to learning from television news. *Journal of Communication, 40*(3), 134–155.

Greenberg, B. (1988). Some uncommon television images and the Drench Hypothesis. In S. Oskamp (Ed.), *Television as a social issue* (pp. 88–102). Newbury Park, CA: Sage.

Greenberg, B., & Busselle, R. (1996). Soap operas and sexual activity: A decade later. *Journal of Communication, 46*(4), 153–160.

Greenberg, B. S. (1982). Television and role socialization. In D. Pearl, L. Bouthilet, & J. Lazer (Eds.), *Television and behavior: Ten years of scientific progress and implications for the eighties: Vol. 2. Technical reviews* (pp. 179–190). Rockville, MD: NIMH.

Greenberg, B. S., Sherry, J. L., Busselle, R. W., Hnilo, L. R., & Smith, S. W. (1997). Daytime television talk shows: Guests, content and interactions. *Journal of Broadcasting and Electronic Media, 41*(3), 412–426.

Greene, R. W. (1998, September 21). Internet addiction: Is it just this month's hand-wringer for worry-warts, or a genuine problem? *Computerworld, 32,* 78–79.

Greenwald, A. G. (1981). Self and memory. In G. H. Bower (Ed.), *The psychology of learning and motivation* (Vol. 15, pp. 201–236). New York: Academic Press.

Greenwald, A. G., & Leavitt, C. (1984). Audience involvement in advertising: Four levels. *Journal of Consumer Research, 11,* 581–592.

Griffiths, M. D., & Shuckford, G. L. J. (1989). Desensitization to television violence: A new model. *New Ideas in Psychology, 7*(1), 85–89.

Grimes, T. (1990). Encoding TV news messages into memory. *Journalism Quarterly, 67*(4), 757–766.

Grimes, T., & Meadowcroft, J. (1995). Attention to television and some methods for its measurement. In B. Burleson (Ed.), *Communication Yearbook 18.* Thousand Oaks, CA: Sage.

Guillund, G., & Shiffrin, R. C. (1984). A retrieval model for both recognition and recall. *Psychological Review, 91,* 1–67.

Gunter, B. (1987). *Poor reception: Misunderstanding and forgetting broadcast news.* Hillsdale, NJ: Lawrence Erlbaum Associates.

Hall, S. (1980). Encoding/decoding. In Hall et al. (Eds.), *Culture, media, language* (pp. 128–138). London: Hutchinson.

Hallin, D. C. (1992). Sound bite news: Television coverage of elections, 1968–1988. *Journal of Communication, 42,* 5–25.

Hamilton, J. (1999, February 22). When cupid uses a cursor. *Business Week,* p. 26.

Harkins, S. G., & Petty, R. E. (1981). Effects of source magnification of cognitive effort on attitudes: An information-processing view. *Journal of Personality and Social Psychology, 40,* 401–413.

Harris, R. J. (1999). *A cognitive psychology of mass communication* (3rd ed.). Mahwah, NJ: Lawrence Erlbaum Associates.

Hastie, R. (1981). Schematic principles in human memory. In E. T. Higgins, C. P. Herman, & M. P. Zanna (Eds.), *Social cognition: The Ontario Symposium* (Vol. 1, pp. 39–88). Hillsdale, NJ: Lawrence Erlbaum Associates.

Hastie, R. (1986). A primer of information processing theory for the political scientist. In R. R. Lau & D. O. Sears (Eds.), *PoliticalcCognition: The 19th Annual Carnegie symposium on cognition* (pp. 11–40). Hillsdale, NJ: Lawrence Erlbaum Associates.

Hastie, R., & Carlston, D. (1980). Theoretical issues in person memory. In R. Hastie, T. M. Ostrom, E. B. Ebbesen, R. S. Wyer, D. Hamilton, & D. E. Carlston (Eds.), *Person memory: The cognitive basis of social perception* (pp. 1–53). Hillsdale, NJ: Lawrence Erlbaum Associates.

Hawkins, R. P., Yong-Ho, K., & Pingree, S. (1991). The ups and downs of attention to television. *Communication Research, 18*(1), 53–76.

Hayes-Roth, B., & Hayes-Roth, F. (1977). Concept learning and the recognition and classification of exemplars. *Journal of Verbal Learning and Verbal Behavior, 16,* 321–338.

Head, S., Sterling, C., & Schofield, L. (1994). *Broadcasting in America* (7th ed.). New York: Houghton Mifflin.

Hearn, G. (1989). Active and passive conception of the television audience: Effects of a change in viewing routine. *Human Relations, 42,* 857–875.

Heath, R. P. (1998, February). Tuning in to talk. *American Demographics,* pp. 48–53.

Heider, F. (1946). Attitudes and cognitive organization. *Journal of Psychology, 21,* 107–112.

Heider, F. (1958). *The psychology of interpersonal relations.* New York: Wiley.

Herbst, S. (1995). On electronic public space: Talk shows in theoretical perspective. *Political Communication, 12,* 263–274.

Himmelstein, H. (1984). *Television myth and the American mind.* New York: Praeger.

Hintzman, D. L. (1986). "Schema abstraction" in a multiple-trace memory model. *Psychological Review, 93,* 411–428.

Hofstetter, R. C. (1976). *Bias in news: Network television coverage of the 1972 election campaign.* Dayton, OH: Ohio State University Press.

Hofstetter, R. C., Donovan, M. C., Klauber, M. R., Cole, A., Huie, C. J., & Yuasa, T. (1994). Political talk radio: A stereotype reconsidered. *Political Research Quarterly, 47,* 467–479.

Hofstetter, R. C., & Gianos, C. L. (1997). Political talk radio: Actions speak louder than words. *Journal of Broadcasting & Electronic Media, 41*(4), 501–515.

Hoijer, B. (1989). Television-evoked thoughts and their relation to comprehension. *Communication Research, 16*(2), 179–203.

Hollander, B. A. (1996). Talk radio: Predictors of use and effects on attitudes about government. *Journalism and Mass Communication Quarterly, 73,* 102–113.

Hovland, C. I., Janis, I. L., & Kelley, H. H. (1953). *Communication and persuasion.* New Haven, CT: Yale University Press.

Huesmann, L. R. (1986). Psychological processes promoting the relations between exposure to media violence and aggressive behavior by the viewer. *Journal of social issues, 42*(3), 125–139.

Huesmann, L. R., & Eron, L. D. (Eds.). (1986). *Television and the aggressive child: A cross national comparison.* Hillsdale, NJ: Lawrence Erlbaum Associates.

Huesmann, L. R., Eron, L. D., Lefkowitz, M. M., & Walder, L. O. (1986). The stability of aggression over time and generations. *Developmental Psychology, 20*(6), 1120–1134.

Huesmann, L. R., Lagerspetz, K., & Eron, L. D. (1984). Intervening variables in the TV violence-aggression relation: Evidence from two countries. *Developmental Psychology, 20*(5), 746–775.

Humm, A. (1997). Not politically incorrect, just tasteless. *Social Policy, 28*(1), 52–54.

Huston, A. C., & Wright, J. C. (1998). Television and the informational and educational needs of children. *The Annals of the American Academy of Political and Social Science, 557,* 9–23.

Isenberg, D. J. (1986). Group polarization. A critical review and meta-analysis. *Journal of Personality and Social Psychology, 50,* 1141–1151.

Iyengar, S. (1991). *Is anyone responsible? How television frames political issues.* Chicago: University of Chicago Press.

Jackson-Beeck, M., & Robinson, J. P. (1981). Television nonviewers: An endangered species? *Journal of Consumer Research, 7,* 356–359.

Jamieson, K. H. (1992). *Packaging the Presidency* (2nd ed.). New York: Oxford University.

Jamieson, K. H., & Campbell, K. K. (1992). *The interplay of influence: News, advertising, politics, and the mass media* (3rd ed.). Belmont, CA: Wadsworth.

Jeffries, L. (1997). *Mass media effects* (2nd ed.). Prospect Heights, IL: Waveland.

Johnson, B. T., & Eagly, A. H. (1989). The effects of involvement on persuasion: A meta-analysis. *Psychological Bulletin, 106,* 290–314.

Johnson, B. T., & Eagly, A. H. (1990). Involvement and persuasion: Types, traditions, and the evidence. *Psychological Bulletin, 107,* 375–384.

Johnson, N. (1970). *How to talk back to your television set.* New York: Bantam Books.

Johnson, P. (1999, November 9). Lewinsky back for chat with Barbara Walters. *USA Today,* p. 3D.

Jones, S. G. (1998). *Cybersociety: Revisiting computer-mediated communication and community.* Thousand Oaks, CA: Sage.

Jones, S. G. (1997). *Virtual culture: Identity and communication in cybersociety.* Thousand Oaks, CA: Sage.

Jost, K. (1995, April 19). Talk show democracy. *The CQ Researcher,* pp. 372–375.

Just, M. R., Crigler, A. N., Alger, D. E., Cook, T. E., Kern, M., & West, D. M. (1996). *Crosstalk: Citizens, candidates, and the media in a presidential campaign.* Chicago: University of Chicago Press.

Kahneman, D. (1973). *Attention and effort.* Englewood Cliffs, NJ: Prentice-Hall.

Kaid, L. L., & Bystrom, D. (1998). *The electronic election: Perspectives on the 1996 campaign communication.* Mahwah, NJ: Lawrence Erlbaum Associates.

Katz, E. (1957). The two-step flow of communication: An up-to-date report. *Public Opinion Quarterly, 21*(1), 61–78.

Katz, E., Adoni, H., & Parness, P. (1977). Remembering the news: What the pictures add to recall. *Journalism Quarterly, 54*(2), 231–239.

Katz, E., Blumler, J. G., & Gurevitch, M., (1974). Utilization of mass communication by the individual. In J. G. Blumler & E. Katz (Eds.), *The uses of mass communication: Current perspectives on gratifications research* (pp. 19–31). Beverly Hills, CA: Sage.

Katz, J. E., & Aspden, P. (1997). A nation of strangers? *Communications of the ACM, 40*(12), 81–86.

Katz, J. L. (March, 1991). The power of talk. *Governing, 4,* 38–42.

Kelleher, T., & Blonska, J. (1998, September 21). *Tube, People,* p. 27.

Keller, T. (1993). Trash TV. *Journal of Popular Culture, 26*(4), 195–206.

Kellermann, K. (1985). Memory processes in media effects. *Communication Research, 12*(1), 83–131.

Kelman, H. C., & Hovland, C. I. (1953). Reinstatement of the communicator in delayed measurement of opinion change. *Journal of Abnormal and Social Psychology, 48,* 327–335.

Kern, M. (1989). *30-second politics: Political advertising in the eighties.* New York: Praeger.

Kern, M., & Wicks, R. H. (1994). Television news and the advertising-driven new mass media election: A more significant role in 1992? In R. Denton (Ed.), *The 1992 presidential campaign: A communication perspective* (pp. 189–206). Westport, CT: Praeger.

Kiernan, V. (1998, May 29). Some scholars question research methods of expert on Internet addiction. *The Chronicle of Higher Education, 44*(38), A25–A27.

Kiesler, S. (1997). *Culture of the Internet.* Mahwah, NJ: Lawrence Erlbaum Associates.

Kintsch, W. (1972). Notes on the structure of semantic memory. In E. Tulving, & W. Donaldson (Eds.), *Organization of memory* (pp. 247–308). New York: Academic Press.

Kintsch, W. (1978). Comprehension and memory of text. In W. K. Estes (Ed.), *Handbook of learning and cognitive processes: Vol. 6. linguistic functions in cognitive processes* (pp. 57–86). Hillsdale, NJ: Lawrence Erlbaum Associates.

Klapper, J. T. (1960). *The effects of mass communication.* New York: The Free Press.

Kohut, A. (1994). *The role of technology in American life.* Los Angeles: Times Mirror Center for the People and the Press.

Kohut, A., Zukin, C., & Bowman, C. (1993). *The vocal minority in American politics.* Washington, DC: Times Mirror Center for the People and the Press.

Kokmen, L. (1998, November 30). Internet commerce maturing slowly. *Denver Post,* p. E1.

Krackhardt, D. (1992). The strength of strong ties: The importance of Philos in organizations. In N. Nohria & R. Eccles (Eds.), *Networks and organizations: Structure, form, and action* (pp. 216–239). Boston, MA: Harvard Business School Press.

Kraus, S., & Davis, D. (1976). *The effects of mass communication on political behavior.* University Park, PA: Pennsylvania State University Press.

Kraut, R., Mukopadhyay, T., Szczypula, J., Kiesler, S., & Scherlis, W. (1998). Communication and information: Alternative uses of the Internet in households. In *Proceedings of the CHI 98* (pp. 368–383). New York: ACM.

Kraut, R., Patterson, M., Lundmark, V., Kiesler, S., Mukopadhyay, T., & Scherlis, W. (1998, September). Internet paradox: A social technology that reduces social involvement and psychological well-being? *American Psychologist, 53*(9), 1017–1031.

Krippendorff, K. (1980). *Content analysis: An introduction to its methodology.* Beverly Hills, CA: Sage.

Kubey, R., & Csikszentmihalyi, M. (1990). *Television and the quality of life: How viewing shapes everyday experience.* Hillsdale, NJ: Lawrence Erlbaum Associates.

Kuhn, T. (1962). *The structure of scientific revolutions.* Chicago: University of Chicago Press.

Kunkel, D. (1992). Children's television advertising in the multichannel environment. *Journal of Communication, 38*(3), 134–152.

LaBerge, D. (1975). Acquisition of automatic processing in perceptual and associative learning. In P. M. A. Rabbitt & S. Dornic (Eds.), *Attention and performance* (Vol. 5, pp. 50–64). New York: Academic Press.

Lafayette, J. (1998, May 18). Who owns the spectrum? Ownership ranks rapidly thinned by consolidation. *Electronic Media,* p. 1A.

Lang, A. (1990). Involuntary attention and physiological arousal evoked by structural features and emotional content in TV commercials. *Communication Research, 17,* 275–299.

Lang, A., Geiger, S., Strickwerda, M., & Sumner, J. (1993). The effects of related and unrelated cuts on television viewers; attention, processing capacity, and memory. *Communication Research, 20,* 4–29.

Lang, A., Newhagen, J., & Reeves, B. (1996). Negative video as structure: Emotion, attention, capacity and memory. *Journal of Broadcasting and Electronic Media, 40*(4), 460–478.

Lasswell, H. D. (1927). *Propaganda technique in the World War.* New York: Alfred A. Knopf.

Lasswell, H. D. (1934). *World politics and personal insecurity. A contribution to political psychiatry.* Chicago: University of Chicago Press.

Lasswell, H. D. (1948). The structure and function of communication in society. In L. Bryson (Ed.), *The communication of ideas* (pp. 37–51). New York: Harper.

Lawrence, J. M. (1999, August 23). Internet proves a Web of addiction for 11 million worldwide; Study claims millions addicted to the Internet. *Boston Herald, Inc.,* p. 1.

Lazarsfeld, P., Berelson, B., & Gaudet, H. (1968). *The peoples' choice: How the voter makes up his mind in a presidential campaign* (3rd ed.). New York: Columbia University Press.

Lazarsfeld, P., & Merton, R. (1948). Mass communication, popular taste and organized social action. In L. Bryson (Ed.), *The communication of ideas* (pp. 95–108). New York: Institute for Religious and Social Studies.

Lazarus, R. S. (1980). The stress and coping paradigms. In C. Eisdorfer, D. Cohen, A. Klienmen, & P. Maxim (Eds.), *Theoretical bases for psychopathology* (pp. 177–214). New York: Spectrum.

Lefkowitz, M. M., Eron, L. D., Walder, L. Q., & Huesmann, L. R. (1977). *Growing up to be violent: A longitudinal study of the development of aggression.* New York: Pergamon.

Leiby, R. (1995, December 3). Movie madness; Does screen violence trigger copycat crimes? *The Washington Post,* Sunday Arts, p. G–01.

Levin, M. B. (1987). *Talk radio and the American dream.* Lexington, MA: Lexington Books.

Lieberman, D. (1998, August 6). Wall Street picks up pieces and keeps going Cable channel gets static over impact. *USA Today,* p. 3b.

Linz, D., Donnerstein, D., & Penrod, S. (1984). The effects of multiple exposures to filmed violence against women. *Journal of Communication, 34*(3), 130–147.

Lippmann, W. (1922). *Public opinion.* New York: Macmillan.

Livingstone, S. M. (1990a). *Making sense of television: The psychology of audience interaction.* Oxford, England: Butterworth-Heinemann.

Livingstone, S. M. (1990b). Interpreting a television narrative. How different viewers see a story. *Journal of Communication, 40,* 72–85.

Lowery, S. A., & DeFleur, M. D. (1988). *Milestones in communication research.* White Plains, NY: Longman.

Lundmark, V., Kiesler, S., Kraut, R., Scherlis, W., & Mukopadhyay, T. (1998). *How the strong survive: Patterns and significance of competence, commitment, and requests for external technical support in families on the Internet.* Unpublished manuscript.

Maccoby, E. E. (1951). Television: It's impact on school children. *Public Communication Quarterly, 15,* 421–444.

Maguire, T. (1998, December). Web nets the masses. *American Demographics, 20,* 12–18

Mander, J. M. (1978). *Four arguments for the elimination of television.* New York: Morrow.

Markus, H., & Zajonc, R. B. (1985). The cognitive perspective in social psychology. In G. Lindzey & E. Aronson (Eds.), *The handbook of social psychology* (3rd ed., Vol. 1, pp. 137–230). New York: Random House.

Matson, L. D. (1998, October-November). Caught in the net: How to recognize the signs of internet Addiction—and a winning strategy for recovery. *Weston, 21*(5), 89.

Mayeux, P. (1991). *Broadcast news: Writing and reporting.* Dubuque, IA: Wm. C. Brown.

Mazzocco, D. W. (1994). *Networks of power: Corporate TV's threat to democracy.* Boston, MA: South End Press.

McChesney, R. W. (1999). *Rich media, poor democracy: Communication politics in dubious times.* Urbana, IL: University of Illinois Press.

McCombs, M. E., & Shaw, D. L. (1972). The agenda-setting function of mass media. *Public Opinion Quarterly, 36,* 176–187.

McGuire, W. J. (1969). Nature of attitudes and attitude change. In G. Lindzey & E. Aronson (Eds.), *The handbook of social psychology* (2nd ed., Vol. 3, pp. 136–314). Reading, MA: Addison-Wesley.

McGuire, W. J. (1989). Public communication campaigns: The American experience. In R. E. Rice & C. K. Atkin (Eds.), *Political communication campaigns* (2nd ed., pp. 15–38). Thousand Oaks, CA: Sage.

McLuhan, M. (1964). *Understanding media.* New York: American Library.

McNeil, A. (1991). *Total television: A comprehensive guide to programming from 1948 to the present* (3rd ed.). New York: Penguin.

McQuail, D., Blumler, J. G., & Brown, J. R. (1972). The televised audience: A revised perspective. In D. McQuail (Ed.), *Sociology of mass communications* (pp. 135–165). Middlesex, UK: Penguin.

Meadowcroft, J. M., & Olson, B. (1995, August 11). *Television viewing vs. reading: Testing information processing assumptions.* Paper presented at the annual meeting of the Association for Education in Journalism and Mass Communication, Washington, DC.

Meadowcroft, J. M., & Reeves, B. (1989). Influence of story schema development on children's attention to television. *Communication Research, 16*(3), 352–374.

Meadowcroft, J. M., & Zillmann, D. (1987). Women's comedy preference during the menstrual cycle. *Communication Research, 14,* 204–218.

Mifflin, L. (1998, September, 28). News and young minds. *The New York Times,* Section E; p. 9.

Miller, G. (1998, December, 25). Computer age enters maturity; revolutionary Internet goes mainstream. *Los Angeles Times,* Business; Part C; Page 1; Financial Desk.

Miller, G. A. (1956). The magical number seven, plus or minus two: Some limits on our capacity for processing information. *Psychological Review, 63,* 81–97.

Milliot, J. (1998, March 2). '97 book sales up 2% as weak trade sales offset gains in ed'n. *Publishers Weekly, 245*(9), p. 11.

Minsky, M. (1975). A framework for representing knowledge. In P. H. Winston (Ed.), *The psychology of computer vision* (pp. 211–277). New York: McGraw-Hill.

Mitra, A. (1997). Diasporic web sites: Ingroup and outgroup discourse. *Critical Studies in Mass Communication, 14*(2), 158–181.

Morgan, M., & Signorielli, N. (1990). Cultivation analysis: Conceptualization and methodology. In N. Signorielli & M. Morgan (Eds.), *Cultivation analysis: New directions in media effects research* (pp. 13–34). Newbury Park, CA: Sage

Morin, R., & Dean, C. (1998, September 14). Poll finds approval of job, not of person. *Washington Post,* p. A1.

Mundorf, N., Drew, D., Zillmann, D., & Weaver, J. (1990). Effects of disturbing news of recall of subsequently presented news. *Communication Research, 17*(5), 601–615.

Mundorf, N., & Zillmann, D. (1991). Effects of story sequencing on affective reactions to broadcast news. *Journal of Broadcasting and Electronic Media, 35*(2), 197–211.

Murdock, B. B., Jr. (1961). The retention of individual items. *Journal of Experimental Psychology, 62,* 618–625.

Murdock, B. B., Jr., (1982). A theory for the storage and retrieval of item and associative information. *Psychological Review, 89,* 609–626.

National Television Violence Study 3. (1998). Thousand Oaks, CA: Sage.

Neisser, U. (1976). *Cognition and reality: Principles and implications of cognitive psychology.* New York: W. H. Freeman.

Nelson, J. (1887). *The perfect machine: Television in the nuclear age.* Toronto: Between the Lines.

Neuman, S. B. (1991). *Literacy in the television age: The myth of the TV effect.* Norwood, NJ: Ablex.

Neuman, W. R. (1976). Patterns of recall among television news viewers. *Public Opinion Quarterly 40,* 115–123.

Neuman, W. R., Just, M. R., & Crigler, A. N. (1992). *Common knowledge: News and the construction of political meaning.* Chicago: University of Chicago Press.

Newhagen, J. E. (1994a). Effects of censorship disclaimers in Persian Gulf War television news on negative thought elaboration. *Communication Research, 21*(2), 232–248.

Newhagen, J. E. (1994b). Effects of televised government censorship disclaimers on memory and thought elaboration during the Gulf War. *Journal of Broadcasting & Electronic Media, 38*(3), 339–352.

Newhagen, J., & Reeves, B. (1992). The evenings bad news: Effects of compelling negative television news images on memory. *Journal of Communication, 42*(2), 25–41.

Nielsen Media Research. (1995). *Nielsen television information.* New York: Author.

Nimmo, D. (1977). Political communication research and theory: An overview. In B. D. Ruben (Ed.), *Communication Yearbook 1* (pp. 441–452) New Brunswick, NJ: Transaction.

Noble, G. (1983). Social learning from everyday television. In M. J. Howe (Ed.), *Learning from television: Psychological and educational research* (pp. 101–124). New York: Academic Press.

Noelle-Neumann, E. (1984). *The spiral of silence—Our social skin.* Chicago: University of Chicago Press.

Norman, D. A., & Bobrow, D. G. (1976). On the role of active memory processes. In C. Cofer (Ed.), *The structure of human memory* (pp. 114–132). San Francisco, CA: W. H. Freeman.

Obmascik, M. (1999, April 22). Healing begins in Colorado, world mourns deaths at Columbine High. *The Denver Post,* p. A1.

O'Keefe, G. J. (1984). Television exposure, credibility, and public views on crime. In R. Bostrom (Ed.), *Communication Yearbook 8* (pp. 513–536). Newbury Park, CA: Sage.

O'Keefe, G. J. (1985). "Taking a bite out of crime": The impact of a public communication campaign. *Communication Research, 12*(2), 147–178.

O'Keefe, G. J. (1986). The "McGruff" national media campaign: Its public impact and future implications. In D. Rosenbaum (Ed.). *Community crime prevention: Does it work?* Beverly Hills, CA: Sage.

O'Keefe, G. J., & Reid, K. (1989). The McGruff crime prevention campaign. In R. E. Rice & C. K. Atkin (Eds.), *Political communication campaigns* (2nd ed., pp. 210–212). Thousand Oaks, CA: Sage.

Olson, J. M., & Zanna, M. P. (1979). A new look at selective exposure. *Journal of Experimental Social Psychology, 15,* 1–15.

Owen, D. (1997). Talk radio and evaluations of President Clinton. *Political Communication, 14*(3), 333–353.

Page, B. I., & Tannenbaum, J. (1996). Populist deliberation and talk radio. *Journal of Communication, 46,* 33–54.

Paige, S., Danitz, T., Hickey, J. G., & Russell, K. (1998, February 9). Talking the talk. *Insights on the News, 14*(5), 9–14.

Paik, H., & Comstock, G. (1994). The effects of television violence on antisocial behavior: A meta-analysis. *Communication Research, 21*(4), 516–546.

Palmgreen, P., Wenner, L. A., & Rosengren, K. E. (1985). Uses and gratifications research: The past ten years. In K. E. Rosengren, L. A. Wenner & P. Palmgreen (Eds.), *Media gratifications research: Current perspectives* (pp. 11–37). Beverly Hills, CA: Sage.

Pan, Z., & Kosicki, G. M. (1993). Framing analysis: An approach to news discourse. *Political Communication, 10,* 55–75.

Pan, Z., & Kosicki, G. M. (1997). Talk show exposure as opinion activity. *Political Communication, 14,* 371–388.

Patterson, T. (1980). *The mass media election: How Americans choose their president.* New York: Praeger.

Perse, E. M. (1990a). Involvement with local television news: Cognitive and emotional dimensions. *Human Communication Research, 16*(4), 556–581.

Perse, E. M. (1990b). Cultivation and involvement with local television news. In N. Signorielli & M. Morgan (Eds.), *Cultivation analysis: New directions in media effects research* (pp. 51–69). Newbury Park, CA: Sage.

Perse, E. M., Ferguson, D. A., & McLeod, D. M. (1994). Cultivation in the newer media environment. *Communication Research, 21*(1), 79–104.

Peterson, L. R., & Peterson, M., (1959). Short-term retention of individual items. *Journal of Experimental Psychology, 58,* 193–198.

Petty, R. E., & Cacioppo, J. T. (1979). Issue-involvement can increase or decrease persuasion by enhancing message-relevant cognitive responses. *Journal of Personality and Social Psychology Bulletin, 5,* 1915–1926.

Petty, R. E., & Cacioppo, J. T. (1981). *Attitudes and persuasion: Classic and contemporary approaches.* Dubuque, IA: W. C. Brown.

Petty, R. E., & Cacioppo, J. T. (1984). The effect of involvement on responses to argument quantity and quality: Central and peripheral routes to persuasion. *Journal of Personality and Social Psychology, 46,* 69–81.

Petty, R. E., & Cacioppo, J. T. (1986a). *Communication and persuasion: Central and peripheral routes to attitude change.* New York: Springer-Verlag.

Petty, R. E., & Cacioppo, J. T. (1986b). The elaboration likelihood model of persuasion. In L. Berkowitz (Ed.), *Advances in experimental social psychology* (Vol. 19, pp. 123–205). New York: Academic Press.

Petty, R. E., & Cacioppo, J. T. (1990). Involvement and persuasion: Tradition versus integration. *Psychological Bulletin, 107,* 367–374.

Petty, R. E., Cacioppo, J. T., & Heesacker, M. (1981). Effects of rhetorical questions on persuasion. A cognitive response analysis. *Journal of Personality and Social Psychology, 40,* 432–440.

Petty, R. E., Cacioppo, J. T., & Kasmer, J. A. (1988). The role of affect in the elaboration likelihood model of persuasion. In L. Donohew, H. E. Sypher, & E. T. Higgins (Eds.), *Communication, social cognition and affect* (pp. 117–146). Hillsdale, NJ: Lawrence Erlbaum Associates.

Petty, R. E., Cacioppo, J. T., & Schumann, D. (1983). Central and peripheral routes to advertising effectiveness: The moderating role of involvement. *Journal of Consumer Research, 10,* 134–148.

Petty, R. E., & Priester, J. R. (1994). Mass media attitude change: Implications of the elaboration likelihood model of persuasion. In J. Bryant & D. Zillmann (Eds.), *Media effects: Advances in theory and research* (pp. 91–122). Hillsdale, NJ: Lawrence Erlbaum Associates.

Petty, R. E., Wells, G. L., & Brock, T. C. (1976). Distraction can enhance or reduce yielding to propaganda: Thought disruption versus effort justification. *Journal of Personality and Social Psychology, 34,* 874–884.

Pew Foundation Center for the People and the Press. (1996, May 13). *TV news viewership declines.* Washington, DC: Author.

Pfau, M., Kendall, K. E., Reichert, R., & Hellweg, S. A. (1997). Influence of communication during the distant phase of the 1996 Republican presidential primary campaign. *Journal of Communication, 47*(4), 6–26.

Pfau, M., Moy, P., Holbert, R. L., Szabo, E. A., Lin, W. K., & Zhang, W. (1999). The influence of political talk radio on confidence in Democratic institutions. *Journalism and Mass Communication Quarterly, 75*(4), 730–745.

Pfau, M., Moy, P., Radler, B., & Bridgeman, M. K. (1998). The influence of individual communication media on public confidence in democratic institutions. *The Southern Communication Journal, 63*(2), 91–112.

Plato. (1945). *The New Republic.* New York: Oxford University Press.

Postman, N. (1985). *Amusing ourselves to death.* New York: Viking.

Potter, D., & Gantz, W. (1999, Spring). The shrinking audience for TV News: Why are viewers tuning out? *News Lab Report, 1*(1), 2.

Potter, W. J. (1986). Perceived reality and the cultivation hypothesis. *Journal of Broadcasting and Electronic Media, 30,* 159–174.

Potter, W. J. (1991a). Examining cultivation from a psychological perspective: Component subprocesses. *Communication Research, 18,* 77–102.

Potter, W. J. (1991b). The relationship between first- and second-order measures of cultivation. *Human Communication Research, 18,* 92–113.

Potter, W. J. (1993). Cultivation theory and research: A conceptual critique. *Human Communication Research, 19,* 564–601.

Potter, W. J. (1998). *Media literacy.* Thousand Oaks, CA: Sage.

Powers, K. (1998, September). 10 years of trash TV. *Good Housekeeping, 227*(3), p. 116.

Powers, R. (1977). *The newscasters.* New York: St. Martins.

Putnam, R. (1995, January). Bowling alone: America's declining social capital. *Journal of Democracy, 6,* 65–78.

Raaijmakers, J. G. W., & Shiffrin, R. M (1980). SAM: A theory of probabilistic search of associative memory. In G. H. Bower (Ed.), *The psychology of learning and motivation* (Vol. 14, pp. 207–262). New York: Academic Press.

Raaijmakers, J. G. W., & Shiffrin, R. M. (1981). Search of associative memory. *Psychological Review, 88,* 93–134.

Ratcliff, R. A. (1978). A theory of memory retrieval. *Psychological Review, 85,* 59–108.

Ratcliff, R. A., & McCoon, G. (1989). Memory models, text processing, and cue dependent retrieval. In H. L. Roediger, III & F. I. M. Craik (Eds.), *Varieties of memory and consciousness.* Hillsdale, NJ: Lawrence Erlbaum Associates.

Raugust, K. (1998, September 14). A common thread. *Publishers Weekly, 245*(37), 36.

Reeves, B., & Anderson, D. R., (1991). Media studies and psychology. *Communication Research, 18*(5), 597–600.

Reeves, B. R., Newhagen, J., Maibach, E., Basil, M., & Kurz, K. (1991). Negative and positive television messages: Effects of message type and context on attention and memory. *The American Behavioral Scientist, 34*(6), 679.

Reeves, B., & Thorson, E. (1986). Watching television: Experiments on the viewing process. *Communication Research, 13,* 343–361.

Rehm, D. (1996). A tower of Babel: Talk shows and politics. *Press/Politics, 1,* 138–142.

Rhine, R., & Severance, L (1970). Ego-involvement, discrepancy, source credibility, and attitude change. *Journal of Personality and Social Psychology, 16,* 175–190.

Rice, M. L., Huston, A. C., Truglio, R., & Wright, J. C. (1990). Words from Sesame Street: Learning vocabulary skills while viewing. *Developmental Psychology, 26,* 421–428.

Rice, R. E. (1989). Smokey Bear. In R. E. Rice & C. K. Atkin (Eds.), *Political communication campaigns* (2nd ed., pp. 215–217). Thousand Oaks, CA: Sage.

Rice, R. E., & Atkin, C. (1989). Preface: Trends in communication campaign research. In R. E. Rice & C. Atkin (Eds.), *Public communication campaigns* (2nd ed., pp. 7–11). Thousand Oaks, CA: Sage.

Rice, R. E., & Atkin, C. K. (1994). Principles of successful public communication campaigns. In J Bryant & D. Zillmann (Eds.), *Media effects: Advances in theory and research* (pp. 365–388). Hillsdale, NJ: Lawrence Erlbaum Associates.

Richtel, M. (1998, September 3). Heavy weather: Hurricane Bonnie a big draw. *The New York Times,* p. G3.

Riffe, D., Lacy, S., & Fico, F. G., (1998). *Analyzing media messages: Using quantitative content analysis in research.* Mahwah, NJ: Lawrence Erlbaum Associates.

Roberts, J. C. (1991, May/June). The power of talk radio. *The American Enterprise,* pp. 57–61.

Robinson, J. P., & Davis, D. K. (1990). Television news and the informed public: An information processing approach. *Journal of Communication, 40*(3), 106–119.

Robinson, J. P., & Godbey, G. (1997). *Time for life: The surprising ways Americans use their time.* University Park, PA: The Pennsylvania State University Press.

Robinson, J. P., & Levy, M. (1986). *The main source: Learning from television news.* Beverly Hills, CA: Sage.

Robinson, M. (1975). American political legitimacy in an era of electronic journalism. In D. Cater & R. Adler (Eds.), *Television as a social force: New approaches to TV criticism* (pp. 97–141). New York: Praeger.

Robinson, M. (1976). Public affairs television and the growth of political malaise: The case of "The selling of the Pentagon." *American Political Science Review, 70,* 409–432.

Robinson, M. (1977). Television and American politics: 1956–1976. *Public Interest, 48,* 3–39.

Roediger, H. L., & Challis, B. H. (1989). Hypermnesia: Improvements in recall with repeated testing. In E. Izawa (Ed.), *Current issues in cognitive processes: The Tulane Flowerree Symposium on Cognition* (pp. 175–200). Hillsdale, NJ: Lawrence Erlbaum Associates.

Roediger, H. L., Payne, D. G., Gillespie, G. L., & Lean, D. S. (1982). Hypermnesia as determined by level of recall. *Journal of Verbal Learning and Verbal Behavior, 21,* 635–655.

Roediger, H. L., & Thorpe, L. A. (1978). The role of recall time in producing hypermnesia. *Memory and Cognition, 6,* 296–305.

Rogers, E. M., & Storey, J. D., (1987). Communication campaigns. In C. E. Berger & S. H. Chaffee (Eds.), *Handbook of communication science* (pp. 817–846). Newbury Park, CA: Sage.

Rook, K. S., & Peplau, L. A. (1982). Perspectives on helping the lonely. In L. A. Peplau & D. Perlman (Eds.), *Loneliness: A sourcebook of current theory, research and therapy* (pp. 351–378). New York: Wiley.

Rosch, E. (1978). Principles of categorization. In E. Rosch & B. B. Lloyd (Eds.), *Cognition and categorization* (pp. 27–48). Hillsdale, NJ: Lawrence Erlbaum Associates.

Rosengren, K. E. (1974). Uses and gratifications: A paradigm outlined. In J. G. Blumler & E. Katz (Eds.), *The uses of mass communications: Current perspectives on gratifications research* (pp. 269–286). Beverly Hills, CA: Sage.

Rosengren, K. E., Wenner, L. E., & Palmgreen, P. (1985). *Media gratification's research: Current perspectives.* Beverly Hills, CA: Sage.

Royer, J. M. (1977). Remembering: Constructive or reconstructive? Comments on Chapter 5 by Spiro. In R. C. Anderson & R. J. Spiro (Eds.), *School and the acquisition of knowledge* (pp. 167–177). Hillsdale, NJ: Lawrence Erlbaum Associates.

Rubin, A. M. (1994). Media uses and effects: A uses-and-gratifications perspective. In J. Bryant & D. Zillmann (Eds.), *Media effects: Advances in theory and research* (pp. 417–436). Hillsdale, NJ: Lawrence Erlbaum Associates.

Rubin, A. M., Perse, E. M., & Taylor, D. S. (1988). A methodological examination of cultivation. *Communication Research, 15,* 107–134.

Rubin, A. M., & Windahl, S. (1986). The uses and dependency model of mass communication. *Critical Studies in Mass Communication, 3,* 184–199.

Rubinstein, C., & Shaver, P. (1982). *In search of intimacy.* New York: Delcorte.

Rumelhart, D. E. (1984). Schemata and the cognitive system. In R. S. Wyer, Jr., & T. K. Srull (Eds.), *Handbook of social cognition* (Vol. 1, pp. 161–188). Hillsdale, NJ: Lawrence Erlbaum Associates.

Rumelhart, D. E., Lindsay, P. H. & Norman, D. A. (1972). A process for long-term memory. In E. Tulving & W. Donaldson (Eds.), *Organization of memory* (pp. 197–246). New York: Academic Press.

Rumelhart, D. E., & McClelland, J. L. (1986). *Parallel distributed processing* (Vol. 1). Cambridge: MIT Press.

Rumelhart, D. E., & Ortony, A. (1977). The representation of knowledge in memory. In R. C. Anderson, R. J. Spiro, & W. E. Montague (Eds.), *Schooling and acquisition of knowledge* (pp. 99–136). Hillsdale, NJ: Lawrence Erlbaum Associates.

Rust, M. (1999, February 8). It's so sensational! *Insight on the News, 15*(5), 10–11.

Sabato, L. J. (1991). *Feeding frenzy: How attack journalism has transformed American politics.* New York: The Free Press.

Salomon, G., (1979). *Interaction of media, cognition, and learning.* San Francisco: Jossey-Bass.

Salomon, G. & Leigh, T. (1984). Predispositions about learning from print and television. *Journal of Communication, 34,* 119–135.

Sawyer, A. (1981). Repetition, cognitive response, and persuasion. In R. E. Petty, T. M. Ostrom, & T. C. Brock (Eds.), *Cognitive responses in persuasion* (pp. 237–262). Hillsdale, NJ: Lawrence Erlbaum Associates.

Scarry, E. (1998, April 9). The fall of TWA 800: The possibility of electromagnetic interference. *The New York Review of Books, 45*(6), 59–76.

Schank, R. C., & Abelson, R. P. (1977). *Scripts, plans, goals, and understanding: An inquiry into human knowledge structures.* Hillsdale, NJ: Lawrence Erlbaum Associates.

Schiano, D. J. (1997, May). Convergent methodologies in cyber-psychology: A case study. *Behavior Research Methods, Instruments & Computers, 29*(2), 270–273.

Schleuder, J. D., White, A. V., & Cameron, G. T. (1993). Priming effects of television news bumpers and teasers on attention and memory. *Journal of Broadcasting and Electronic Media, 37*(4), 437–452.

Schneider, W., & Shiffrin, R. M. (1977). Controlled and automatic human information processing: 1. Detection, search, and attention. *Psychological Review, 84,* 1–66.

Schramm, W. (1971). The nature of communication between humans. In W. Schramm & D. Roberts (Eds.), *The process and effects of mass communication* (rev. ed., pp. 3–53). Urbana: University of Illinois Press.

Severin, W. J., & Tankard, J. W. (1992). *Communication theories: Origins, methods and uses in the mass media.* New York: Longman.

Shapiro, M. A. (1991). Memory and decision processes in the construction of social reality. *Communication Research, 18*(1), 3–24.

Shiffrin, R. S., & Schneider, W. (1977). Controlled and automatic human information processing: II. Perceptual learning, automatic attending and a general theory. *Psychological Review, 84,* 127–190.

Shoemaker, P. J., & Reese, S. D. (1996). *Mediating the message: Theories of influences on mass media content* (2nd ed.). New York: Longman.

Shrum, L. J., & O'Guinn, T. (1993). Processes and effects in the construction of social reality: Construct accessibility as an explanatory variable. *Communication Research, 20*(3), 436–471.

Sidney, S., Sternfeld, B., Haskell, W. L., Jacobs, D. R., Chesney, M. A., & Hulley, S. B. (1998). Television viewing and cardiovascular risk factors in young adults: The CARDIA study. *Annals of Epidemiology, 6*(2), 154–159.

Signorielli, N. (1990). *Television's mean and dangerous world: A continuation of the cultural indicators perspective.* Beverly Hills, CA: Sage.

Simon, H. A. (1974). How big is a chunk? *Science, 183,* 482–488.

Singer, J. L. (1980). The power and limitations of television: A cognitive-affective analysis. In P. H. Tannenbaum (Ed.), *The entertainment functions of television* (pp. 31–65). Hillsdale, NJ: Lawrence Erlbaum Associates.

Singer, J. L., & Singer, D. G. (1983). The implications of childhood television viewing for cognition, imagination, and emotion. In J. Bryant & D. R. Anderson (Eds.), *Children's understanding of television* (pp. 265–295). New York: Academic Press.

Singh, S., Gedeon, T. D., & Rho, Y. (1998). Enhancing comprehension of Web information for users with special linguistic needs. *Journal of Communication, 48*(2), 86–108

Smith, E. E., & Medin, D. L. (1981). *Categories and concepts.* Cambridge, MA: Harvard University Press.

Smith, M. C., & Magee, L. E. (1980). Tracing the time-course of picture-word processing. *Journal of Experimental Psychology: General, 109,* 373–392.

Smith, S. L., & Wilson, B. J. (1995, May). *Children's comprehension of and emotional reactions to TV news.* Paper presented at the International Communication Association, Albuquerque, NM.

Snow, S. (1998, August 22). Morning report; arts and entertainment reports from the times, national and international news services and the nation's press. *Los Angeles Times.* p. F2.

Sperling, G. A. (1960). The information available in brief visual presentations. *Psychological Monographs, 74,* Whole No. 498.

Spiro, R. J. (1980). Accommodative reconstruction in prose recall. *Journal of Verbal Learning and Verbal Behavior, 19,* 84–95.

Sproull, L. S., & Kiesler, S. (1991). *Connections: New ways of working in the networked organization.* Cambridge, MA: MIT Press.

Stark, P. (1995, June 18). Country radio levels off; news/talk keeps growing. *Billboard,* 89.

Stauffer, J., Frost, R., & Rybolt, W. (1983). The attention factor in recalling network television news. *Journal of Communication, 33*(1), 29–36.

Stephen, A. (1998, June 19). An Internet addict confesses. *New Statesman, 11* (509), 26.

Stephens, M. (1993). *Broadcast news.* Fort Worth, TX: Harcourt, Brace Javanovich College Publishers.

Sternthal, B., Dholakia, R., & Leavitt, C. (1978). The persuasive effect of source credibility: A test of cognitive response analysis. *Journal of Consumer Research, 4,* 252–260.

Stoll, C. (1995). *Silicon snake oil.* New York: Doubleday.

Stone, V. (2000). *Supply, demand and entry-level pay in television and radio news.* http://web.missouri.edu/~jourvs/entrypay.html.

Suls, J. M., & Wills, T. A. (1991). *Social comparison: Contemporary theory and research.* Hillsdale, NJ: Lawrence Erlbaum Associates.

Tamborini, R. (1991). Responding to horror: Determinants of exposure and appeal. In J. Bryant & D. Zillmann (Eds.), *Responding to the screen: Reception and reaction processes* (pp. 305 – 328). Hillsdale, NJ: Lawrence Erlbaum Associates.

Tan, A. S. (1986). Social learning of aggression from television. In J. Bryant & D. Zillmann (Eds.), *Perspectives on media effects* (pp. 41–55). Hillsdale, NJ: Lawrence Erlbaum Associates.

Taylor, S. E., & Crocker, J. (1981). Schematic bases of social information processing. In E. T. Higgins, C. P. Herman, & M. P. Zanna (Eds.), *Social cognition: The Ontario symposium* (Vol. 1, pp. 89–134). Hillsdale, NJ: Lawrence Erlbaum Associates.

Technology Forecast: 1997 (1997, January). Menlo Park, CA: Price Waterhouse.

Tesser, A., & Leone, C. (1977). Cognitive schemas and thought as determinants of attitude change. *Journal of Experimental Psychology, 13,* 340–356.

Thomas, D. (1999, June 13). Aggressively studying violence an Iowa State psychologist's research takes aim at popular notions about aggression. *Omaha World-Herald,* p. 1E.

Thomas, K. (1998, November 4). Teen cyberdating is a new wrinkle for parents, too. *USA Today,* p. 9D.

Thorndyke, P. W., & Yekovich, F. R. (1979). A critique of schemata as a theory of human memory. *Rand Series Collection # P–6307.*

Thorson, E., Reeves, B., & Schleuder, J. (1987). Attention to local and global complexity in television messages. In M. L. McGlaughlin (Ed.), *Communication Yearbook 10* (pp. 366–383). Newbury Park, CA: Sage.

Traugott, M., Berinsky, A., Cramer, K., Howard, M., Mayer, R., Schuckman, H. P., Tewksbury, D., & Young, M., (1996, July). *The impact of talk radio on its audience.* Paper presented at the annual meeting of the International Society of Political Psychology, Vancouver, British Columbia, Canada.

Tuchman, G. (1978). *Making news: A study in the construction of reality.* New York: The Free Press.

Tulving, E. (1972). Episodic and semantic memory. In E. Tulving & W. Donaldson (Eds.), *Organization of memory* (pp. 381–403). New York: Academic Press.

Tulving, E. (1974). Cue-dependent forgetting. *American Scientist, 62,* 74–82.

Tulving, E., & Pearlstone, Z. (1966). Availability versus accessibility of information in memory for words. *Journal of Verbal Learning and Verbal Behavior, 87,* 1–8.

Turkle, S. (1996, Winter). Virtuality and its discontents: Searching for community in cyberspace. *The American Prospect, 24,* 50–57.

Turkle, S. (1997). Constructions and reconstructions of self in virtual reality: Playing in the MUDs. In S. Kiesler (Ed.), *Culture of the Internet* (pp. 143–155). Mahwah, NJ: Lawrence Erlbaum Associates.

Tversky, A. (1977). Features of similarity. *Psychological Review, 84*(4), 327–352.

Van der Voort, T. H. A. (1986). *Television violence: A child's eye view.* Amsterdam: North-Holland.

Vanderwart, M. (1984). Priming by pictures in lexical decision. *Journal of Verbal Learning and Verbal Behavior, 23,* 67–83.

Van Evra, J. (1998). *Television and child development* (2nd ed.). Mahwah, NJ: Lawrence Erlbaum Associates.

Vatz, R. E., & Weinberg, L. S. (1998, September). Television's assault on civility. *USA Today, 127*(2640), 62–63.

Venkatesh, A., & Vitalari, N. (1992). An emerging distributed work arrangement: An investigation of computer-based supplemental work at home. *Management Science, 38*(12), 1687–1706.

Vidmar, N., & Rokeach, M., (1974). Archie Bunker's bigotry: A study in selective perception and exposure. *Journal of Communication, 24*(1), 36–47.

Vinzant, C. (1998, July 6). Electronic books are coming at last! *Fortune, 138*(1), 119–124.

Vitalari, N. P., Venkatesh, A., & Gronhaug, K. (1985). Computing in the home: Shifts in time allocation patterns of households. *Communications of the ACM, 28*(5), 512–522.

Warnick, B. (1998). Appearance or reality? Political parody on the Web in campaign '96. *Critical Studies in Mass Communication, 15*(3), 306–324.

Weaver, J. (1991). Responding to erotica. Perceptual processes and dispositional implications. In J. Bryant & D. Zillmann (Eds.), *Responding to the screen: Reception and reaction processes* (pp. 329–354). Hillsdale, NJ: Lawrence Erlbaum Associates.

Weaver, P. H. (1972). Is television news biased? *Public Interest, 26,* 57–74.

Webster, J. G., & Phalen, P. F. (1997). *The mass audience: Rediscovering the dominant model.* Mahwah, NJ. Lawrence Erlbaum Associates.

Wells, W., Burnett, J., & Moriarity, S., (1995). *Advertising principles and practices.* Englewood Cliffs, NJ: Prentice-Hall.

Wheeler, L. (1991). A brief history of social comparison theory. In J. Suls & T. A. Wills (Eds.), *Social comparison processes: Contemporary theory and research* (pp. 3–21). Hillsdale, NJ: Lawrence Erlbaum Associates.

Wheeling and Dealing. (1998, September 21). *Forbes, 162*(6), p. 222.

White, D. M. (1950). The "gatekeeper": A case study in the selection of news. *Journalism Quarterly, 27,* 383–390.

Wicks, R. H. (1989a). Product matching in television news using benefit segmentation. *Journal of Advertising Research, 29*(5), 64–71.

Wicks, R. H. (1989b). Segmenting broadcast news audiences in the new media environment. *Journalism Quarterly, 66*(3), 383–390.

Wicks, R. H. (1992a). Improvement over time in recall of media information: An exploratory study. *Journal of Broadcasting and Electronic Media, 36*(3), 287–302.

Wicks, R. H. (1992b). Schema theory and measurement in mass communication research: Theoretical and methodological issues in news information processing. In S. Deetz (Ed.), *Communication Yearbook 15* (pp. 115–145). Beverly Hills, CA: Sage.

Wicks, R. H. (1995). Remembering the news: Effects of medium and message discrepancy on news recall over time. *Journalism and Mass Communication Quarterly, 72*(3), 666–681.

Wicks, R. H., & Drew, D. (1991). Learning from the news: Effects of message consistency and medium on recall and inference making. *Journalism Quarterly, 68*(1 & 2), 155–164.

Wicks, R. H., & Kern, M. (1993). Cautious optimism: A new proactive role for local television news departments in local election coverage? *American Behavioral Scientist, 37*(2), 262–271.

Wicks, R. H., & Kern, M. (1995). Factors influencing decisions by local television news directors to develop new reporting strategies during the 1992 political campaign. *Communication Research, 22*(2), 237–255.

Wicks, R. H, Scheide, F. M., & Smith, S. A. (1999). The construction of political meaning by native Americans in the 1996 election: The case of the Cherokees & Keetoowahs. In L. Kaid & D. Bystrom (Eds.), *The electronic election: Perspectives on the campaign communication* (pp. 275–292). Mahwah, NJ: Lawrence Erlbaum Associates.

Winn, M. (1977). *The plug-in drug.* New York: Viking Press.

Wilcox, C., & Williams, L. (1990). Taking stock of schema theory. *Social Science Journal, 27*(4), 373–393.

Wood, J. V. (1989). Theory and research concerning social comparisons of personal attributes. *Personality Bulletin, 106*(2), 231–248.

Wood, J. V., & Taylor, K. L. (1991). Serving self-referent goals through social comparison. In J. Suls & T. A. Wills (Eds.), *Social comparison processes: Contemporary theory and research* (pp. 261–285). Hillsdale, NJ: Lawrence Erlbaum Associates.

Wright, J. C., & Huston, A. C. (1981). Children's understanding of the forms of television. In H. Kelly & H. Gardner (Eds.), *Viewing children through television* (pp. 73–88). San Francisco: Jossey Bass.

Wyer, R. S., & Srull, T. K. (1980). The processing of social stimulus material: A conceptual integration. In R. Hastie, T. M. Ostrom, E. B. Ebbesen, R. S. Wyer, D.

Hamilton, & D. E. Carlston (Eds.), *Person memory: The cognitive basis of social perception* (pp. 227–300). Hillsdale, NJ: Lawrence Erlbaum Associates.

Wyer, R. S., & Srull, T. K. (1981). Category accessibility: Some theoretical and empirical issues concerning the processing of social stimulus information. In E. T. Higgins, C. P. Herman, & P. Zanna (Eds.), *Social cognition: The Ontario Symposium* (Vol. 1, pp. 161–197). Hillsdale, NJ: Lawrence Erlbaum Associates.

Yekovich, F. R., & Thorndyke, P. W. (1981). An evaluation of alternative functional models of narrative schemata. *Journal of Verbal Learning and Verbal Behavior, 20,* 454–469.

Young, K. S. (1996). Pathological Internet use: A case that breaks the stereotype. *Psychological Reports, 79*(3, Pt. 1), 899–902.

Young, K. S. (1998). *Caught in the Net: How to recognize the signs of Internet addiction and a winning strategy for recovery.* New York: Wiley.

Zajonc, R. B. (1980). Feeling and thinking: Preferences need no inferences. *American Psychologist, 35,* 151–175.

Zillmann, D. (1983a). Disparagement humor. In P. E. McGhee & J. H. Goldstein (Eds.), *Handbook of humor research: Vol. 1, Basic issues* (pp. 85–107). New York: Springer-Verlag.

Zillmann, D. (1983b). Transfer of excitation in emotional behavior. In J. T. Cacioppo & R. E. Petty (Eds.), *Social psychophysiology: A sourcebook* (pp. 215–240). New York: Guilford.

Zillmann, D. (1991a). Television viewing and physiological arousal. In J. Bryant & D. Zillmann (Eds.), *Responding to the screen: Reception and reaction processes* (pp. 103–134). Hillsdale, NJ: Lawrence Erlbaum Associates.

Zillmann, D. (1991b). The logic of suspense and mystery. In J. Bryant & D. Zillmann (Eds.), *Responding to the screen: Reception and reaction processes* (pp. 281–304). Hillsdale, NJ: Lawrence Erlbaum Associates.

Zillmann, D., & Bryant, J. (1985). Selective exposure phenomena. In D. Zillmann & J. Bryant (Eds.), *Selective exposure to communication* (pp. 1–10). Hillsdale, NJ: Lawrence Erlbaum Associates.

Zillmann, D., & Bryant, J. (1986). Exploring the entertainment experience. In J. Bryant & D. Zillmann (Eds.), *Perspectives on media effects* (pp. 303–324). Hillsdale, NJ: Lawrence Erlbaum Associates.

Author Index

Subject Index